FLY TIER'S

Handbook

GENE KUGACH

0 11557 02611 5

STACKPOLE
BOOKS

Published by
STACKPOLE BOOKS
5067 Ritter Road
Mechanicsburg, PA 17055

Printed in the United States of America

10 9 8 7 6 5 4 3 2 1

First edition

Cover photo by Michael Radencich

Library of Congress Cataloging-in-Publication Data

Kugach, Gene.
   Fly tier's handbook / Gene Kugach.—1st ed.
     p. cm.
   ISBN 0-8117-2611-8 (paperback)
   1. Fly tying—Handbooks, manuals, etc. I. Title

   SH451 .K843 2001
   688.7'9—dc21   00-054138

To the members of The Chicago Fly Fishers,
with whom I spent many enjoyable hours
learning the skill of fly tying

CONTENTS

CONTENTS

CONTENTS

PREFACE

The hobby of fly tying is centuries old and is currently practiced more than ever. On the following pages, I have tried to list the various materials both old and new that are used in the construction of the many patterns available today.

Even as I write this, new materials and tools are added to the fly tier's bench every day. To list all of them would be impossible: however, I hope that my efforts help simplify the selection.

ACKNOWLEDGMENTS

It would be impossible to identify and credit all the sources on which I relied for the information in this book. Much of the factual data came from a variety of sources, including knowledgeable fishing individuals, fishing books, manufacturers' catalogs, monthly magazines, and so forth. If I were to list each one of them, the list would be a book in itself, but I would like to mention just a few that were extremely helpful.

Books and Pamphlets

Fly Tying (John F. McKim)

Complete Fly Tying Instruction Book (Hobby Bait Industries)

Practical Flies and Their Construction (Gee and Sias)

Publications by the Illinois Department of Conservation

Manufacturers' Catalogs

O. Mustad and Sons Inc., Wright & McGill-Eagle Claw Hook Co., Tiemco Hook Co., Kamasan Hook Co., Partridge of Redditch Ltd., VMC Inc., Gamakatsu Hook Co., Hunters, The Fly Shop, Fly & Field, Kaufmann's Streamborn, Thomas & Thomas, Orvis, Madison River Fishing Co., Frontier Anglers, E. Hille Co., and The Hook & Hackle Co.

CHAPTER 1

Tools of the Trade

The following pages list the various tools required for fly tying. The primary tools are the basic tools necessary to get started, while the secondary tools help simplify some of the procedures during the tying process.

Whether you own inexpensive tools or you spend a lot of money to buy the best, there is only one thing to remember: The tools don't make the tier. To become an excellent tier requires practice, practice, and more practice.

Primary Tools

The following items and illustrations are examples of the primary tools necessary for fly tying. Most, if not all, of them can be purchased through mail-order catalogs or most fly shops.

Vise

The basic function of the vise is to hold the hook securely in a fixed position while various materials are added to the hook shank. Most vises can be purchased as pedestal models or with bench clamps that allow the tier to secure it to some type of table or bench top. The more expensive vises include a rotary function that allows the tier to rotate the secured hook 90 degrees. This function is used when adding material such as ribbing or dubbing to the hook shank. In addition, many expensive vises have interchangeable jaws (Midge Jaws, Saltwater Jaws, etc.) that can be purchased separately. The following are a few of the more popular vise manufacturers: Sunrise "A," Renzetti, HMH, Dyna-King, Regal Thompson.

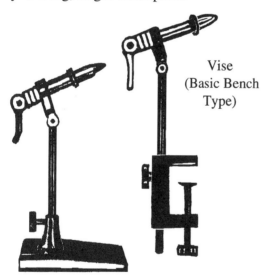

Vise
(Basic Bench
Type)

Vise (Pedestal Type)

Bobbins

Bobbins are designed to hold the thread when adding material to the hook shank. They are available with stainless steel or ceramic tubes.

Threader

A threader is used to thread bobbins and remove wax buildup from the bobbin tube.

Whip-Finisher

This device makes it easy to finish off a fly with a whip-finish knot. Manufacturers include Thompson, Sunrise, and Matarelli.

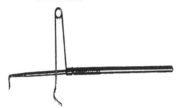

Bodkin

The bodkin is another basic tool used when dubbing or tying off. It is often available with a half-hitch tool on one end.

Scissors

This is a basic tool used to trim material. More than one pair is recommended, one for fine cuts and another for coarse materials.

Hackle Pliers

Hackle pliers are used to palmer hackles around the hook shank. They are available in different shapes and sizes.

Hair Stacker

This device is designed to even up the tips of hair fibers or other synthetic materials. It is available in various sizes.

Secondary Tools

The following items and illustrations are examples of additional (secondary) tools used for fly tying. They are used to simplify some of the steps during the tying process. Most of these tools can also be purchased through mail-order catalogs or in fly shops.

Waste-Trol, Gar-Bag, or Trim Bag

This device is used to collect tying scraps and waste material during the tying process. It attaches to the vise shaft and hangs below the tying surface.

Material Holder (Spring) or Material Clip

This device is used to hold material that will be used later in the pattern construction away from the hook.

Tweezers

Tweezers are used to remove unwanted materials on small flies or around the hook eye.

Floss Bobbin

This device is designed specifically for holding all sizes of floss.

Forceps

Forceps are used to hold the hook when trimming hair patterns or can be used as a streamside vise.

Hackle Gauge

This neat little device slides onto most vise stems, taking the guesswork out when selecting dry-fly hackles.

Wing Cutter or Burner

This device is used to provide a realistic wing pattern from a large feather for both mayfly and caddis patterns. It is available in assorted sizes.

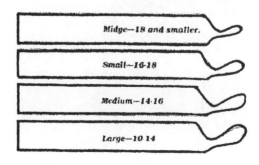

Secondary Tools

Hackle Guard

This device is used to hold back hackle collars on both wet and dry flies when finishing off the pattern. They are sold as sets in different sizes.

Head Cement Applicator
(Squeeze Bottle)

This excellent container is used to apply cement to the head of a finished pattern or in various tight locations during pattern construction.

Half-Hitch Tool

This is a simple tool used with the thread to form a half hitch. They are sold as sets in different sizes.

Dubbing Blender

A dubbing blender is a very useful item for tiers who want to blend their own dubbing combinations.

Dubbing Twister

Use this device to spin a dubbing loop during the tying process.

Opti-Visor

This precision binocular headband magnifier is made for close work or for tiers with limited vision.

Profile Plate

This device can be attached to most vise stems to provide an unobstructed tying background. It comes in various colors.

Bobbin Cradle

Designed to fit on most vise stems, a bobbin cradle allows the tier to keep the bobbin out of the way or serves as a bobbin rest during the tying procedure.

CHAPTER 2

Pattern Categories

The first thing a fly tier determines prior to putting a hook into a vise is the type of pattern he or she will attempt to construct or create. Will it be a dry fly, a wet fly, a nymph, a streamer, or one of the many other categories that exist today? Will it be a standard dry fly, a traditional, a fan-wing, or a dun or quill pattern? What do each of them look like, and what do they attempt to represent? These are only a few of the questions a tier asks prior to selecting the hook and the materials necessary to accomplish the job.

The following pages list the majority of the various pattern categories and subcategories that exist. To help simplify the selection process, information is given regarding what each pattern type attempts to represent, what type and size hook to use, the basic construction, and an illustration of the pattern. Also included are the names of the more popular patterns in each category or subcategory, along with an illustrated example.

Pattern Categories

DRY FLIES
- Traditionals
- Fan-wings
- Duns and Quills
- Variants
- Bivisibles
- Parachutes and Paraduns
- Spinners
- Thoraxes
- Irresistibles and Hair Bodies
- Long and Large Bodies
- Extended Bodies
- Midges and Tiny Dry Flies
- Caddis and Sedges
- No Hackles
- Wulffs and Humpies
- Spiders and Skaters
- Compara-duns
- Cut-Wings (Iwamasa)

NYMPH FLIES
- Standards or Classics
- Mayfly Nymphs
- Stonefly Nymphs
- Floating or Emerger Nymphs
- Caddis or Sedges
- Midge Nymphs
- Damselflies
- Dragonflies
- Mosquito Larvae
- Hellgrammites
- Water Beetles
- All-Purpose Nymphs

WET FLIES
- Standards or Classics
- Soft Hackles
- Woolly Worms
- Woolly Buggers

STREAMERS
- Standards or Traditionals
- Trolling Streamers
- Matukas
- Bucktails

SALMON AND STEELHEAD FLIES
- Classics
- Standards
- Hairwings
- Low-Water
- Double-Hook
- Tube Flies

BASS FLIES
- Hair Patterns
- Divers
- Keel Hook Patterns
- Poppers
- Lures
- Standard Bass Flies

BAITFISH FLIES
- Muddlers
- Sculpins
- Thunder Creek Patterns
- Zonkers
- Minnows

TERRESTRIAL FLIES
- Ants
- Crickets
- Grasshoppers
- Beetles

CRUSTACEAN FLIES
- Crayfish
- Scuds or Shrimp

MISCELLANEOUS FLIES
- Eggs
- Leeches
- Worms
- Shad

SALTWATER FLIES
- Baitfish
- Shrimp
- Squid
- Crabs

Dry Flies

Dry flies are designed to represent adult insects found floating or touching down on the water surface. They usually represent imitations of aquatic insects such as mayflies, caddisflies, stoneflies, black flies, and so forth. However, some patterns are designed as attractors that are not representative of any specific insect. The following are a few of the major categories and subcategories of dry flies.

Traditional Dry-Fly Patterns

Adams

Traditional patterns have been around for many years and are still being used today. They are considered a mainstay for most dry-fly fishing enthusiasts.

Some of the more popular traditional patterns include the Adams, Black Gnat, Mosquito, Royal Coachman, Coachman, White Miller, March Brown, Light or Dark Cahill, Dark Blue or Brown Sedge, Gray Fox, Light or Dark Coty, Gordon, Beverkill, Brown or Gray Hackle, Grey Fox, and Light or Dark Hendrickson.

Recommended Hook Sizes

Most traditional dry-fly patterns can be tied on hook sizes 10, 12, 14, 16, 18, and 20, using hooks made of fine-gauge wire.

Recommended Hook Numbers

The following are a few of the more popular hooks (by manufacturer) used for tying traditional dry-fly patterns. For alternative or additional hook selections, see Chapter 3.

Mustad: 94840, 94842 **Eagle Claw:** 59, L059, 159, L159 **Tiemco:** TMC100, TMC9300

Kamasan: B-400, B-830 **Partridge:** L2A, L3A, L3B **Daiichi:** 1100, 1170, 1330

VMC: 9280, 9281, 9288 **Gamakatsu:** S10, P10

Typical Traditional Dry-Fly Construction

The following proportions and material options can be used when tying traditional dry-fly patterns.

Wings: Height equal to shank
Materials: Hair fibers, feather segments, or feather tips

Body: Equals shank less head
Materials: Thread, floss, dubbing, or tinsel

Hackle: Fibers equal to body length.
Materials: Hackle wound in front and behind wing

Tail: 1½ times body length
Materials: Hair or feather fibers

Fan-wing Dry-Fly Patterns

Fan Wing
Royal Coachman

Like the traditionals, fan-wings have also been around for a long time. They are designed to represent various adult flying insects. The patterns are tied with the wings formed by using two duck breast feathers that sit like two fans on top of the hook.

Some of the more popular fan-wing patterns include the Fan Wing Royal Coachman, Fan Wing Cahill, Fan Wing Gordon, and Fan Wing Ginger Quill.

Recommended Hook Sizes

All the above patterns can be tied on hook sizes 10, 12, or 14, using hooks made of fine-gauge wire.

Recommended Hook Numbers

The following are a few of the more popular hooks (by manufacturer) used for tying fan-wing dry-fly patterns. For alternative or additional hook selections, see Chapter 3.

Mustad: 94840, 94842   **Eagle Claw:** 59, L059, 159, L159   **Tiemco:** TMC100, TMC9300

Kamasan: B-400, B-830   **Partridge:** L2A, L3A, L3B   **Daiichi:** 1100, 1170, 1330

VMC: 9280, 9281, 9288   **Gamakatsu:** S10, P10

Typical Fan-wing Dry-Fly Construction

The following proportions and material options can be used when tying fan-wing dry-fly patterns.

Wings: Height equal to shank
Materials: Duck breast feather tips

Hackle: Fibers equal to body length
Materials: Hackle wound in front and behind wing

Center Joint (optional): 2 or 3 wraps
Materials: Peacock or ostrich herl

Butt (optional): 2 or 3 wraps
Materials: Peacock or ostrich herl

Tail: 1½ times body length
Materials: Hair or feather fibers

Body: Equals shank less head
Materials: Thread, floss, dubbing, or tinsel

Dun and Quill Dry-Fly Patterns

Quill Gordon

Dun and quill patterns represent adult mayfly hatches (*Baetis*), which are widely distributed and occur throughout the year.

Dun patterns represent winged mayflies that emerge from the nymphal stage. The wings on mayfly duns are usually a dull gray or grayish brown.

Quill patterns represent adult mayflies with pronounced body markings that are imitated by using stripped quills in the body construction.

Dun patterns include the Blue Wing Olive, Blue Dun, Olive Dun, Pale Evening, and Morning Dun.

Quill patterns include the Ginger Quill, Blue Quill, Olive Quill, Red Quill, Black Quill, and Quill Gordon.

Recommended Hook Sizes

Most dun and quill patterns can be tied on hook sizes 10, 12, 14, 16, 18, and 20, using hooks made of fine wire.

Recommended Hook Numbers

The following are a few of the more popular hooks (by manufacturer) used for tying dun or quill dry-fly patterns. For alternative or additional hook selections, see Chapter 3.

Mustad: 94840, 94842   **Eagle Claw:** 59, L059, 159, L159   **Tiemco:** TMC100, TMC9300

Kamasan: B-400, B-830   **Partridge:** L2A, L3A, L3B   **Daiichi:** 1100, 1170, 1330

VMC: 9280, 9281, 9288   **Gamakatsu:** S10, P10

Typical Dun and Quill Dry-Fly Construction

The following proportions and material options can be used when tying dun and quill dry-fly patterns.

Wings: Height equal to shank
Materials: Hair fibers, feather segments, or feather tips

Body: Equals shank less head
Materials:
Duns—Dun-colored dubbing
Quills—Stripped quill ribbed with fine wire

Tail: 1 1/2 times body length
Materials: Hair or feather fibers

Hackle: Fibers equal to body length
Materials: Hackle wound in front and behind wing

Variant Dry-Fly Patterns

H & L Variant

Variant patterns represent a wide variety of adult insects and are usually tied using oversized hackle collars that are two to three times larger than a standard hackle. Variant patterns have bodies, and some also include wings. The oversized hackles make them good floaters and easy to see on the water.

Variants include the Cream Variant, Dun Variant, Gray Fox Variant, Brown Variant, and H & L Variant.

Recommended Hook Sizes

All the above patterns can be tied on hook sizes 10, 12, 14, 16, 18, 20, or 22, using hooks made of fine-gauge wire.

Recommended Hook Numbers

The following are a few of the more popular hooks (by manufacturer) used for tying variant patterns. For alternative or additional hook selections, see Chapter 3.

Mustad: 94840, 94842   **Eagle Claw:** 59, L059, 159, L159   **Tiemco:** TMC100, TMC9300

Kamasan: B-400, B-830   **Partridge:** L2A, L3A, L3B   **Daiichi:** 1100, 1170, 1330

VMC: 9280, 9281, 9288   **Gamakatsu:** S10, P10

Typical Variant Dry-Fly Construction

The following proportions and material options can be used when tying variant dry-fly patterns.

Hackle: Oversized, tied in at the front 1/3 of the body
Materials: Oversized hackle feather or feathers wound in collar style
Note: Feathers can be mixed colors

Body: Equals shank less head
Materials: Stripped hackle stem (quill)

Tail: 1½ times body length
Materials: Hair or feather fibers

Bivisible Dry-Fly Patterns

Brown Bivisible

Bivisible patterns are representative of adult insects. They are similar to a variant pattern using an oversized white or cream hackle near the hook eye, followed by several hackles wound with close turns over the body. Bivisible patterns generally do not have wings. The oversized hackles make them good floaters and easy to see on the water.

Bivisibles include the Black Bivisible, Badger Bivisible, Brown Bivisible, Ginger Bivisible, Grizzly Bivisible, and Gray Bivisible.

Recommended Hook Sizes

All the above patterns can be tied on hook sizes 10, 12, 14, 16, 18, and 20, using hooks made of fine wire.

Recommended Hook Numbers

The following are a few of the more popular hooks (by manufacturer) used for tying bivisible dry-fly patterns. For alternative or additional hook selections, see Chapter 3.

Mustad: 94840, 94842   **Eagle Claw:** 59, L059, 159, L159   **Tiemco:** TMC100, TMC9300

Kamasan: B-400, B-830   **Partridge:** L2A, L3A, L3B   **Daiichi:** 1100, 1170, 1330

VMC: 9280, 9281, 9288   **Gamakatsu:** S10, P10

Typical Bivisible Dry-Fly Construction

The following proportions and material options can be used when tying bivisible dry-fly patterns.

Hackle: Covers 1/16 of the body area
Material: Oversized white or cream hackle wound in behind the hook eye in front of the body hackles

Body: Equals shank less head
Materials: Thread base, wound with hackles increasing in size from the back of the hook to the front

Tail: $1^{1}/_{2}$ times body length
Materials: Hair or feather fibers

Parachute and Paradun Dry-Fly Patterns

Elk Wing Paradun

Hare's Ear Parachute

These patterns are designed to represent the first stages of a maturing winged insect. The hackle is wound on the horizontal plane rather than the vertical plane.

Paraduns include the Adams Paradun, Tan Paradun, Olive Paradun, Elk Wing Paradun, and Loopwing Quill Paradun.

Parachutes include the Hare's Ear Parachute, Schroeder's Caddis Parachute, Adams Parachute, Cahill Parachute, Dun Parachute, Coachman Parachute, Black Gnat Parachute, Pale Evening Dun Parachute, and Blue Wing Olive Parachute.

Recommended Hook Sizes

All the above patterns can be tied on hook sizes 10, 12, 14, 16, 18, or 20.

Recommended Hook Numbers

The following are a few of the more popular hooks (by manufacturer) used for tying parachute or paradun dry-fly patterns. For alternative or additional hook selections, see Chapter 3.

Mustad: 94840, 94842   **Eagle Claw:** 59, L059, 159, L159   **Tiemco:** TMC100, TMC9300

Kamasan: B-400, B-830   **Partridge:** L2A, L3A, L3B   **Daiichi:** 1100, 1170, 1330

VMC: 9280, 9281, 9288   **Gamakatsu:** S10, P10

Typical Parachute and Paradun Dry-Fly Construction

The following proportions and material options can be used when tying parachute and paradun dry-fly patterns.

Wings: Height equal to shank
Materials: Hair fibers, feather segments, or feather tips

Body: Equals shank less head
Materials: Dubbing, clipped hair

Hackle: Fibers equal to body length
Materials: Hackle wound in on the horizontal plane.

Tail: Equal to body length
Materials: Hair or feather fibers

Spinner Dry-Fly Patterns

Poly Quill

These patterns are designed to represent the final wing stage of a mayfly (order Ephemeroptera).

Some of the more popular spinner patterns are the White/Black Spinner, Dun/Brown Spinner, Dun/Cream Spinner, Partridge Spinner, Slate/Olive Spinner, Red/Brown Spinner, White/Yellow Spinner, Antron Spinner, and Poly Quill.

Recommended Hook Sizes
Most spinner patterns can be tied on hook sizes 14, 16, 18, 20, 22, and 24.

Recommended Hook Numbers
The following are a few of the more popular hooks (by manufacturer) used for tying spinner patterns. For alternative or additional hook selections, see Chapter 3.

Mustad: 94840, 94842   **Eagle Claw:** 59, L059, 159, L159   **Tiemco:** TMC100, TMC9300

Kamasan: B-400, B-830   **Partridge:** L2A, L3A, L3B   **Daiichi:** 1100, 1170, 1330

VMC: 9280, 9281, 9288   **Gamakatsu:** S10, P10

Typical Spinner Dry-Fly Construction
The following proportions and material options can be used when tying spinner dry-fly patterns.

Body: Equals shank less head
Materials: Fur, dubbing, poly dubbing, stripped quill
Note: Body can also be ribbed using floss or fine wire

Wings: Length equal to shank
Materials: Polywing material tied in in the spent position (horizontal)
Note: Some older patterns use hackle tips, calf tail, or other types of feather or hair fibers for the wing

Tail: Equal to body length
Materials: Hackle fibers (forked)

Thorax (optional): Equal to 1/2 body length
Materials: Fur or dubbing

Thorax Dry-Fly Patterns

Thorax

These patterns are designed to represent an assortment of adult insects. They are tied with the hackle and wings placed near the center of the hook.

Some of the more common thorax patterns include the Pale Morning Dun, White/Black Dun, Mahogany Dun, Callibeatis, and Slate/Olive Dun.

Recommended Hooks Sizes

All the above patterns can be tied on hook sizes 14, 16, 18, and 20.

Recommended Hook Numbers

The following are a few of the more popular hooks (by manufacturer) used for tying thorax patterns. For alternative or additional hook selections, see Chapter 3.

Mustad: 94840, 94842   **Eagle Claw:** 59, L059, 159, L159   **Tiemco:** TMC100, TMC9300

Kamasan: B-400, B-830   **Partridge:** L2A, L3A, L3B   **Daiichi:** 1100, 1170, 1330

VMC: 9280, 9281, 9288   **Gamakatsu:** S10, P10

Typical Thorax Dry-Fly Construction

The following proportions and material options can be used when tying thorax dry-fly patterns.

Wings: Height equal to shank
Materials: Hair fibers, feather segments, or feather tips

Body: Equals shank less head
Materials: Dubbing

Hackle: Fibers equal to body length
Materials: Hackle wound in front and behind wing

Tail: Equal to body length
Materials: Hair or feather fibers

15

Irresistible and Hair Body Dry-Fly Patterns

Adams Irresistible

These patterns are designed to represent adult insects and are tied using a variety of clipped hair (deer, moose, elk, caribou, or antelope) for the body, which gives them excellent floatability.

Irresistible and hair body patterns include the Adams Irresistible, Rat Face McDougal, Blue Dun Irresistible, Wulff Irresistible, and Bomber.

Recommended Hook Sizes
All the above patterns can be tied on hook sizes 8, 10, 12, and 14.

Recommended Hook Numbers
The following are a few of the more popular hooks (by manufacturer) used for tying irresistible or hair body dry-fly patterns. For alternative or additional hook selections, see Chapter 3.

Mustad: 94840, 94842   **Eagle Claw:** 59, L059, 159, L159   **Tiemco:** TMC100, TMC9300

Kamasan: B-400, B-830   **Partridge:** L2A, L3A, L3B   **Daiichi:** 1100, 1170, 1330

VMC: 9280, 9281, 9288   **Gamakatsu:** S10, P10

Typical Irresistible and Hair Body Dry-Fly Construction
The following proportions and material options can be used when tying irresistible and hair body dry-fly patterns.

Wings: Height equal to shank
Materials: Hair fibers, feather segments, or feather tips

Body: Equals shank less head
Materials: Clipped hair (deer, moose, elk, caribou, or antelope)

Hackle: Fibers equal to body length
Materials: Hackle wound in front and behind wing

Tail: Equal to body length
Materials: Hair or feather fibers

Long- and Large-Body Dry-Fly Patterns

Henryville Special

Long- and large-body patterns are designed to represent adult insects and are tied on long shanked or larger size hooks. Most patterns are representative of stoneflies or large mayflies.

This category includes the Sofa Pillow; Hornberg Special (also considered a wet fly); Bird's Stone; Elk Hair Salmon; Yellow, Brown, or Golden Stones; and Henryville Special.

Recommended Hook Sizes

All the above patterns can be tied on hook sizes 4, 6, 8, and 10.

Recommended Hook Numbers

The following are a few of the more popular hooks (by manufacturer) used for tying long- and large-body patterns. For alternative or additional hook selections, see Chapter 3.

Mustad: 9671   **Eagle Claw:** 63   **Tiemco:** TMC2312
Kamasan: B-170   **Partridge:** L3A   **Daiichi:** 1280
VMC: 9288   **Gamakatsu:** S10

Typical Long and Large Body Dry-Fly Construction

The following proportions and material options can be used when tying long and large-body dry-fly patterns.

Wings: Length equal to shank + tail if it's included in the recipe
Materials: Hair, feather tips, or feather segments, depending on pattern recipe

Hackle: Fibers equal to hook gape
Materials: Hackles tied in collar style or full

Tail (not shown): Some patterns call for a tail, which in most cases is equal to the gape of the hook
Materials: Hackle fibers or hair

Body: Equal to shank less head
Materials: Base can be fur, dubbing, poly dubbing, or floss, palmered with a hackle
Note: Some patterns call for wire ribbing

Extended-Body Dry-Fly Patterns

Stammet Damsel

These patterns are designed to represent adult insects with long tails that extend beyond the hook (e.g., damselflies, dragonflies, mayflies).

A few examples of extended-body patterns include the Green/Brown Drake, Lawson's Paradrake, Hexagenia Paradun, and Stammet Damsel.

Recommended Hook Sizes
All the above patterns can be tied on hook sizes 8, 10, 12, 14, 16, and 18.

Recommended Hook Numbers
The following are a few of the more popular hooks (by manufacturer) used for extended-body patterns. For alternative or additional hook selections, see Chapter 3.

Mustad: 94838	**Eagle Claw:** 57	**Tiemco:** TMC2487
Kamasan: B-170	**Partridge:** E6A	**Daiichi:** 1640
VMC: 8527	**Gamakatsu:** S10	

Typical Extended-Body Dry-Fly Construction
The following proportions and material options can be used when tying extended-body dry-fly patterns.

Hackle: Fibers equal to hook gape
Materials: Rooster hackles
Note: Hackles can be tied in collar style, parachute style (horizontally), or full

Tail: Length varies, depending on pattern; most tails are equal to hook length
Materials: Clump of deer, moose, or elk hair fibers or poly yarn fibers, secured with thread to form a tight bundle

Wings: If included in the pattern, height equal to shank
Materials: Hair, feather tips, or feather segments, depending on pattern recipe

Body: Equal to shank less head
Materials: Base can be hair fibers used for tail, fur, dubbing, poly dubbing, etc.

Midge and Tiny Dry-Fly Patterns

Black Midge

Adams Midge

These patterns are designed to represent tiny adult insects floating on the water surface.

This category includes the Adams Midge, Olive Midge, Cream Midge, Brown Midge, Black Midge, Grizzly Midge, and Blue Dun Midge. It can also include other patterns such as the Black Gnat and the Mosquito.

Recommended Hook Sizes

All the above patterns can be tied on hook sizes 20, 22, 24, 26, and 28.

Recommended Hook Numbers

The following are a few of the more popular hooks (by manufacturer) used for tying midge or tiny dry-fly patterns. For alternative or additional hook selections, see Chapter 3.

Mustad: 540L   **Eagle Claw:** 59   **Tiemco:** TMC500
Kamasan: B-170   **Partridge:** K1A   **Daiichi:** 1480
VMC: 9288   **Gamakatsu:** S13S-M

Typical Midge and Tiny Dry-Fly Construction

The following proportions and material options can be used when tying midge or tiny dry-fly patterns.

Wings: Most midge patterns exclude the wing; on tiny dry-fly patterns, wing height equals shank
Materials: Hair fibers, feather segments, or feather tips

Body: Equals shank length less head
Materials: Thread, floss, dubbing, or tinsel

Hackle: Fibers equal to body length
Materials: Hackle wound in front and behind wing

Tail: Equal to body length
Materials: Hair or feather fibers

Caddis and Sedge Dry-Fly Patterns

Goddard Caddis

Sofa Pillow

These patterns are designed to represent aquatic insects, particularly large caddis or sedge flies (order Trichoptera) in their adult stage.

Caddis or sedge patterns include the Elk Hair Caddis, Bucktail Caddis, Goddard Caddis, King's River Caddis, Henryville Special, October Caddis, Dark Blue Sedge, Brown Sedge, Sofa Pillow, Stimulator, and Peacock Caddis.

Recommended Hook Sizes

Most caddis or sedge patterns can be tied on hook sizes 4, 6, 8, 10, 12, 14, 16, and 18. However, there are some exceptions, depending on the type of caddis and various pattern recipes.

Recommended Hook Numbers

The following are a few of the more popular hooks (by manufacturer) used for caddis or sedge dry-fly patterns. For alternative or additional hook selections, see Chapter 3.

Mustad: 9671	**Eagle Claw:** 59	**Tiemco:** TMC102Y
Kamasan: B-170	**Partridge:** L2A	**Daiichi:** 1170
VMC: 9288	**Gamakatsu:** S10	

Typical Caddis and Sedge Dry-Fly Construction

The following proportions and material options can be used when tying caddis dry-fly patterns.

Hackle: Fibers equal to hook gape
Materials: Hackles tied in collar style or full

Wings: Equal to body length + tail, if it's included in the recipe
Materials: Hair, feather tips, or feather segments, depending on pattern recipe

Body: Equals shank less head
Materials: Base can be fur, dubbing, poly dubbing, or floss, palmered with a hackle
Note: Some patterns call for wire ribbing

Tail: Some patterns call for a tail, which in most cases is equal to the gape of the hook
Materials: Hackle fibers or hair fibers

No-Hackle Dry-Fly Patterns

No Hackle

These patterns are exactly what the category name implies. They are insect imitations with a minimum of material dressing.

Some of the more popular no-hackle patterns include the Compara-dun, Gray, Olive, Gray/Yellow, White/Black, Rust, and Slate/Tan.

Recommended Hook Sizes

All the above patterns can be tied on hook sizes 16, 18, 20, 24, and 26.

Recommended Hook Numbers

The following are a few of the more popular hooks (by manufacturer) used for tying no-hackle dry-fly patterns. For alternative or additional hook selections, see Chapter 3.

Mustad: 94840, 94842   **Eagle Claw:** 59, L059, 159, L159   **Tiemco:** TMC100, TMC9300

Kamasan: B-400, B-830   **Partridge:** L2A, L3A, L3B   **Daiichi:** 1100, 1170, 1330

VMC: 9280, 9281, 9288   **Gamakatsu:** S10, P10

Typical No-Hackle Dry-Fly Construction

The following proportions and material options can be used when tying no-hackle dry-fly patterns.

Tail: Equal to body length
Materials: Hair or feather fibers (divided)

Wings: Height equal to shank
Materials: Mallard wing quill segments, tied in the upright position and divided

Body: Equals shank less head
Materials: Poly or fur dubbing

Wulff and Humpy Dry-Fly Patterns

Royal Wulff

Humpy
Goofus Bug

These patterns are designed to represent adult insect imitations, using hair as the wing material.

Humpys include the Royal, Red, Yellow, Orange, Black, Adams, Blue Dun, and Goofus Bug.

Wulffs include the Royal, Irresistible, White, Blonde, Gray, and Grizzly.

Recommended Hooks Sizes
All the above patterns can be tied on hook sizes 8, 10, 12, 14, 16, and 18.

Recommended Hook Numbers
The following are a few of the more popular hooks (by manufacturer) used for tying Wulff and Humpy dry-fly patterns. For alternative or additional hook selections, see Chapter 3.

Mustad: 94840, 94842   **Eagle Claw:** 59, L059, 159, L159   **Tiemco:** TMC100, TMC9300

Kamasan: B-400, B-830   **Partridge:** L2A, L3A, L3B   **Daiichi:** 1100, 1170, 1330

VMC: 9280, 9281, 9288   **Gamakatsu:** S10, P10

Typical Wulff and Humpy Dry-Fly Construction
The following proportions and material options can be used when tying Wulff and Humpy patterns.

Body: Equals shank less head
Materials: Thread, floss, dubbing, or tinsel

Tail: Equal to body length
Materials: Hair or feather fibers

Wings: Height equal to shank
Materials: Hair fibers,
formed from the tips of the hair used to make the body

Hackle: Fibers equal to body length
Materials: Hackle wound in front and behind wing

Wulff Patterns

Humpy Patterns

Wings: Height equal to shank
Materials: Hair fibers

Hackle: Fibers equal to body length
Materials: Hackle wound in front and behind wing.

Body: Equals shank less head
Materials: Dubbing or thread underbody with hair pulled over the top like a nymph wing case

Tail: 1½ times body length
Materials: Hair or feather fibers

Spider and Skater Dry-Fly Patterns

Spider Pattern

Skater Pattern

Spider and skater patterns are tied similar to a variant pattern using oversized hackles for the body. Spider patterns use long hackle fibers for the tail, while the skater pattern is tied without a tail. Spider or skater patterns are never tied with a wing, but some patterns do have fur dubbing or peacock herl underbodies.

Both spider and skater patterns with their oversized hackles are good floaters and easy to see on the water. Some examples of spider patterns include the Badger Spider, Black Spider, Blue Dun Spider, and Ginger Spider. Examples of skater patterns include the Never Sink Skater and Troth's Super Skater.

Recommended Hook Sizes

Most spider and skater patterns can be tied on hook sizes 14 and 16, using hooks made of fine wire.

Recommended Hook Numbers

The following are a few of the more popular hooks (by manufacturer) used for tying spider and skater patterns. For alternative or additional hook selections, see Chapter 3.

Mustad: 94838   **Eagle Claw:** 59   **Tiemco:** TMC100
Kamasan: B-170   **Partridge:** L2A   **Daiichi:** 1100
VMC: 9288   **Gamakatsu:** S10

Typical Spider and Skater Dry-Fly Construction

The following proportions and material options can be used when tying spider or skater patterns.

Typical Spider

Tail: 1½ times body length
Materials: Feather fibers

Typical Skater

Tail: None

Body: None

Body: Equals shank less head
Materials: Thread base with an oversized hackle palmered along the hook shank
***Note:** Some patterns call for a peacock herl or dubbing underbody*

Materials: Thread base with two oversized hackles palmered about midshank using tight wraps, with the rear hackle fibers going forward and the front hackle fibers going rear toward the bend

Compara-dun Dry-Fly Patterns

Compara-dun Pattern

The name Compara-dun was coined by Al Caucci and Bob Nastasi for a type of dry fly that uses deer hair spread fanlike on the shank at 180 degrees. This eliminates the use of a hackle to support the fly on the water. These patterns are designed to represent the first stages of a maturing winged insect.

Some examples of Compara-dun patterns include the Compara-dun Blue-Winged Olive, Compara-dun Dun Variant, Compara-dun Gray Fox, Compara-dun Green Drake, and Compara-dun Hendrickson.

Recommended Hooks Sizes
All the above patterns can be tied on hook sizes 8, 10, 12, 14, 16, and 18.

Recommended Hook Numbers
The following are a few of the more popular hooks (by manufacturer) used for tying Compara-dun patterns. For alternative or additional hook selections, see Chapter 3.

Mustad: 94840, 94842   **Eagle Claw:** 59, L059, 159, L159   **Tiemco:** TMC100, TMC9300

Kamasan: B-400, B-830   **Partridge:** L2A, L3A, L3B   **Daiichi:** 1100, 1170, 1330

VMC: 9280, 9281, 9288   **Gamakatsu:** S10, P10

Typical Compara-dun Dry-Fly Construction
The following proportions and material options can be used when tying Compara-dun patterns.

Wings: Height equal to shank
Materials: Deer-hair fibers tied on top of the shank, which fan upward and outward to form an arc or fan-shaped wing of 180 degrees

Tail: 1½ times body length
Materials: Hair or feather fibers divided and flared outward at a 45-degree angle

Body: Equals shank less head
Materials: Fur dubbing

Cut-Wing (Iwamasa) Dry-Fly Patterns

Typical Cut or Burned
Wing Pattern

These patterns, developed by Ken Iwamasa, are designed to represent a more realistic winged imitation of various adult insects. The wings are made from neck or body feathers using a wing cutting or burning tool that can be purchased in assorted sizes. Cut-wing flies are highly visible on the water, and the wing construction makes them always land in the upright position. Cut-wings can be used for traditional, quill, spinner, extended-body, midge, and no-hackle patterns.

Some of the more popular cut-wing patterns include the Western Green Drake, Mahogany Dun, Brown Drake, Pale Morning Dun, Blue-Winged Olive, Baetis Dun, Callibaetis Dun, Callibaetis Spinner, and Rusty Spinner.

Recommended Hook Sizes

Most cut patterns can be tied on the same hook sizes recommended for traditional, quill, spinner, extended-body, midge, and no-hackle patterns.

Recommended Hook Numbers

Refer to the patterns for traditional, quill, spinner, extended-body, midge, and no-hackle flies for recommended hook numbers.

Typical Cut-Wing (Iwamasa) Dry-Fly Construction

The following proportions and material options can be used when tying cut-wing dry-fly patterns based on a traditional pattern. Cut-wing patterns can also be tied the same way that quill, spinner, extended-body, midge, and no-hackle patterns are tied.

Body: Equals shank less head
Materials: Thread, floss, dubbing, or tinsel

Wings: Height equal to shank
Materials: Feather segments formed into wings using a burning tool or cut to shape

Tail: 1½ times body length
Materials: Hair or feather fibers

Hackle (optional): Fibers equal to body length.
Materials: Hackle wound in front of wing

Nymphs

Nymph patterns are designed to represent immature aquatic insects in various stages of development. Included are mayflies, caddisflies, stoneflies, black flies, and midges. Following are a few of the many categories representing nymph flies and some of the more popular patterns included in each of them.

Standard or Classic Nymph Patterns

Prince Nymph

Zug Bug

The standard or classic nymph patterns have been around for a great number of years and are considered mainstays for most fly-fishing enthusiasts. They represent a wide variety of aquatic insects, mostly mayflies or stoneflies in their nymphal stages.

Some of the more popular standard or classic nymph patterns include the Prince Nymph, Gold Rib Hare's Ear Nymph, Pheasant Tail Nymph, Beaver Nymph, Martinez, Light Cahill Nymph, March Brown Nymph, Tellico Nymph, Zug Bug, Mossback Nymph, and Casual Dress Nymph.

Recommended Hook Sizes

Most standard nymphs can be tied on hook sizes 4, 6, 8, 10, 12, 14, and 16.

Recommended Hook Numbers

The following are a few of the more popular hooks (by manufacturer) used for tying standard nymph patterns. For alternative or additional hook selections, see Chapter 3.

Mustad: 3906, 3906B, 3908, 7948A, 9672   **Eagle Claw:** 57, L057, 63, L063

Tiemco: TMC3761, TMC5210   **Kamasan:** B-170, B-400, B-830

Partridge: D4A, E1A, G3A, L2A   **Daiichi:** 1170, 1530, 1560, 1710

VMC: 8526, 8527, 9281, 9282, 9283   **Gamakatsu:** L10-2H, P10-2L1H, S10, S10-2S, S10S

Typical Standard or Classic Nymph Construction

The following proportions and material options can be used when tying standard or classic nymph patterns. These are only suggestions, however; a large variety of sizes and shapes fall into this catagory. *Note: Most nymph patterns can be weighted using lead wire prior to adding the materials listed below.*

Body: Equals shank less head, including thorax and abdomen
Materials: See thorax and abdomen

Wing Case: Equal to thorax
Materials: Feather segment or swiss straw, tied in over the top

Tail: 1 1/2 times body length
Materials: Hair or feather fibers

Legs: Equal to body length
Materials: Hackle wound around thorax

Thorax: Equal to 1/3 body length
Materials: Dubbing, chenille, yarn, etc.

Abdomen: Equal to 2/3 body length
Materials: Dubbing, chenille, stripped quill, floss, etc. *Note: Some patterns are ribbed with wire, tinsel, or floss*

Mayfly Nymph Patterns

These patterns are representative of mayflies in ther nymphal stage prior to emerging as adults. Because of the large variety of sizes and shapes that fall into the mayfly catagory, there are a vast number of patterns available.

Some of the more popular mayfly patterns include the Green Drake Nymph, Arbona Wiggle Nymph, Cate's Turkey Nymph, Gold Rib Hare's Ear Nymph, Baetis Nymph, Filoplume Mayfly Nymph, March Brown Nymph, Ostrich Nymph, and A.P. Nymph.

A.P. Mayfly Nymph

Recommended Hook Sizes
Most mayfly nymphs can be tied on hook sizes 2, 4, 6, 8, 10, and 12.

Recommended Hook Numbers
The following are a few of the more popular hooks (by manufacturer) used for tying mayfly nymph patterns. For alternative or additional hook selections, see Chapter 3.

Mustad: 3906, 3906B, 3908, 7948A, 9672
Tiemco: TMC3761, TMC5210
Partridge: D4A, E1A, G3A, L2A
VMC: 8526, 8527, 9281, 9282, 9283

Eagle Claw: 57, L057, 63, L063
Kamasan: B-170, B-400, B-830
Daiichi: 1170, 1530, 1560, 1710
Gamakatsu: L10-2H, P10-2L1H, S10, S10-2S, S10S

Typical Mayfly Nymph Construction
The following proportions and material options can be used when tying mayfly patterns. Because of the large variety of sizes and shapes that fall into the mayfly category, tiers have the option of creating their own representations using the proportions specified below. *Note: Most nymph patterns can be weighted using lead wire prior to adding the materials listed below.*

Abdomen: Equal to 2/3 body length
Materials: Dubbing, chenille, quill, floss, etc. *Note: Some patterns are ribbed with wire, tinsel, or floss*

Tail: 1½ times body length
Materials: Hair, feather fibers, rubber hackle, or biots

Body: Equals shank less head, including thorax and abdomen
Materials: See thorax and abdomen

Wing Case: Equal to thorax
Materials: Feather segment, swiss straw, tied in over the top

Thorax: Equal to 1/3 body length
Materials: Dubbing, chenille, yarn, etc.

Legs: Equal to body length
Materials: Hackle, rubber hackle, biots
Note: Hackle is palmered around the thorax, or it can also be tied in collar style

Stonefly Nymph Patterns

Kaufmann Dark Stone

Stoneflies come in a variety of sizes and shapes. Their nymph stage prior to emerging as adults takes place as a aquatic form in many rivers, lakes, and streams. Because of the large variety of stoneflies, it is very difficult to standardize their proportions.

Some of the more popular stonefly patterns include the Brooks Stone Nymph, Montana Stone Nymph, Ted's Stone Nymph, Bitch Creek Nymph, Matt's Fur Nymph, Rubber Legs Nymph, Grindle Bug Nymph, Doc Spratley Nymph, Carey Special Nymph, Kaufmann Dark Stone Nymph, and Mossbacks.

Recommended Hook Sizes

Most stonefly nymphs can be tied on hook sizes 2, 4, 6, 8, 10, and 12.

Recommended Hook Numbers

The following are a few of the more popular hooks (by manufacturer) used for tying stonefly nymph patterns. For alternative or additional hook selections, see Chapter 3.

Mustad: 3906, 3906B, 3908, 7948A, 9672

Tiemco: TMC3761, TMC5210

Partridge: D4A, E1A, G3A, L2A

VMC: 8526, 8527, 9281, 9282, 9283

Eagle Claw: 57, L057, 63, L063

Kamasan: B-170, B-400, B-830

Daiichi: 1170, 1530, 1560, 1710

Gamakatsu: L10-2H, P10-2L1H, S10, S10-2S, S10S

Typical Stonefly Nymph Construction

The following are suggested proportions and material options that can be used when tying stonefly patterns.

Abdomen: Equal to 2/3 body length
Materials: Dubbing, chenille, quill, floss, etc. *Note: Some patterns are ribbed with wire or tinsel*

Tail: 1½ times body length
Materials: Hair, feather fibers, rubber, or biots

Body: Equals shank less head, including thorax and abdomen
Materials: See thorax and abdomen

Wing Case: Equal to thorax
Materials: Feather segment, swiss straw, tied in over the top

Antennae: Equal to 1/2 body length
Materials: Hair, biots, rubber

Thorax: Equal to 1/3 body length
Materials: Dubbing, chenille, yarn, etc.

Legs: Equal to body length
Materials: Hackle, rubber, biots *Note: Hackle is wound around the thorax, or it can also be tied in collar style*

Floating or Emerger Nymph Patterns

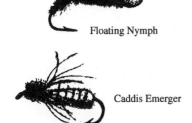

Floating Nymph

Caddis Emerger

These patterns are representative of aquatic insects emerging from their nymph stage and floating on or just below the water surface prior to becoming adults.

Some of the more popular floating nymph patterns include the Brown, Black, Gray, Yellow, and Olive Floating Nymphs.

Some of the more popular emerger nymphs are the Gray Emerger, Olive Emerger, Gray-Yellow Emerger, White-Black Emerger, and Slate-Tan Emerger.

Recommended Hook Sizes

Most floating nymphs can be tied on hook sizes 12, 14, 16, 18, and 20. Emerger patterns can be tied on hook sizes 2, 4, 6, 8, 10, and 12.

Recommended Hook Numbers

The following are a few of the more popular hooks (by manufacturer) used for tying floating nymph patterns. For alternative or additional hook selections, see Chapter 3.

Mustad: 3906, 3906B, 3908, 7948A, 9672

Tiemco: TMC3761, TMC5210

Partridge: D4A, E1A, G3A, L2A

VMC: 8526, 8527, 9281, 9282, 9283

Eagle Claw: 57, L057, 63, L063

Kamasan: B-170, B-400, B-830

Daiichi: 1170, 1530, 1560, 1710

Gamakatsu: L10-2H, P10-2L1H, S10, S10-2S, S10S

Typical Floating or Emerger Nymph Construction

The following proportions and material options can be used when tying floating or emerger nymph patterns.

Body: Equals shank less head, tapered to the rear
Materials: Fur or synthetic dubbing

Wing Bulge: Tied in behind the hook eye on top of the shank where the wing case normally appears on a nymph
Materials: Poly dubbing, tied in over the top

Thorax: Equal to 1/3 body length
Materials: Dubbing, chenille, yarn, herl, etc.

Floating

Body: Includes thorax and abdomen
Materials: See thorax and abdomen

Abdomen: Equal to 2/3 body length
Materials: Dubbing, chenille, quill, floss, etc.
Note: Some patterns are ribbed with wire, tinsel, or floss

Emerger

Legs (optional): Tied beard style not quite to the hook point
Materials: Hackle fibers

Legs: Equal to body length
Materials: Hackle, rubber, biots
Note: Hackle is tied in collar style

Caddis or Sedge Larvae/Pupae Patterns

Peeking Caddis
Pupal Stage

Larval Stage

These patterns are representative of caddis or sedge flies in their larval or pupual stages. These flies have a complete metamorphosis, and the young are known as larvae rather than nymphs. The larva builds itself a shell or house from sand, bark, or stones and lives in it until the pupal stage, at which time it grows wings. When it finishes the pupal stage, it leaves the shell, swims to the surface, and becomes an adult.

Some of the more popular larvae/pupae caddis or sedge patterns include the Micro Caddis, Laytex Caddis Pupa, Cate's Turkey Caddis, Caddis Larva, Sparkle Pupa, Diving Caddis, and Peeking Caddis.

Recommended Hook Sizes
Most larvae/pupae caddis patterns can be tied on hook sizes 2, 4, 6, 8, 10, and 12.

Recommended Hook Numbers
The following are a few of the more popular hooks (by manufacturer) used for tying larvae/pupae caddis patterns. For alternative or additional hook selections, see Chapter 3.

Mustad: 3906, 3906B, 3908, 7948A, 9672
Tiemco: TMC3761, TMC5210
Partridge: D4A, E1A, G3A, L2A
VMC: 8526, 8527, 9281, 9282, 9283

Eagle Claw: 57, L057, 63, L063
Kamasan: B-170, B-400, B-830
Daiichi: 1170, 1530, 1560, 1710
Gamakatsu: L10-2H, P10-2L1H, S10, S10-2S, S10S

Typical Caddis or Sedge Larvae or Pupae Construction
The following proportions and material options can be used when tying larvae/pupae caddis or sedge patterns. *Note: Most nymph patterns can be weighted using lead wire prior to adding the materials listed below.*

Body Case: Equals shank less head
Materials: Gray spun deer hair trimmed to shape or gray yarn covered with epoxy cement with sprinkles of sand and small, chopped up pieces of sticks, raffia, or reed material

Larval Stage

Tail (optional):
1/2 body length
Materials:
Feather fibers

Legs (optional): Equal to body length
Materials: Hackle fibers
Note: Hackle is tied in collar style

Abdomen: Equal to 2/3 body length
Materials: Dubbing, chenille, yarn, etc.
Note: Some patterns are ribbed with wire, tinsel, or floss

Pupal Stage

Legs: Equal to body length
Materials: Hackle
Note: Hackle is tied in collar style

Thorax: Equal to 1/3 body length
Materials: Dubbing, chenille, yarn, herl, etc.

Midge Nymph Patterns

Tochihara's OTR

Jenni's Caddis Nymph

These patterns are representative of midges in their larval stage. The larvae of midges live in water and are very important fish food. Many of the larvae are blood red in color.

Some of the more popular midge nymph patterns include the Midge Nymph, Sparkle Midge Pupa, Mini Midge Pupa, Bead Head Midge, and Midge.

Recommended Hook Sizes

Most midge nymph patterns can be tied on hook sizes 14, 16, 18, 20, 22, 24, and 26.

Recommended Hook Numbers

The following are a few of the more popular hooks (by manufacturer) used for tying midge nymph patterns. For alternative or additional hook selections, see Chapter 3.

Mustad: 3906, 3906B, 3908, 7948A, 9672

Tiemco: TMC3761, TMC5210

Partridge: D4A, E1A, G3A, L2A

VMC: 8526, 8527, 9281, 9282, 9283

Eagle Claw: 57, L057, 63, L063

Kamasan: B-170, B-400, B-830

Daiichi: 1170, 1530, 1560, 1710

Gamakatsu: L10-2H, P10-2L1H, S10, S10-2S, S10S

Typical Midge Nymph Construction

The following proportions and material options can be used when tying midge nymph patterns.

Thorax: Equal to 1/4 body length
Materials: Fur dubbing, chenille, yarn, hackle clipped top and bottom

Head (optional): 1/4 body length
Materials: Small glass, brass, or copper bead

Body: Equals shank less head, including thorax and abdomen
Materials: See thorax and abdomen

Abdomen: Equal to 1/2 body length
Materials: Stripped quill, floss, copper wire, stripped peacock

Tail (optional): Most patterns exclude the tail; if desired, the tail should be $1\frac{1}{2}$ times body length
Materials: Hair, feather fibers

Damselfly Nymph Patterns

These patterns are designed to represent the nymph stage of the damselfly. Damselflies lay their eggs at the base of water-growing plants, and nymphs hatch from these eggs. During this stage, the insects are eaten by a large variety of fish species, including trout, bass, and panfish.

Some of the more popular damselfly nymph patterns include the Marabou Damsel and Whit's Damsel.

Recommended Hook Sizes
Most damselfly nymph patterns can be tied on hook sizes 2, 4, 6, 8, 10, and 12.

Recommended Hook Numbers
The following are a few of the more popular hooks (by manufacturer) used for tying damselfly nymph patterns. For alternative or additional hook selections, see Chapter 3.

Mustad: 3906, 3906B, 3908, 7948A, 9672

Tiemco: TMC3761, TMC5210

Partridge: D4A, E1A, G3A, L2A

VMC: 8526, 8527, 9281, 9282, 9283

Eagle Claw: 57, L057, 63, L063

Kamasan: B-170, B-400, B-830

Daiichi: 1170, 1530, 1560, 1710

Gamakatsu: L10-2H, P10-2L1H, S10, S10-2S, S10S

Typical Damselfly Nymph Construction
The following proportions and material options can be used when tying damselfly nymph patterns. *Note: Most nymph patterns can be weighted using lead wire prior to adding the materials listed below.*

Abdomen: Equal to 2/3 body length
Materials: Dubbing, chenille, yarn, etc.
Note: Some patterns are ribbed with wire, tinsel, or floss

Body: Equals shank less head, including thorax and abdomen
Materials: See thorax and abdomen

Wing Case: Equal to thorax
Materials: Feather segment, swiss straw, tied in over the top

Eyes: Various sizes
Materials: Bead chain, lead eyes

Thorax: Equal to 1/3 body length
Materials: Dubbing, chenille, yarn, etc.

Legs: Equal to body length
Materials: Hackle, rubber, biots
Note: Hackle is palmered around the thorax, or it can also be tied in collar style

Dragonfly Nymph Patterns

These patterns are designed to represent the nymph stage of the dragonfly. Like damselflies, dragonflies also lay their eggs in water and are eaten by a large variety of fish species in both the nymph and adult stages.

Some of the more popular dragonfly nymphs include the Assam Dragon, Filoplume Dragon, Floating Dragon, Lake Dragon, Simulator, and Whit's Dragon.

Recommended Hook Sizes
Most dragonfly nymph patterns can be tied on hook sizes 2, 4, 6, 8, 10, and 12.

Recommended Hook Numbers
The following are a few of the more popular hooks (by manufacturer) used for tying dragonfly nymph patterns. For alternative or additional hook selections, see Chapter 3.

Mustad: 3906, 3906B, 3908, 7948A, 9672

Tiemco: TMC3761, TMC5210

Partridge: D4A, E1A, G3A, L2A

VMC: 8526, 8527, 9281, 9282, 9283

Eagle Claw: 57, L057, 63, L063

Kamasan: B-170, B-400, B-830

Daiichi: 1170, 1530, 1560, 1710

Gamakatsu: L10-2H, P10-2L1H, S10, S10-2S, S10S

Typical Dragonfly Nymph Construction
The following proportions and material options can be used when tying dragonfly nymph patterns. *Note: Most nymph patterns can be weighted using lead wire prior to adding the materials listed below.*

Wing Case: Equal to thorax
Materials: Feather segment, swiss straw, tied in over the top

Thorax: Equal to 1/3 body length
Materials: Dubbing, chenille, yarn, etc.

Legs: Equal to body length
Materials: Hackle, rubber, biots

Body: Equals shank less head, including thorax and abdomen
Materials: See thorax and abdomen

Tail: 1¹/₂ times body length
Materials: Hair, feather fibers, rubber, or biots

Abdomen: Equal to 2/3 body length
Materials: Dubbing, chenille, quill, floss, etc.

Mosquito Larvae Patterns

These patterns represent a mosquito larva and emerger, which are a primary source of food for many fish species. Both are found in streams, lakes, ponds, and rivers throughout the spring, summer, and fall seasons.

Patterns include the Mosquito Larva and Mosquito Emerger.

Recommended Hook Sizes

Most mosquito larvae or pupae patterns can be tied on hook sizes 14, 16, 18, and 20.

Recommended Hook Numbers

The following are a few of the more popular hooks (by manufacturer) used for tying mosquito larvae or pupae patterns. For alternative or additional hook selections, see Chapter 3.

Mustad: 9672, 9671, 94840   **Eagle Claw:** 63   **Tiemco:** TMC3761
Kamasan: B-830   **Partridge:** H1A   **Daiichi:** 1710
VMC: 8527   **Gamakatsu:** P10-2L1H

Typical Mosquito Larvae or Pupae Construction

The following proportions and material options can be used when tying mosquito larvae or pupae patterns. *Note: Most nymph patterns can be weighted using lead wire prior to adding the materials listed below.*

Wing (not shown): Emerger patterns have a short wing (1/2 shank length) tied flat over the thorax
Materials: Grizzly hackle tip

Abdomen: Equal to 2/3 body length
Materials: Stripped quill or floss
Note: Some patterns are ribbed with wire

Antennae: Equal to body length
Materials: Grizzly hackle tip

Tail: 1½ times body length
Materials: Hair, hackle fibers

Thorax: Equal to 1/3 body length
Materials: Peacock herl

Hellgrammite Nymph Patterns

These patterns are designed to imitate the nymph stage of the dobsonfly. Hellgrammites are found throughout the United States in many streams and rivers under rocks. They are a primary food source for many fish species.

Hellgrammite patterns include Whit's Hellgrammite and the Hellgrammite Nymph.

Recommended Hook Sizes

Most hellgrammite nymph patterns can be tied on hook sizes 2, 4, 6, 8, 10, and 12.

Recommended Hook Numbers

The following are a few of the more popular hooks (by manufacturer) used for tying hellgrammite nymph patterns. For alternative or additional hook selections, see Chapter 3.

Mustad: 3906, 3906B, 3908, 7948A, 9672
Tiemco: TMC3761, TMC5210
Partridge: D4A, E1A, G3A, L2A
VMC: 8526, 8527, 9281, 9282, 9283

Eagle Claw: 57, L057, 63, L063
Kamasan: B-170, B-400, B-830
Daiichi: 1170, 1530, 1560, 1710
Gamakatsu: L10-2H, P10-2L1H, S10, S10-2S, S10S

Typical Hellgrammite Nymph Construction

The following proportions and material options can be used when tying hellgrammite nymph patterns.
Note: Most nymph patterns can be weighted using lead wire prior to adding the materials listed below.

Abdomen: Equal to 2/3 body length
Materials: Dubbing, chenille, Swannundaze
Note: Some patterns are ribbed with a hackle over the Swannundaze

Tail: 1/3 or 1/2 times body length
Materials: Goose biots

Legs: 1¹/₂ times hook gape
Materials: Hackle, rubber, biots
Note: Hackle is palmered around the thorax

Wing Case: Equal to thorax
Materials: Feather segment, swiss straw, tied in over the top

Antennae: 1/3 body length
Materials: Goose biots

Thorax: Equal to 1/3 body length
Materials: Dubbing, chenille, yarn, etc.

Water Beetle Nymph Patterns

Silver Corixa

These patterns are designed to represent water beetle larvae. Included are the water boatman, back swimmer, chomper, and yellow and silver corixa beetles. The nymph stages of each of these beetles can be found in weed beds and are often eaten by a variety of fish species.

Water beetle patterns include the Silver Corixa, Yellow Corixa, Chomper, Backswimmer, and Waterboatman.

Recommended Hook Sizes

Most water beetle nymph patterns can be tied on hook sizes 10, 12, and 14.

Recommended Hook Numbers

The following are a few of the more popular hooks (by manufacturer) used for tying water beetle nymph patterns. For alternative or additional hook selections, see Chapter 3.

Mustad: 3906, 3906B, 3908, 7948A, 9672　　**Eagle Claw:** 57, L057, 63, L063

Tiemco: TMC3761, TMC5210　　**Kamasan:** B-170, B-400, B-830

Partridge: D4A, E1A, G3A, L2A　　**Daiichi:** 1170, 1530, 1560, 1710

VMC: 8526, 8527, 9281, 9282, 9283　　**Gamakatsu:** L10-2H, P10-2L1H, S10, S10-2S, S10S

Typical Water Beetle Nymph Construction

The following proportions and material options can be used when tying water beetle nymph patterns. *Note: Most nymph patterns can be weighted using lead wire prior to adding the materials listed below.*

Shellback: Equal to body
Materials: Feather segment, swiss straw, tied in over the top

Paddles (optional): Equal to 1/3 body length
Materials: Feather fibers

Body: Equals shank less head
Materials: Floss, tinsel, ostrich herl, or chenille

Legs (optional): Equal to body length
Materials: Hackle palmered around the body

All-Purpose Nymph Patterns

These patterns are designed to represent multiple insect species rather than any specific insect nymph.

All-purpose patterns include the Casual Dress, Witt's Damsels, and Fuzzy Nymphs.

Recommended Hook Sizes

Most all-purpose nymph patterns can be tied on hook sizes 2, 4, 6, 8, 10, and 12.

Recommended Hook Numbers

The following are a few of the more popular hooks (by manufacturer) used for tying all-purpose nymph patterns. For alternative or additional hook selections, see Chapter 3.

Mustad: 3906, 3906B, 3908, 7948A, 9672
Tiemco: TMC3761, TMC5210
Partridge: D4A, E1A, G3A, L2A
VMC: 8526, 8527, 9281, 9282, 9283

Eagle Claw: 57, L057, 63, L063
Kamasan: B-170, B-400, B-830
Daiichi: 1170, 1530, 1560, 1710
Gamakatsu: L10-2H, P10-2L1H, S10, S10-2S, S10S

Typical All-Purpose Nymph Construction

The following proportions and material options can be used when tying all-purpose nymph patterns. *Note: Most nymph patterns can be weighted using lead wire prior to adding the materials listed below.*

Abdomen: Equal to 2/3 body length
Materials: Dubbing, chenille, quill, floss, etc.
Note: Some patterns are ribbed with wire, tinsel, or floss

Wing Case: Equal to thorax
Materials: Feather segment, swiss straw, tied in over the top

Thorax: Equal to 1/3 body length
Materials: Dubbing, chenille, yarn, etc.

Tail: 1½ times body length
Materials: Hair, feather fibers, rubber, or biots

Legs: Equal to body length
Materials: Hackle, rubber, biots
Note: Hackle is palmered around the thorax, or it can also be tied in collar style

Wet Flies

Wet flies are designed to represent various types of aquatic insects and are fished below the water surface. Following are a few of the subcategories of wet flies, with some of the more popular patterns in each of them.

Standard or Classic Wet-Fly Patterns

Rio Grand King

These patterns have been around for many years and are considered mainstays for most fly-fishing enthusiasts.

Some of the more popular standard wet-fly patterns include the Adams, Black Gnat, Cahill, Red Carey, Coachman, Lead Wing Coachman, Royal Coachman, Hare's Ear, March Brown, McGinty, Mosquito, Professor, Renegade, and Rio Grand King.

Recommended Hook Sizes
Most standard wet-fly patterns can be tied on hook sizes 10, 12, or 14, using hooks made of regular-gauge wire.

Recommended Hook Numbers
The following are a few of the more popular hooks (by manufacturer) used for tying standard wet-fly patterns. For alternative or additional hook selections, see Chapter 3.

Mustad: 3906, 3906B, 3908, 7958	**Eagle Claw:** 57, L057, 59, L059	**Partridge:** G3A, L2A, H1A
Tiemco: TMC102, TMC3761	**Kamasan:** B-170, B-400	**Gamakatsu:** S10, S10-3F, P10
Daiichi: 1170, 1550	**VMC:** 8526, 8527, 9288	

Typical Standard Wet-Fly Construction
The following proportions and material options can be used when tying standard wet-fly patterns.

Tail: Equals body length
Materials: Hair or feather fibers

Wings: Equals hook length
Materials: Feather segments or hair fibers

Tag (optional): 3 to 4 wraps
Materials: Tinsel, mylar, or floss

Beard: Equals the distance from head to hook point
Materials: Hair or feather fibers

Body: Equals shank length less head
Materials: Thread, floss, dubbing, tinsel, herl, chenille, or yarn
Note: Can also be ribbed

42

Soft-Hackle Wet-Fly Patterns

Soft Hackle

These patterns are similar to the standard patterns, but they are sparsely dressed and tied with soft hackles such as hen, partridge, or pheasant. This type of pattern was popularized in recent years by Sylvester Nemus.

Examples of soft-hackle patterns include the Nemus Soft Hackle, Partridge and Orange Soft Hackle, Partridge and Yellow Soft Hackle, Pheasant Tail Soft Hackle, March Brown Soft Hackle, Olive Soft Hackle, and Hare's Ear Soft Hackle.

Recommended Hook Sizes

Most soft-hackle patterns can be tied on hook sizes 10, 12, or 14, using hooks made of regular-gauge wire.

Recommended Hook Numbers

The following are a few of the more popular hooks (by manufacturer) used for tying soft-hackle patterns. For alternative or additional hook selections, see Chapter 3.

Mustad: 3906, 3906B, 3908, 7958   **Eagle Claw:** 57, L057, 59, L059   **Partridge:** G3A, L2A, H1A

Tiemco: TMC102, TMC3761   **Kamasan:** B-170, B-400   **Gamakatsu:** S10, S10-3F, P10

Daiichi: 1170, 1550   **VMC:** 8526, 8527, 9288

Typical Soft-Hackle Wet-Fly Construction

The following proportions and material options can be used when tying soft-hackle wet-fly patterns.

Hackle: Fibers slightly longer than hook gape, tied in collar style
Materials: Hen hackle, partridge hackle, pheasant hackle

Body: Equals shank less head
Materials: Thread, floss, dubbing, tinsel, herl, or yarn
Note: Can also be ribbed

Woolly Worm Wet-Fly Patterns

Woolly Worm

These patterns are designed to represent almost any type of aquatic insect in the nymph stage. Because they are not considered true nymph patterns, they are grouped with the wet flies.

These are simple patterns to tie, requiring only a few pieces of chenille and a few hackle feathers. When fished, they produce an undulating, kicking, swimming motion that makes them very effective.

Woolly worm patterns are too numerous to list due to the many color and material variations.

Recommended Hook Sizes

Most woolly worm patterns can be tied on hook sizes 10, 12, or 14, using hooks made of regular-gauge wire.

Recommended Hook Numbers

The following are a few of the more popular hooks (by manufacturer) used for tying woolly worm patterns. For alternative or additional hook selections, see Chapter 3.

Mustad: 3906B   **Eagle Claw:** 57   **Tiemco:** TMC3761
Kamasan: B-170   **Partridge:** G3A   **Daiichi:** 2546
VMC: 8527   **Gamakatsu:** S10

Typical Woolly Worm Construction

The following proportions and material options can be used when tying woolly worm patterns.

Hackle: Saddle hackle with fibers twice the hook gape
Materials: Saddle hackle palmered over body

Body: Equals shank length less head
Materials: Dubbing, herl, chenille, or yarn

Tail (optional): Equals body length
Materials: Hair or feather fibers

Woolly Bugger Wet-Fly Patterns

Woolly Bugger

These patterns are similar to the woolly worm in their design, with the exception of hook size and tail, which is usually tied with marabou. They also represent the nymph stage of a variety of nonspecific aquatic insects. Because they are not considered true nymph patterns, they are grouped with the wet flies.

As with the woolly worm, there are many variations of woolly buggers. A few examples are the Flash-A-Buggers and the Brown, Olive, and Black Woolly Buggers.

Recommended Hook Sizes

Woolly bugger patterns can be tied on hook sizes 4, 6, 8, 10, and 12.

Recommended Hook Numbers

The following are a few of the more popular hooks (by manufacturer) used for tying woolly bugger patterns. For alternative or additional hook selections, see Chapter 3.

Mustad: AC80000   **Eagle Claw:** 59   **Tiemco:** TMC5210
Kamasan: B-400   **Partridge:** L2A   **Daiichi:** 1170
VMC: 9288   **Gamakatsu:** P10

Typical Woolly Bugger Construction

The following proportions and material options can be used when tying woolly bugger patterns.

Hackle: Saddle hackle with fibers slightly longer than the hook gape, palmered over the entire length of the body
Materials: Saddle hackle

Body: Equals shank length less head
Materials: Dubbing, herl, chenille, or yarn
Note: Woolly buggers are almost always tied weighted, using fine lead wire over the forward 1/3 of the hook

Tail: Equals 1½ times body length
Materials: Marabou

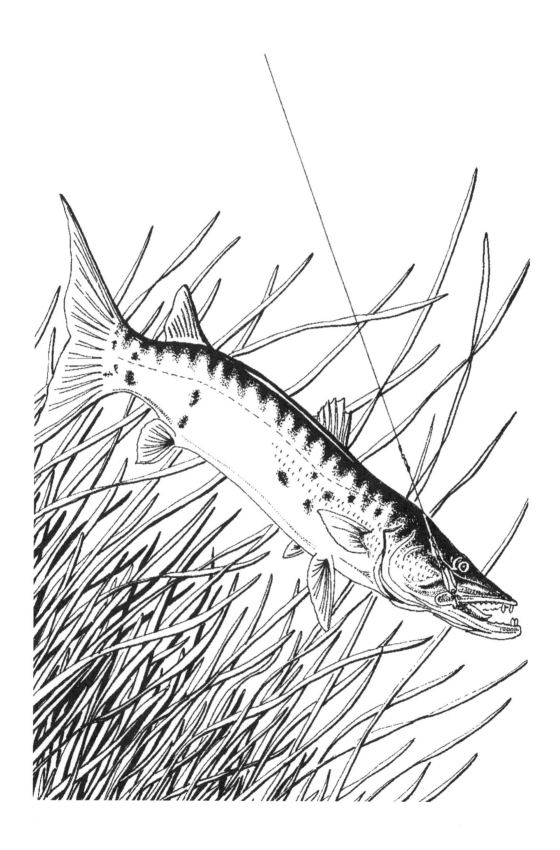

Streamers

Streamer flies are designed to represent various types of baitfish or to serve as attractors and are fished below the water surface. Following are a few of the subcategories of streamer flies and some of the more popular patterns in each of them.

Standard or Traditional Streamer Patterns

Standard or Traditional Streamer

Standard or traditional streamer patterns have been around for many years. Most of them are designed to represent baitfish. Some of the more popular standard or traditional streamers include the Black, Gray, Green, and Lady Ghosts; Supervisor; Silver Doctor; Light and Dark Edison Tiger; Light and Dark Spruce; Joe's Smelt; Nine Three; and the Royal Coachman.

Recommended Hook Sizes

Standard or traditional patterns can be tied on hook sizes 6, 8, 10, and 12, with 3X, 4X, 5X, or 6X long shanks.

Recommended Hooks

The following are a few of the more popular hooks (by manufacturer) used for tying standard or traditional streamers. For alternative or additional hook selections, see Chapter 3.

Mustad: 9575   **Eagle Claw:** 281, L281   **Tiemco:** TMC300

Kamasan: B-800   **Partridge:** CS17   **Daiichi:** 2340

VMC: 9284   **Gamakatsu:** S11-4L2H

Typical Standard or Traditional Streamer Construction

The following proportions and material options can be used when tying standard or traditional streamer patterns.

Tag (optional, not shown): 3 to 4 wraps at the hook bend
Materials: Tinsel, mylar, or floss

Tail: Equal to 1/2 body length
Materials: Hair or feather fibers

Body: Equal to shank length less head
Materials: Thread, floss, dubbing, tinsel, herl, chenille, or yarn

Rib (optional): Equally spaced wraps from the back to the front
Materials: Tinsel, mylar, or floss

Wings: Equal tail plus body length
Materials: Hackle feathers or hair fibers

Shoulder (optional, not shown): Equal to the 1/3 of the body, tied in over the wing
Materials: Pheasant or duck body feathers

Cheek (optional, not shown): Equal to 2/3 of the shoulder, tied in over the shoulder
Materials: Jungle cock

Beard: Equal to hook gape
Materials: Hair or feather fibers

Trolling Streamer Patterns

Trolling Streamer

Tandem Style

These patterns also represent baitfish or attractors and are tied basically the same way as standards or traditionals. However, they are typically tied on larger and extra long shanked hooks. *Note: They can also be tied tandem style using shorter shanked hooks.*

Trolling streamer patterns include the Big Horn Special; Black, Gray, Green, and Lady Ghosts; Supervisor; Black-Nose Dace; Little Brown; Brook and Rainbow Trout; Silver Doctor; Light and Dark Edison Tiger; Light and Dark Spruce; Joe's Smelt; Hornberg; Nine Three; and Royal Coachman.

Recommended Hook Sizes

Trolling streamers can be tied on hook sizes 6, 8, 10, and 12, with 3X, 4X, 5X, or 6X long shanks.

Recommended Hooks

The following are a few of the more popular hooks (by manufacturer) used for tying trolling streamers. For alternative or additional hook selections, see Chapter 3.

Mustad: 94720   **Eagle Claw:** 74   **Tiemco:** None
Kamasan: None   **Partridge:** CS15   **Daiichi:** J171
VMC: 9148   **Gamakatsu:** None

Typical Trolling Streamer Construction

The following proportions and material options can be used when tying trolling streamer patterns.

Tail (optional, not shown): Equal to 1/2 body length
Materials: Hair or feather fibers

Tag (optional): 3 to 4 wraps
Materials: Tinsel, mylar, or floss

Trailers (optional): Equal to length of the wing
Materials: Hair fibers

Rib (optional): Equally spaced wraps from the back to the front
Materials: Tinsel, mylar, or floss

Wings: Equal tail plus body length
Materials: Hackle feathers or hair fibers

Shoulder (optional): Equal to 1/3 of the body.
Materials: Pheasant, duck body feathers

Cheek (optional): Equal to 2/3 of the shoulder.
Materials: Jungle cock

Beard (optional): Equal to hook gape
Materials: Hair or feather fibers

Body: Equal to shank length less head
Materials: Thread, floss, dubbing, tinsel, herl, chenille, or yarn

Matuka Streamer Patterns

Matuka Streamer

Matukas are another baitfish imitation. These patterns are tied with the wing (which can be fur strips or feathers) bound to the top of the hook shank. Examples of Matukas are the Marabou Matuka, Olive Matuka, Black Matuka, Brown Matuka, Badger Matuka, Olive Matuka Sculpin, and Marabou Matuka Sculpin.

Recommended Hook Sizes

Matuka patterns can be tied on hook sizes 6, 8, 10, and 12, with 3X, 4X, 5X, or 6X long shanks.

Recommended Hook Numbers

The following are a few of the more popular hooks (by manufacturer) used for tying Matuka patterns. For alternative or additional hook selections, see Chapter 3.

Mustad: 3906B   **Eagle Claw:** 57, L057   **Tiemco:** TMC3761
Kamasan: B-170   **Partridge:** G3A   **Daiichi:** 2546
VMC: 8527   **Gamakatsu:** S10

Typical Matuka Streamer Construction

The following proportions and material options can be used when tying Matuka streamer patterns.

Wings: Equal to twice body length
Materials: Four hackle feathers or a fur strip tied down (back to front) to the top of the body with fine wire or tinsel

Rib (optional): Equally spaced wraps over the body from the back to the front
Materials: Wire, tinsel, mylar, or floss

Beard: Equal to hook gape
Materials: Hair or feather fibers

Body: Equal to shank length less head
Materials: Dubbing, chenille, or yarn

Bucktail Streamer Patterns

Bucktail Streamer

Bucktail streamers are designed to imitate baitfsh or attractors. Bucktail patterns are tied using various colored bucktail for the wings rather than hackle feathers. Some examples of the many bucktail patterns include the Mickey Finn, Black-Nose Dace, Little Brown Trout, Little Brook Trout, and Little Rainbow Trout.

Recommended Hook Sizes

Bucktail streamer patterns can be tied on hook sizes 6, 8, 10, and 12, with 3X, 4X, 5X, or 6X long shanks.

Recommended Hook Numbers

The following are a few of the more popular hooks (by manufacturer) used for tying bucktail streamer patterns. For alternative or additional hook selections, see Chapter 3.

Mustad: 9575   **Eagle Claw:** 57, L057   **Tiemco:** TMC3761
Kamasan: B-170   **Partridge:** G3A   **Daiichi:** 2546
VMC: 8527   **Gamakatsu:**S10

Typical Bucktail Streamer Construction

The following proportions and material options can be used when tying bucktail streamer patterns.

Tail (optional, not shown): Equal to 1/2 body length
Materials: Hair or feather fibers

Wings: Equal twice body length
Materials: Hair fibers (deer, squirrel, fox, etc.)

Beard (optional, not shown): Equal to hook gape
Materials: Hair or feather fibers

Tag (optional): 3 to 4 wraps of material at the end of the body or the bend of the hook
Materials: Tinsel, mylar, or floss

Rib (optional): Equally spaced wraps from the back to the front
Materials: Tinsel, mylar, or floss

Body: Equal to shank length less head
Materials: Thread, floss, dubbing, tinsel, herl, chenille, yarn, or mylar piping

Salmon and Steelhead Flies

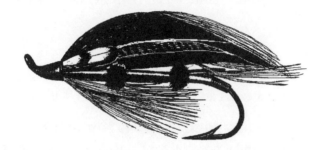

Salmon and steelhead flies are probably the most colorful flies you can tie. They are attractor patterns rather than any specific insect or baitfish imitation. Following are a few of the categories of salmon and steelhead flies.

Classic Salmon Patterns

The following patterns are by far the most beautiful flies ever designed. They require special materials (mostly unique feathers) and tying techniques and a lot of experience to be tied properly. They are most often tied for display purposes rather than actual fishing, and in many cases they become collector items.

Classic patterns (full-dress versions) include the Jock Scott, Green Highlander, Silver Doctor, Black Dose, Silver Wilkinson, Dunkeld, Thunder and Lightning, Torrish, Night Hawk, Sweep, Cosseboom, Durham Ranger, Popham, Dusty Miller, Blue Charm, Lady Amherst, and Black Prince.

Recommended Hooks Sizes
Most classic patterns can be tied on hook sizes 6/0 through 12.

Recommended Hook Numbers
The following are a few of the more popular hooks (by manufacturer) used for tying classic salmon patterns. For alternative or additional hook selections, see Chapter 3.

Mustad: 36890, 9049   **Eagle Claw:** None   **Tiemco:** TMC7999
Kamasan: B-180   **Partridge:** M, N, CS10   **Daiichi:** 2441
VMC: None   **Gamakatsu:** T10-6H

Typical Classic Salmon Fly Construction
The following proportions and material options can be used when tying classic salmon fly patterns.

Cheek: 1/2 body length
Materials: Jungle cock or equivalent

Shoulder (not shown): 1/2 body length
Materials: Feather tip

Body: Equals shank less head
Materials: Tinsel, silk, floss, etc.
Ribbing: Equally spaced wraps
Materials: Tinsel or hackle

Center Joint (optional): 1 or 2 turns of herl
Materials: Peacock or ostrich herl

Horns (optional): Equal to body plus tail
Materials: Macaw feather

Hackle (Beard): Equal to body length
Materials: Hackle tied beard style
Butt: 1 or 2 turns of herl
Materials: Peacock or ostrich herl

Topping: Equal to wing, to tip of tail
Materials: Golden pheasant crest

Wings: Equal to shank plus tail
Materials: Various feather segments

Tail: 1/2 body length
Materials: Feather fibers
Tail Topping: 1/2 tail length
Materials: Feather fibers

Tag: 3 to 4 close wraps of material
Materials: Tinsel, wire, or Flashabou

Tip: Twice length of tag
Materials: Floss, silk, or tinsel

Standard Salmon and Steelhead Patterns

Green Butt Skunk

These patterns are the most recent designs for both salmon and steelheads.

Standard patterns include the Boss Series (Black/Yellow/Red/Purple), Comet Series (Silver/Orange), Babine Special, Rusty Squirrel Optic, Orange Demon, Polar Shrimp, Cowichan, Karluk Flash, Coho Streamer, Chinook Special, Wiggle Tail, Fall Favorite, Thor, Skunk, Brindle Bug, Silver Hilton, McCleod Ugly, Butterfly, Skykomish Sunrise, and Purple Peril.

Recommended Hooks Sizes
Most standard patterns can be tied on hook sizes 6/0 through 12.

Recommended Hook Numbers
The following are a few of the more popular hooks (by manufacturer) used for tying standard salmon or steelhead patterns. For alternative or additional hook selections, see Chapter 3.

Mustad: 36890, 9049	**Eagle Claw:** None	**Tiemco:** TMC7999
Kamasan: B-180	**Partridge:** M, N, CS10	**Daiichi:** 2441
VMC: None	**Gamakatsu:** T10-6H	

Typical Standard Salmon Fly Construction
The following proportions and material options can be used when tying standard salmon and steelhead fly patterns. Due to the large number of patterns and material variations, the following are basic suggestions.

Wings: Equal to shank plus tail
Materials: Hair fibers or feather segments

Hackle: Equal to body length
Materials: Hackle tied in beard style

Body: Equals shank less head
Materials: Chenille, yarn, or tinsel

Ribbing: Equally spaced wraps
Materials: Tinsel, hackle

Tail (optional): 1½ times body length
Materials: Hair or feather fibers

Tag (not shown): 3 to 4 close wraps of material.
Materials: Tinsel, wire, or Flashabou

Tip (not shown): Twice the length of the tag
Materials: Floss, silk, or tinsel

Butt (optional): 1 or 2 turns of selected material
Materials: Peacock or ostrich herl, chenille

Hairwing Salmon and Steelhead Patterns

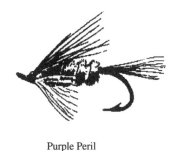

Purple Peril

Hairwing patterns are tied with bucktail or other types of hair rather than feathers and in many cases are simplified versions of the classics.

Hairwing patterns include the Jock Scott, Green Highlander, Silver Doctor, Black Dose, Silver Wilkinson, Dunkeld, Thunder and Lightning, Torrish, Night Hawk, Sweep, Cosseboom, Durham Ranger, Popham, Blue Charm, Lady Amherst, Rusty Rat, Green Butt Skunk, Skykomish Sunrise, Umpqua Special, Thor, Fright Train, Polar Shrimp, Black Prince, Fall Favorite, and Brad's Brat.

Recommended Hooks Sizes

Most hairwing patterns can be tied on hook sizes 6/0 through 12.

Recommended Hook Numbers

The following are a few of the more popular hooks (by manufacturer) used for tying hairwing salmon or steelhead patterns. For alternative or additional hook selections, see Chapter 3.

Mustad: 36890, 9049	**Eagle Claw:** None	**Tiemco:** TMC7999
Kamasan: B-180	**Partridge:** M, N, CS10	**Daiichi:** 2441
VMC: None	**Gamakatsu:** T10-6H	

Typical Hairwing Construction

The following proportions and material options can be used when tying hairwing salmon or steelhead fly patterns.

Tag (not shown): 3 to 4 close wraps of material prior to tying in the tail
Materials: Tinsel, wire, Flashabou

Wing: Equal to the hook bend
Note: Some patterns include the tail
Materials: Hair fibers

Tail (optional): 1 1/2 times body length
Materials: Hair or feather fibers

Tip (not shown): Twice the length of the tag and tied in after the tail
Materials: Floss, silk, or tinsel

Hackle: Equal to body length
Materials: Hackle tied in beard or collar style

Body: Equals shank less head
Materials: Chenille, yarn, or tinsel

Ribbing: Equally spaced wraps
Materials: Tinsel or hackle

Low-Water Salmon and Steelhead Patterns

These patterns are sparsely dressed versions of the classics or hairwings.

Low-water patterns include the Jock Scott, Green Highlander, Silver Doctor, Black Dose, Silver Wilkinson, Dunkeld, Thunder and Lightning, Torrish, Night Hawk, Sweep, Cosseboom, Durham Ranger, Popham, Blue Charm, Lady Amherst, Rusty Rat, Green Butt Skunk, Skykomish Sunrise, Umpqua Special, Thor, Fright Train, Polar Shrimp, Black Prince, Fall Favorite, Brad's Brat, Purple Peril, and Coho Streamer.

Recommended Hooks Sizes

Most low-water patterns can be tied on hook sizes 6/0 through 12.

Recommended Hook Numbers

The following are a few of the more popular hooks (by manufacturer) used for tying low-water salmon or steelhead patterns. For alternative or additional hook selections, see Chapter 3.

Mustad: 36890, 9049
Kamasan: B-180
VMC: None

Eagle Claw: None
Partridge: M, N, CS10
Gamakatsu: T10-6H

Tiemco: TMC7999
Daiichi: 2441

Typical Low-Water Construction

The following proportions and material options can be used when tying low-water salmon or steelhead fly patterns.

Tag (not shown): 3 to 4 close wraps of material
Materials: Tinsel, wire, or Flashabou
Tail: Length extends to the hook bend
Materials: Hair or feather fibers
Tip (not shown): Twice the length of the tag
Materials: Floss, silk, or tinsel

Wings: Equal to shank
Materials: Hair fibers, formed from the tips of the hair used to make the body

Cheek: 1/2 times body length
Materials: Jungle cock or equivalent

Hackle (Beard): Equal to body length
Materials: Hackle wound in front and behind wing

Ribbing: Equally spaced wraps
Materials: Tinsel or hackle

Body: Equals 2/3 shank less head
Materials: Chenille, yarn, or tinsel

Double-Hook Salmon and Steelhead Patterns

These patterns can be dressed the same as most hairwing versions.

Double-hook patterns can be tied to represent the Jock Scott, Green Highlander, Silver Doctor, Black Dose, Silver Wilkinson, Dunkeld, Thunder and Lightning, Torrish, Night Hawk, Sweep, Cosseboom, Durham Ranger, Popham, Blue Charm, Lady Amherst, Rusty Rat, Green Butt Skunk, Skykomish Sunrise, Umpqua Special, Thor, Fright Train, Polar Shrimp, Black Prince, Fall Favorite, Brad's Brat, Purple Peril, and Coho Streamer.

Recommended Hook Sizes

Most double-hook patterns can be tied on hook sizes ranging from #2 through #12.

Recommended Hook Numbers

The following are a few of the more popular hooks (by manufacturer) used for tying double-hook salmon or steelhead patterns. For alternative or additional hook selections, see Chapter 3.

Mustad: 3582, 3582C, 3582F	**Eagle Claw:** None	**Tiemco:** None
Kamasan: None	**Partridge:** R1A, R2A, R3HF, P, Q, 02	**Daiichi:** 7131
VMC: None	**Gamakatsu:** None	

Typical Double-Hook Construction

The following proportions and material options can be used when tying double-hook salmon or steelhead fly patterns.

Wing: Equal to hook bend
Materials: Hair fibers

Tail (optional): 1$\frac{1}{2}$ times body length
Materials: Hair or feather fibers

Tip (not shown): Twice the length of the tag and tied in after the tail
Materials: Floss, silk, or tinsel

Ribbing: Equally spaced wraps
Materials: Tinsel or hackle

Body: Equals shank less head
Materials: Chenille, yarn, or tinsel

Hackle: Equal to body length
Materials: Hackle tied in beard or collar style

Tag: 3 to 4 close wraps of material prior to tying in the tail
Materials: Tinsel, wire, or Flashabou

Tube Fly Salmon and Steelhead Patterns

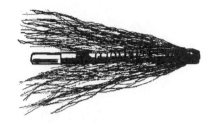

Tube flies can be dressed the same as most hairwing or standard patterns using a variety of materials.

This type of fly doesn't use a hook. The material is tied onto a tube rather than a hook shank. The finished fly is fished by slipping it onto the leader or line and tying on a double or triple hook behind the tube.

The tubes used to tie these patterns can be small-diameter plastic straws, the hollow plastic stems of cotton swabs, or plastic tubes made specifically for tube fly patterns sold through catalogs or local fly shops. Tube flies have become very popular in recent years, and a number of manufacturers have developed tube fly adapter jaws for vises to secure the tubing.

As mentioned earlier, tube flies can be dressed using a multitude of materials. They can also be tied using a standard vise by inserting a nail through the tubing and grasping the tubing and nail with the vise jaws. When using this technique, be careful about the amount of tension applied to the thread when tying on the material, so as not to collapse the tubing around the nail.

Typical Tube Fly Construction

The following proportions and material options can be used when tying tube fly salmon or steelhead fly patterns.

Wing: Equal to tube length
Materials: Hair fibers, feathers, or synthetic materials

Tube: Small diameter
Materials: Plastic or aluminum

Tag: 3 to 4 close wraps of material
Materials: Tinsel, wire, or Flashabou

Tip (not shown): Twice the length of the tag
Materials: Floss, silk, or tinsel

Tail: None

Hackle (not shown): Equal to 1/2 body length
Materials: Hackle tied in collar style

Head: Thread

Body: 1/4-inch short of tube length, excluding head
Materials: Chenille, yarn, or tinsel

Ribbing: Equally spaced wraps over the body
Materials: Tinsel or hackle

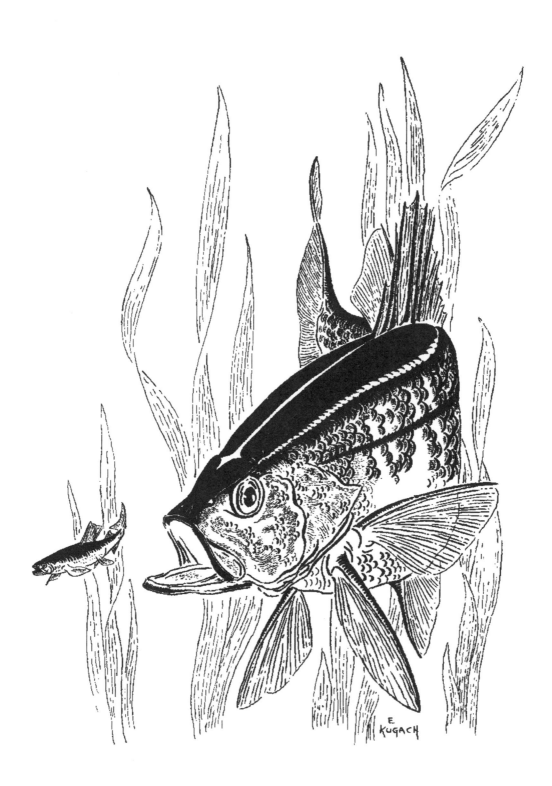

Bass Flies and Lures

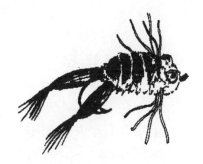

Bass flies and lures are designed to represent an assortment of creatures (fish, frogs, birds, insects, crustaceans, leeches) in both the largemouth and smallmouth bass food chain. Following are a few of the subcategories of bass flies and lures and some of the patterns in each of them.

Hair Patterns

Whit's Mouse Rat

Wiggle Legs Frog

Hair patterns are designed to represent a wide varity of creatures, including such things as frogs, snakes, mice, rats, and most anything else you can think of. The basic material used to create most of them is spun deer hair, and in most cases, the patterns are fished on the water surface.

Examples of hair patterns include the Snakey, Whit's Hair Bug, Whit's Mouse Rat, Wiggle Legs Frog, Dahlberg's Frog, Whit's Near-Nuff Frog, Kicker Frog, Dahlberg's Slider, Sneaky Slider, Hair Poppers, and Hair Mouse.

Recommended Hook Sizes
Most bass hair fly patterns can be tied on hook sizes 5/0, 3/0, 1/0, 2, 6, and 10.

Recommended Hook Numbers
The following are a few of the more popular hooks (by manufacturer) used for tying hair patterns. For alternative or additional hook selections, see Chapter 3.

Mustad: 37187	**Eagle Claw:** None	**Tiemco:** None
Kamasan: None	**Partridge:** None	**Daiichi:** 2720
VMC: None	**Gamakatsu:** None	

Typical Hair Fly Construction
There are many variations in the construction of hair patterns. This is only one example of the many proportions and material options that can be used.

Tail: Equal to hook shank
Materials: Hair fibers, feathers, or rubber hackle

Body: Equal to hook shank
Materials: Spun hair fibers (deer, antelope, caribou, elk, etc.) trimmed to shape

Note: Underside of body should be trimmed close to hook shank

Diver Patterns

This type of pattern was designed (by Larry Dahlberg) to dive when retrieved with a quick line pull. The basic material in the body construction is spun deer hair. The hair is shaped in such a fashion that it causes the diving effect, forcing the pattern to submerge below the water surface.

Diver patterns include the Purple Dahlberg Diver; Black Dahlberg Diver; Frog Dahlberg Diver; and Black, Yellow, White, or Olive Rabbit Strip Divers.

Recommended Hook Sizes

Most diver fly patterns can be tied on hook sizes 5/0, 3/0, 1/0, 2, 6, and 10.

Recommended Hook Numbers

The following are a few of the more popular hooks (by manufacturer) used for tying diver patterns. For alternative or additional hook selections, see Chapter 3.

Mustad: 37187	**Eagle Claw:** None	**Tiemco:** None
Kamasan: None	**Partridge:** None	**Daiichi:** 2720
VMC: None	**Gamakatsu:** None	

Typical Diver Construction

The following proportions and material options can be used when tying diver patterns.

Wings: Equal to body + tail
Overwing Material: Hair fibers
Underwing Material: Hair fibers

Collar: Equal to 1/4 of hook shank
Materials: Spun hair fibers (deer, antelope, caribou, elk, etc.) trimmed to shape

Head: Equal to 1/4 of hook shank
Materials: Spun hair fibers (deer, antelope, caribou, elk, etc.) trimmed to shape

Trailers: Twice the wing length
Materials: Krystal Flash, tinsel, Flashabou, etc.

Tail: Equal to the hook length
Materials: Hair fibers, feathers, rubber hackle

Body: Equal to 1/2 of hook shank
Materials: Dubbing, chenille, tinsel, yarn, etc.

Keel Hook Patterns

These patterns are tied on Keel Hooks using an assortment of materials. Keel Hook patterns include the Yellow, Green, or Natural Keel Bug; Frog Keel Popper, Bee Keel Popper, Black Keel Popper, Pearl Keel Popper, and Chartreuse Keel Popper.

Recommended Hook Sizes
Most Keel Hook patterns can be tied on hook sizes 6, 8, 10, and 12.

Recommended Hook Numbers
The following are a few of the more popular hooks (by manufacturer) used for tying Keel Hook patterns. For alternative or additional hook selections, see Chapter 3.

Mustad: 38972, 79666   **Eagle Claw:** None   **Tiemco:** None
Kamasan: None   **Partridge:** None   **Daiichi:** None
VMC: None   **Gamakatsu:** None

Typical Keel Hook Construction
The following proportions and material options can be used when tying Keel Hook patterns.

Wings: Equal to hook length
Materials: Hair fibers

Hackle: Tied in front of tail
Materials: Feather collared back or spun deer hair collared back

Head: Equal to horizontal front portion of hook shank
Materials: Spun hair fibers trimmed to shape, wool, etc.

Body: Equal to 1/2 of hook shank; can be weighted with lead wire
Materials: Dubbing, chenille, tinsel, yarn, etc. over the optional lead wire

Ribbing: Equally spaced over body
Materials: Tinsel

Tail: Equal to hook length
Materials: Saddle hackles

Popper Patterns

These patterns are exactly what the category name implies. They are surface patterns that create a popping noise when retrieved in a quick, jerking fashion because of the body's shape. The bodies of these patterns can be constructed using spun deer hair, cork, balsa wood, old sandals, or Styrofoam.

Popper patterns include the Sneaky Pete, Peeper Popper, Bass Buster, Pencil Popper, Keel Poppers (see Keel Hook Patterns), Shoe Fly Poppers, and Hair Poppers.

Recommended Hook Sizes

Most popper patterns are tied on hook sizes 6, 8, 10, and 12, with 3X, 4X, 5X, or 6X long shanks. However, larger ones such as the Pencil Popper require sizes 3/0, 1/0, or 2–4, with long shanks.

Recommended Hook Numbers

The following are a few of the more popular hooks (by manufacturer) used for tying popper patterns. For alternative or additional hook selections, see Chapter 3.

Mustad: 32669CT, 33900, 33903, 37190   **Eagle Claw:** L200   **Tiemco:** TMC511S
Kamasan: None   **Partridge:** None   **Daiichi:** None
VMC: 8527   **Gamakatsu:** None

Typical Popper Construction

The following proportions and material options can be used when tying popper patterns.

Tail: Equal to hook length
Materials: Saddle hackles

Hackle: Tied in front of tail
Materials: Feather collared back

Head: Size depends on hook type
Materials: Cork or closed-cell foam (sandal plug)

Eyes: Size depends on head size
Materials: Movable doll eyes, Styrofoam eyes, or painted eyes

Lure Patterns

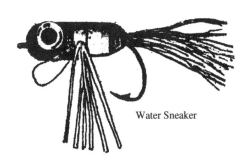
Water Sneaker

These patterns are a category in themselves. Many of these patterns are a combination of hair, fur strips, feathers, and other materials. Some of them represent specific creatures, while others are nondescriptive.

Lure patterns include the Water Sneaker, Calcasien Pig Boat, Wobbler Fly, Edge Water Wiggle Bug, Widow Maker, and Prismatic Shad.

Recommended Hook Sizes

Most lure patterns can be tied on hook sizes 6, 8, 10, and 12, with 3X, 4X, 5X, or 6X long shanks.

Recommended Hook Numbers

The following are a few of the more popular hooks (by manufacturer) used for tying lure patterns. For alternative or additional hook selections, see Chapter 3.

Mustad: 37187	**Eagle Claw:** 57	**Tiemco:** TMC3761
Kamasan: B-170	**Partridge:** G3A	**Daiichi:** 2546
VMC: 8527	**Gamakatsu:** S10	

Typical Lure Construction

There are many variations in the construction of lure patterns. This is only one example of the proportions and material options that can be used.

Eyes: 7mm
Materials: Movable doll eyes, Styrofoam eyes, or painted eyes

Body: 3/8-inch diameter sandal plug (rounded at both ends), multicolored
Materials: Cork or closed-cell foam (sandal plug)

Lip: Length and shape variable (tier's choice)
Materials: Clear plastic

Legs: Equal to body length, pushed through the body with a needle
Materials: Green and white rubber hackles

Tail: Equal to hook length
Materials: Green and white rubber hackles, silver and blue Flashabou strands

Standard Bass Fly Patterns

These patterns are large wet flies and streamers designed specifically for bass fishing.

Bass fly patterns include the Olive Bunny Bugger, Yellow or Black Moth Bug, and Gold or Pearl Flash Dancer.

Recommended Hook Sizes

Most bass fly patterns can be tied on hook sizes 6, 8, 10, and 12, with 3X, 4X, 5X, or 6X long shanks.

Recommended Hook Numbers

The following are a few of the more popular hooks (by manufacturer) used for tying bass fly patterns. For alternative or additional hook selections, see Chapter 3.

Mustad: 3906B	**Eagle Claw:** 57	**Tiemco:** TMC3761
Kamasan: B-170	**Partridge:** G3A	**Daiichi:** 2546
VMC: 8527	**Gamakatsu:** S10	

Typical Standard Bass Fly Construction

The following proportions and material options can be used when tying bass fly patterns.

Wings: Equal to hook length
Materials: Feather segments or feather tips

Body: Equals shank length less head
Materials: Thread, floss, dubbing, tinsel, herl, chenille, or yarn
Note: Can also be ribbed

Tail: Equal to 1/2 the body length
Materials: Feather fibers or segments

Beard: Equals about 1/2 body length
Materials: Feather fibers or hackle collared back

Ribbing: Equally spaced wraps over the body
Materials: Tinsel or mylar

Baitfish Flies

B aitfish patterns are designed to represent various types of minnows, muddlers, and sculpin, as well as young fish fry found in ponds, lakes, streams, and rivers. Following are a few of many subcategories of baitfish, with some of the more popular patterns in each of them.

Muddler Patterns

Muddler Minnow

These patterns are designed to represent a variety of minnows found throughout the world in various streams, lakes, and rivers. The original muddler was designed by Don Gapen and became a standard for fly tiers and fishermen throughout the world. Muddler patterns can be tied in assorted color patterns and variations.

Muddler patterns include the Muddler Minnow Black, Golden, Green, Orange, White, and Yellow.

Recommended Hook Sizes
Most muddler patterns can be tied on hook sizes 2 to 14.

Recommended Hook Numbers
The following are a few of the more popular hooks (by manufacturer) used for tying muddler patterns. For alternative or additional hook selections, see Chapter 3.

Mustad: 9672, 38941, 79580   **Eagle Claw:** 63, L063, 58, L058   **Tiemco:** TMC5263
Kamasan: B-830   **Partridge:** H1A   **Daiichi:** 1720
VMC: 9283   **Gamakatsu:** P19-2L1H

Typical Muddler Construction
There are many variations in the construction of muddler patterns. The following is only one example of the proportions and material options that can be used.

Tail: Length equal to hook gape, or slightly shorter
Materials: Mottled turkey wing quill segment

Body: Rear 2/3 of hook shank wrapped with material
Materials: Tinsel
Note: Body can be weighted with lead wire prior to wrapping if desired

Underwing: Body length + tail
Wing: Body length + tail
Materials:
Underwing—Squirrel or calf tail
Overwing—Paired sections of speckled turkey quill segments tied on edge

Head: Spun hair, trimmed to shape
Materials: Deer, caribou, elk, or wool

Collar: Equal to body
Materials: Spun hair fibers

Sculpin Patterns

These patterns are designed to represent freshwater sculpins found throughout rivers, lakes, and streams. They are an important forage for game fish, particularly trout and smallmouth bass.

There are about 129 species that occur in the United States and Canada. Sculpin patterns can be tied in assorted color patterns and variations.

Sculpin patterns include the Whitlocks Sculpin, Marabou Matuka Sculpin, and Wool Head Sculpin.

Recommended Hook Sizes
Most sculpin patterns can be tied on the hook sizes 1/0 to 8.

Recommended Hook Numbers
The following are a few of the more popular hooks (by manufacturer) used for tying sculpin patterns. For alternative or additional hook selections, see Chapter 3.

Mustad: 7979, 9672   **Eagle Claw:** 57   **Tiemco:** TMC5263
Kamasan: B-170   **Partridge:** H1A, J1A   **Daiichi:** 1720
VMC: 9283   **Gamakatsu:** P19-2L1H

Typical Sculpin Construction
The following proportions and material options can be used when tying sculpin patterns.

Wings: Twice hook length tied Matuka style
Materials: Feathers or feather tips, fur strips

Collar: Spun hair fibers
Materials: Deer, elk, caribou

Head: Equal to 1/3 body length
Materials: Spun hair fibers or wool trimmed to shape

Eyes: Optional
Materials: Movable doll eyes glued on each side of head

Body: Wrap 2/3 of the hook shank with red dubbed throat
Materials: Dubbing, chenille, or yarn
Note: Body can also be weighted with lead wire
Ribbing: Equally spaced wraps over body
Materials: Tinsel or mylar

Cheeks: Curved out feather on each side shank
Materials: Breast feather from hen pheasant or duck

Thunder Creek Patterns

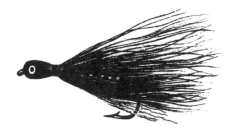

Originally designed by Keith C. Fulsher to represent various members of the minnow family, Thunder Creek patterns can also be tied to represent young trout fry.

Thunder Creek patterns include the Black-Nose Dace, Golden Shiner, Red Fin Shiner, Emerald Minnow, Spot-Tailed Minnow, Smelt, Brown Trout, Rainbow Trout, and Brook Trout.

Recommended Hook Sizes

Thunder Creek patterns can be tied on hook sizes 2 to 10.

Recommended Hook Numbers

The following are a few of the more popular hooks (by manufacturer) used for tying Thunder Creek patterns. For alternative or additional hook selections, see Chapter 3.

Mustad: 36620, 79580   **Eagle Claw:** 74   **Tiemco:** TMC300

Kamasan: B-800   **Partridge:** CS17, D4A   **Daiichi:** J171

VMC: 9283   **Gamakatsu:** S11-4L3H

Typical Thunder Creek Construction

There are many variations in the construction of Thunder Creek patterns. The following is only one example of the proportions and material options that can be used.

Eyes: 7mm or smaller (assorted colors)
Materials: Movable doll eyes, Styrofoam eyes, or painted eyes

Head and Wing: Bucktail hair fibers in assorted colors tied in as separate bunches behind the hook eye at the butt ends, with the tips going forward over the hook eye, then pulled over the shank and secured about 1/4 to 3/8 inch behind the hook eye with a band of thread
Materials: Bucktail fibers (assorted colors)

Body: Hook shank covered to within 1/4 or 3/8 inch behind hook eye
Materials: Tinsel

Zonker Patterns

This type of pattern is a streamer lure designed to represent almost any baitfish. It works well for all trout, salmon, and smallmouth and largemouth bass. It can be tied in various sizes and color combinations.

Zonker patterns include the White Zonker, Yellow Zonker, Black Zonker, and Green Zonker.

Recommended Hook Sizes

Most Zonker patterns can be tied on hook sizes 2 to 6, with 3X, 4X, 5X, or 6X long shanks.

Recommended Hook Numbers

The following are a few of the more popular hooks (by manufacturer) used for tying Zonker patterns. For alternative or additional hook selections, see Chapter 3.

Mustad: 9674, 79580, AC79580   **Eagle Claw:** 58, L058, 281, L281   **Tiemco:** TMC300, TMC5263
Kamasan: B-800   **Partridge:** D4A   **Daiichi:** 2220
VMC: 9283   **Gamakatsu:** S11-4L2H

Typical Zonker Construction

The following proportions and material options can be used when tying Zonker patterns.

Eye: 7mm or smaller
Materials: Movable doll eyes

Wings: Twice the length of the body, tied in at the bend and behind the hook eye
Materials: Rabbit fur strip tied in over the top of the body

Rear Tie-in Point: Thread band
Materials: Thread

Head: Oversize
Materials: Thread

Underbody (optional): Aluminum strip or Zonker Tape folded over the shank and cut to shape
Body: Equals shank length less head
Materials: Mylar tubing slipped over the hook shank and tied in at the hook bend and behind the hook eye

Minnow Patterns

These patterns are designed to represent a multitude of minnows found in lakes, ponds, streams, and rivers. Many of these patterns are a combination of fur, feathers, and other materials. Some of them represent specific minnows, while others are nondescript.

Minnow patterns include the Jenssen Minnow Series, Floating Minnow, George Cik's Minnow, Mylar Fingerling, and Transparent Minnow.

Recommended Hook Sizes

Most minnow patterns can be tied on hook sizes 2 to 6, with 3X, 4X, 5X, or 6X long shanks.

Recommended Hook Numbers

The following are a few of the more popular hooks (by manufacturer) used for tying minnow patterns. For alternative or additional hook selections, see Chapter 3.

Mustad: 9674, 79580, AC79580   **Eagle Claw:** 58, L058, 281, L281   **Tiemco:** TMC300, TMC5263
Kamasan: B-800   **Partridge:** D4A   **Daiichi:** 2220
VMC: 9283   **Gamakatsu:** S11-4L2H

Typical Minnow Construction

There are many variations in the construction of minnow patterns. The following is only one example of the proportions and material options that can be used.

Markings: Colors to match minnow
Materials: Permanent colored markers

Underbody (optional): Aluminum strip or Zonker Tape folded over the shank and cut to shape
Body: Equals shank length
Materials: Mylar tubing slipped over the hook shank and tied in at the hook bend and behind the hook eye

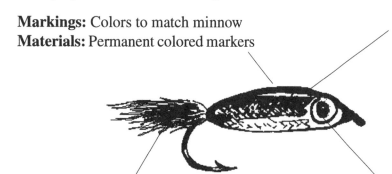

Tail: Equal to hook shank length
Materials: Rubber hackles, Flashabou strands, feather tips, marabou, etc.

Eyes: 7mm
Materials: Movable doll eyes, Styrofoam eyes, or painted eyes

Terrestrial Flies

Terrestrial patterns are designed to represent various types of land insects and are most often fished on the water surface. Following are a few of the subcategories representing terrestrial patterns, with some of the more popular representations in each of them.

Ant Patterns

Typical ant patterns represent flying ants or wingless ants that have fallen into the water and are floating on the surface. Ant patterns are excellent producers and are one of the simpler patterns to tie.

Some of the more popular ant patterns include the Red, Brown, or Black Flying Ant; Black or Rusty Fur Ant; McMurray Ant; Foam Ant; and Red or Black Hard Shell Ant.

Recommended Hook Sizes

Ant patterns can be tied on hook sizes 14, 16, 18, or 20, using hooks made of regular or fine-gauge wire.

Recommended Hook Numbers

The following are a few of the more popular hooks (by manufacturer) used for tying ant patterns. For alternative or additional hook selections, see Chapter 3.

Mustad: 94840, 94842	**Eagle Claw:** 59, L059	**Tiemco:** TMC5210
Kamasan: B-400	**Partridge:** L2A	**Daiichi:** 1170
VMC: 9288	**Gamakatsu:** P10	

Typical Ant Construction

There are many variations in the construction of ant patterns. The following are examples of the proportions and material options that can be used when tying the three different types of ant patterns.

Hackle (Legs): Equal to body length, wound in at the body separation
Materials: Saddle hackle

Wingless Ant

Wings: Equal to hook or body length (extending just beyond the hook bend), tied in flat or spread at the body separation, behind the hackle
Materials: Feather segments or feather tips

Winged Ant

Body: Equal to shank length, tied in two sections that are separated with a wound hackle near or at the center of the body
Materials: Thread, floss, dubbing, herl, chenille, foam, yarn, or McMurray body

Hackle (Legs): Equal to body length, wound in at the body separation
Materials: Saddle hackle

McMurray Ant

Cricket Patterns

These patterns represent crickets that have jumped or fallen into the water and are floating or swimming on the surface. Cricket patterns are excellent producers during the summer season for trout, bass, and panfish.

Some of the more popular cricket patterns include the Letort Cricket, Dave's Cricket, and Field Cricket.

Recommended Hook Sizes

Cricket patterns can be tied on hook sizes 8, 10, and 12, using hooks made of regular or fine-gauge wire.

Recommended Hook Numbers

The following are a few of the more popular hooks (by manufacturer) used for tying cricket patterns. For alternative or additional hook selections, see Chapter 3.

Mustad: 9671	**Eagle Claw:** 63, L063	**Tiemco:** TMC5263
Kamasan: B-830	**Partridge:** H1A	**Daiichi:** 1720
VMC: 9282	**Gamakatsu:** P10	

Typical Cricket Construction

The following proportions and material options can be used when tying cricket patterns.

Wings: Equal to hook or body length (extending just beyond the hook bend)
Materials: Turkey feather segment or goose quill segment cut to shape, laquered, and tied in flat over the body.
Note: Wing segments can be black, brown, or mottled, depending on the type of cricket

Collar (optional): Equal to 2/3 shank length
Materials: Spun deer, elk, or antelope hair tips, used to form the head

Head: Equal to 1/3 shank length
Materials: Spun deer, elk, or antelope hair, clipped to shape

Legs (optional): Equal to twice body length, knotted at the center
Materials: Rubber hackle, hackle segments, deer hair, or hackle quills cut to shape

Body: Equal to 2/3 shank length
Materials: Dubbing, herl, chenille, foam, or yarn
Note: Can also be plamered with a hackle and then clipped; some patterns call for a tail, which can be hair or hackle fibers

Grasshopper Patterns

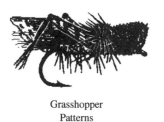

Grasshopper
Patterns

These patterns represent grasshoppers that have jumped or fallen into the water and are floating or swimming on the surface. Grasshopper patterns are excellent producers during the summer season for trout, bass, and panfish.

Some of the more popular grasshopper patterns include the Letort Hopper, Dave's Hopper, Henry's Fork Hopper, Parachute Hopper, and Grasshopper.

Recommended Hook Sizes

Grasshopper patterns can be tied on hook sizes 8, 10, 12, and 14, using hooks made of regular or fine-gauge wire.

Recommended Hook Numbers

The following are a few of the more popular hooks (by manufacturer) used for tying grasshopper patterns. For alternative or additional hook selections, see Chapter 3.

Mustad: 94831, 94840   **Eagle Claw:** 59, L059   **Tiemco:** TMC5210

Kamasan: B-400   **Partridge:** L2A   **Daiichi:** 1170

VMC: 9288   **Gamakatsu:** P10

Typical Grasshopper Construction

The following proportions and material options can be used when tying grasshopper patterns.

Wings: Equal to hook or body length (extending just beyond the hook bend)
Materials: Feather or quill segment cut to shape, laquered, and tied in flat over the body
Note: Wing segments can be brown or mottled, depending on the type of grasshopper

Legs (optional): Equal to twice the body length, knotted at the center
Materials: Feather segments, hair, rubber, or hackle quills cut to shape

Head: Equal to 1/3 shank length
Materials: Spun deer, elk, or antelope hair, clipped to shape
Note: Can also be hair tied bullet shape or a hackle tied collar style and clipped to shape

Body: Equal to 2/3 shank length
Materials: Dubbing, herl, chenille, foam, or yarn
Note: Can also be palmered with a hackle and then clipped; some patterns include a tail, which can be hair or hackle fibers equal to body length

Collar (optional): Equal to 2/3 shank length
Materials: Spun deer, elk, or antelope hair tips, used to form the head

Beetle Patterns

Beetle
Patterns

This category represents an assortment of beetle types that live near or around water. They often jump, fall, or fly into the water and can be seen floating or swimming on the water surface. Beetle patterns are excellent producers during the summer season for trout, bass, and panfish.

Some of the more popular beetle patterns include the Visible Beetle, Black Beetle, Black Crow Beetle, Green Leaf Hopper, Foam Beetle, and Jassid.

Recommended Hook Sizes

Beetle patterns can be tied on hook sizes 8, 10, and 12, using hooks made of regular or fine-gauge wire.

Recommended Hook Numbers

The following are a few of the more popular hooks (by manufacturer) used for tying beetle patterns. For alternative or additional hook selections, see Chapter 3.

Mustad: 94840, 94842	**Eagle Claw:** 59, L059	**Tiemco:** TMC5210
Kamasan: B-400	**Partridge:** L2A	**Daiichi:** 1170
VMC: 9288	**Gamakatsu:** P10	

Typical Beetle Construction

The following proportions and material options can be used when tying beetle patterns.

Shell: Equal to hook or body length
Materials: Turkey feather segment or goose quill segment, tied in at the bend and pulled over the body

Top View

Head: 1/16 inch wide
Materials: Thread or clipped ends of wing material

Side View

Legs: Equal to twice the gape of the hook
Materials: Rubber hackle, black fishing line

Body: Equal to shank length
Materials: Dubbing, herl, chenille, foam, or yarn

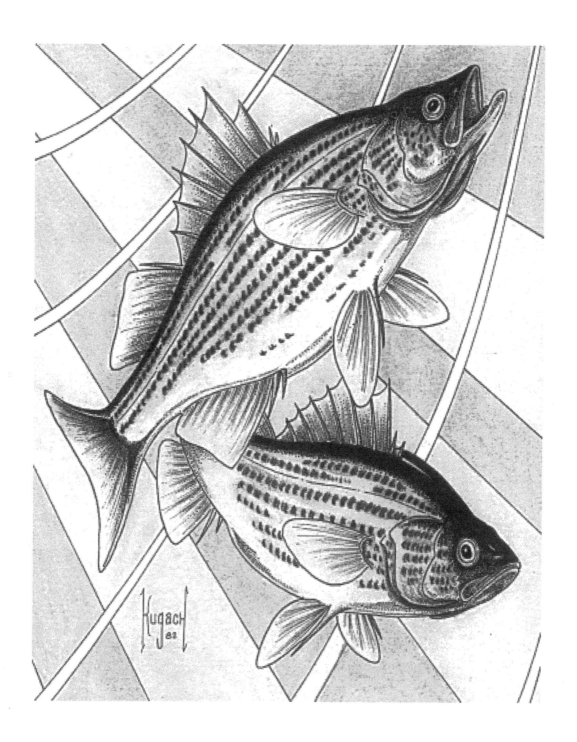

Crustacean (Freshwater) Flies

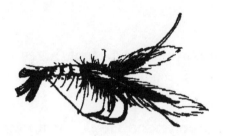

Crustacean patterns are designed to represent either freshwater shrimp (scuds) or freshwater crayfish. All are a major source of food for a variety of game fish. The following pages show examples of shrimp, scud, and crayfish patterns.

Crayfish (Crab) Patterns

Crayfish
Pattern

These patterns are designed to represent a wide variety of freshwater crayfish (crabs). They can vary in color, size, material selection, and construction. They are very effective patterns for smallmouth bass and other game fish when fished near or on the bottom.

Some of the more popular crayfish patterns include the Whitlock Crayfish, NearNuff Crayfish, and Orange Crayfish.

Recommended Hook Sizes
Most crayfish patterns can be tied on hook sizes 2, 4, 6, and 8.

Recommended Hook Numbers
The following are a few of the more popular hooks (by manufacturer) used for tying crayfish patterns. For alternative or additional hook selections, see Chapter 3.

Mustad: 9671, 9672	**Eagle Claw:** 63, L063	**Tiemco:** TMC5263
Kamasan: B-830	**Partridge:** H1A	**Daiichi:** 1720
VMC: 9283	**Gamakatsu:** P10-2L1H	

Typical Crayfish Construction
The following proportions and material options can be used when tying crayfish patterns.

Tail: Equal to 1/3 body length
Materials: Swiss straw, raffia, bucktail, or chamois
Carapace: Equal to body length, ribbed with fine wire
Materials: Swiss straw, raffia, bucktail, or chamois

Body: Equals shank less head
Materials: Dubbing
Note: Body can be weighted with lead wire prior to adding dubbing
Legs: Front 1/2 of body length
Materials: Palmered hackle, rubber hackle

Eyes: Various sizes
Materials: Bead chain, lead eyes, Mono eyes

Antennae: Equal to body length
Materials: Stripped feather quills, moose mane fibers

Weed Guard: Optional
Materials: Mono

Claws: Equal to hook length
Materials: Feather tips, chamois

Scud or Shrimp Patterns

Scud Pattern

Scud patterns are designed to represent a wide variety of freshwater shrimp found throughout the world. They are simple patterns that are very effective for a variety of game fish. Most scud patterns are fished near or on the bottom.

Some of the more popular scud patterns include the Freshwater Scud, Olive Scud, Bighorn Scud, and Flashback Scud.

Recommended Hook Sizes

Most scud or shrimp patterns can be tied on hook sizes 12, 14, and 16.

Recommended Hook Numbers

The following are a few of the more popular hooks (by manufacturer) used for tying scud or shrimp patterns. For alternative or additional hook selections, see Chapter 3.

Mustad: 3906, 3906B   **Eagle Claw:** 57, L057   **Tiemco:** TMC3761
Kamasan: B-170   **Partridge:** L2A   **Daiichi:** 1550
VMC: 8527   **Gamakatsu:** S10-3F

Typical Scud Construction

The following proportions and material options can be used when tying scud patterns.

Rib: Equally spaced wraps
Materials: Fine wire

Carapace (Shell): Equal to body length
Materials: Feather segment, swiss straw, or plastic bag strip tied in over the top

Head: Various sizes
Materials: Thread

Body: Equals shank less head
Materials: Dubbing, yarn, or chenille

Legs: Equal to body length
Materials: Hackle fibers

Miscellaneous Flies

This catch-all category includes egg fly patterns, leeches, shad patterns, and worms.

Egg (Glo-Bug) Patterns

Egg
Pattern

Egg patterns are designed to represent trout or salmon spawn, which are used as bait for fall-run salmon and steelheads.

Egg patterns can be tied in various shades of pink, red, or yellow, and as a single egg or a double.

Recommended Hook Sizes
Egg patterns can be tied on hook sizes 6 and 8.

Recommended Hook Numbers
The following are a few of the more popular hooks (by manufacturer) used for tying egg patterns. For alternative or additional hook selections, see Chapter 3.

Mustad: 3906, 3906B   **Eagle Claw:** 57, L057   **Tiemco:** TMC3761

Kamasan: B-170   **Partridge:** L2A   **Daiichi:** 1550

VMC: 8527   **Gamakatsu:** S10-3F

Typical Egg Construction
The following proportions and material options can be used when tying egg patterns.

Body: Equals shank less head. Two pieces of Glo-Bug Yarn $1\frac{1}{2}$ inches long (Salmon and Fire Orange) are tied in at the center on top midshank, using 3 to 5 wraps.

Lift both ends up above the shank and make an additional 3 or 4 wraps counterclockwise around the binding wraps, and bring the thread forward on the hook.

Next, gather the strands, pulling them tightly up above the hook shank, and trim them to the desired length with a curved scissors. Fluff up and shape the ball, and whip-finish the head.

Materials: Glo-Bug Yarn (Salmon or Fire Orange)

Leech Patterns

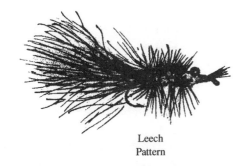

Leech
Pattern

These patterns are designed to represent a freshwater leech. They can vary in color, size, material selection, and construction. They are very effective patterns for smallmouth bass and other game fish, when fished near or on the bottom.

Some of the more popular leech patterns include the RB Leech, Chamois Leech, Egg Sucking Leech, Marabou Matuka Leech, and Dave's Leech.

Recommended Hook Sizes

Most leech patterns can be tied on hook sizes 2, 4, 6, and 8.

Recommended Hook Numbers

The following are a few of the more popular hooks (by manufacturer) used for tying leech patterns. For alternative or additional hook selections, see Chapter 3.

Mustad: 9671, 9672
Kamasan: B-830
VMC: 9283

Eagle Claw: 63, L063
Partridge: H1A
Gamakatsu: P10-2L1H

Tiemco: TMC5263
Daiichi: 1720

Typical Leech Construction

The following proportions and material options can be used when tying leech patterns.

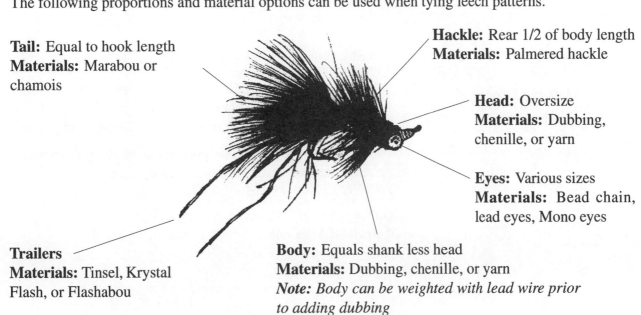

Tail: Equal to hook length
Materials: Marabou or chamois

Hackle: Rear 1/2 of body length
Materials: Palmered hackle

Head: Oversize
Materials: Dubbing, chenille, or yarn

Eyes: Various sizes
Materials: Bead chain, lead eyes, Mono eyes

Trailers
Materials: Tinsel, Krystal Flash, or Flashabou

Body: Equals shank less head
Materials: Dubbing, chenille, or yarn
Note: Body can be weighted with lead wire prior to adding dubbing

Worm Patterns

San Juan Worm
Pattern

For the most part, these patterns are designed to represent annelids (segmented marine worms). However, the category also includes other types of worms such as caterpillars, grubs, and inchworms. They can vary in color, size, material selection, and construction. They are very effective patterns for trout, panfish, and other game fish when fished near or on the bottom.

Some of the more popular worm patterns include the San Juan Worm, Inch Worm, Tochihara's OTR, and Blood Worm.

Recommended Hook Sizes

Most worm patterns can be tied on hook sizes 8 to 14.

Recommended Hook Numbers

The following are a few of the more popular hooks (by manufacturer) used for tying worm patterns. For alternative or additional hook selections, see Chapter 3.

Mustad: AC80200 **Eagle Claw:** 56, L056 **Tiemco:** TMC200, TMC2457
Kamasan: None **Partridge:** K4A, K12ST **Daiichi:** 1130, 1273
VMC: 9283 **Gamakatsu:** C12

Typical Worm Construction

The following proportions and material options can be used when tying worm patterns.

Head: Various sizes
Materials: Peacock herl, glass beads, or bead chain

Tochihara's OTR

Body: Entire shank (less the head) up to the bend
Materials: Silk, floss, thread, or wire

Note: Pattern can be slightly weighted with fine lead wire under the head

Ribbing: Equally spaced wraps over the body
Materials: Fine wire, French tinsel, or stripped quill

Shad Patterns

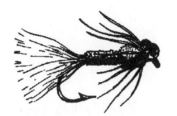

Shad fly patterns vary in color, size, material selection, and construction. They are very effective when fished near or on the bottom.

Some of the more popular shad patterns include the Shad Dart, Connecticut River, Narragansett Bay, and Chesapeake Bay.

Recommended Hook Sizes

Most shad patterns can be tied on hook sizes 4, 6, and 8.

Recommended Hook Numbers

The following are a few of the more popular hooks (by manufacturer) used for tying shad patterns. For alternative or additional hook selections, see Chapter 3.

Mustad: 3906, 3906B   **Eagle Claw:** 57, L057   **Tiemco:** TMC3761
Kamasan: B-170   **Partridge:** L2A   **Daiichi:** 1550
VMC: 8527   **Gamakatsu:** S10-3F

Typical Shad Construction

There are many variations of shad patterns. The following proportions and material options are only one example.

Tail: Equal to hook length
Materials: Marabou, feather segments, or Krystal Flash

Wing (not shown): Equal to body + tail
Materials: Hackle segments or tips, bucktail

Hackle: Collared
Materials: Palmered hackle

Eyes: Various sizes
Materials: Bead chain, lead eyes, or Mono eyes

Body: Equals shank less head
Materials: Dubbing, chenille, or yarn
Note: Body can be weighted with lead wire prior to adding dubbing

Head: Oversize
Materials: Dubbing, chenille, or yarn

Saltwater Flies

Saltwater patterns are designed to represent various baitfish, shrimp, squid, and crabs, which are the main diet of most saltwater species.

Saltwater Baitfish Patterns

Saltwater baitfish patterns are designed to represent a variety of saltwater species found throughout the world. The more common species are pinfish, sardines, silversides, herring, smelt, shad, mullet, needlefish, and ballyhoo.

Baitfish patterns include the Deceiver Series, Cuda Fly, Marabou Needlefish, Janssen's Half Beak, Seducer, Joe Brooks Blonde Series, and Whistler Series.

Recommended Hook Sizes

Most baitfish patterns can be tied on hook sizes 8/0 to1/0.

Recommended Hook Numbers

The following are a few of the more popular hooks (by manufacturer) used for tying baitfish patterns. For alternative or additional hook selections, see Chapter 3.

Mustad: 3406, 3407, 3408B	**Eagle Claw:** L054SS	**Tiemco:** TMC811S
Kamasan: None	**Partridge:** None	**Daiichi:** 2451, 2546
VMC: 9255	**Gamakatsu:** None	

Typical Saltwater Baitfish Construction

There are many variations in the construction of baitfish patterns. The following is only one example of the proportions and material options that can be used.

Tail: Four feathers 6 to 8 inches long
Materials: Saddle hackles

Half Beak Pattern

Head: Oversize
Materials: Thread or floss

Body/Beak: Hook shank wrapped with material
Materials: Thread or loss

Collar: Equal to body
Materials: Marabou

Eyes: Size and color vary
Materials: Painted or Styrofoam

Saltwater Shrimp Patterns

Shrimp patterns are designed to swim backwards with the hook riding up and are fished on or just off the bottom. They can vary in color, size, and shape, as well as in the materials used in their construction. They can be simple in design or realistic looking.

Shrimp patterns include Pflueger Hair Shrimp, Phillip's Pink Shrimp, Tom's Buggy Shrimp, and Gene's Shrimp.

Recommended Hook Sizes
Most shrimp patterns can be tied on hook sizes 1/0 to 2.

Recommended Hook Numbers
The following are a few of the more popular hooks (by manufacturer) used for tying shrimp patterns. For alternative or additional hook selections, see Chapter 3.

Mustad: 3406, 3407, 3408B

Kamasan: None

VMC: 9255

Eagle Claw: L054SS

Partridge: None

Gamakatsu: None

Tiemco: TMC811S

Daiichi: 2451, 2546

Typical Saltwater Shrimp Construction
There are many variations in the construction of shrimp patterns. The following is only one example of the proportions and material options that can be used.

Tail: Body bucktail tips spread out (fan shape) and coated with clear silicone cement
Materials: Bucktail

Body: Bucktail hair fibers tied in on top of the shank with the butt ends tapered to a point extending slightly past the bend and the tips extending over the hook eye and wrapped with thread to form an extended body; body should be weighted with lead wire
Materials: Bucktail, thread or floss

Eyes: Black beads glued on copper wire
Materials: Black beads

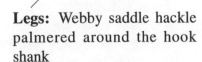

Gene's Shrimp Pattern

Legs: Webby saddle hackle palmered around the hook shank
Materials: Webby saddle hackle

Head/Carapace: 1/2-inch-wide plastic strip, cut to a point at one end and tied in over the body with equally spaced wraps
Materials: Clear, heavy-gauge plastic bag material colored with permanent marker

Feelers: Equal to body
Materials: Stripped quills

Squid Patterns

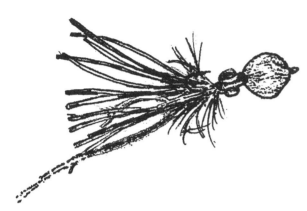

Squid patterns are large flies used for offshore fishing. They can be tied in assorted color patterns and variations.

Squid patterns include Dan Blanton's Sea Arrow Squid, Harry Kim's Tutti Fruti Squid, and Gene's Tinsel Tail Squid.

Recommended Hook Sizes

Most squid patterns can be tied on hook sizes 1/0 to 5/0.

Recommended Hook Numbers

The following are a few of the more popular hooks (by manufacturer) used for tying squid patterns. For alternative or additional hook selections, see Chapter 3.

Mustad: 3406, 3407, 3408B	**Eagle Claw:** L054SS	**Tiemco:** TMC811S
Kamasan: None	**Partridge:** None	**Daiichi:** 2451, 2546
VMC: 9255	**Gamakatsu:** None	

Typical Squid Construction

There are many variations in the construction of squid patterns. The following is only one example of the proportions and material options that can be used.

Tail: Eight 12-inch-long silver Christmas tree tinsel strips doubled over
Materials: Silver Christmas tree tinsel

Tentacles: Six to eight strands of 12-inch-long Krystal Flash
Materials: Marabou

Eyes: 7mm
Materials: Movable doll eyes

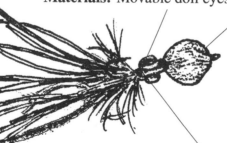

Butt: Chenille or foam covered with the mylar tubing from the body/head and unraveled after being secured with thread
Materials: Chenille or foam

Body/Head: Preshaped plastic or foam head form, with a 3½-inch-long piece of large mylar tubing tied in behind the hook eye and pulled over the head form and secured at the butt
Materials: Preshaped plastic or foam head form, 3½-inch-long piece of large mylar tubing

Crab Patterns

In recent years, crab patterns have become popular with surf fishermen and fly tiers. They can be tied to represent a wide variety of common crabs found along the shoreline and in the surf. Patterns include Nick Curcione's Sand Crab, Jack Montague's Epoxy Crabs, Ben Estes's Epoxy Deer Hair Crab, and Scotty Sanchez's Bunny Crab.

Recommended Hook Sizes

Most crab patterns can be tied on hook sizes 4/0 to 1/0.

Recommended Hook Numbers

The following are a few of the more popular hooks (by manufacturer) used for tying crab patterns. For alternative or additional hook selections, see Chapter 3.

Mustad: 3406, 3407, 3408B   **Eagle Claw:** L054SS   **Tiemco:** TMC811S
Kamasan: None   **Partridge:** None   **Daiichi:** 2451, 2546
VMC: 9255   **Gamakatsu:** None

Typical Crab Construction

There are many variations in the construction of crab patterns. The following is only one example of the proportions and material options that can be used.

Eyes: Black beads glued to copper wire
Materials: Black beads

Body: Spun deer hair cut to shape or molded epoxy
Materials: Deer hair or epoxy

Legs: Six 2- to 3-inch knotted feather fibers, feathers, or rubber hackle
Materials: Knotted feather fibers, feathers, or rubber hackle

Claws: Hair fibers or feather
Materials: Deer-hair fibers or feather tips

Note: Spots and coloring can be added using permanent colored markers

CHAPTER 3

Hooks

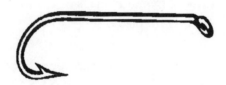

The first and most important material a fly tier starts with to create or tie a pattern is a hook. In many instances, the success of a pattern is directly dependent on the hook type, size, and shape. Which hook to use, what type, which manufacturer, and so forth are questions that tiers have to ask themselves prior to putting a hook into a vise.

In today's tying world, there is a wide assortment of hooks available for experienced or novice fly tiers. This chapter is intended to help tiers better understand what the various hooks are used for. Whether you're an experienced tier or a novice, the information contained here should be useful in your tying endeavors.

Manufacturers

Which hook to use can be a perplexing decision for the novice tier because of the many manufacturers out there and the various types of hooks that each of them offers. The following pages can be used as a guide or reference for hook selection when tying various types of patterns. Listed are the most frequently used manufacturers and the hooks they offer. Included are the manufacturer's hook number, the size ranges, and a standardized description of the hook characteristics. Also included are the manufacturer's recommendations for appropiate hook selection and possible substitutes.

MANUFACTURERS

Following is a list of addresses of the hook manufacturers or their U.S. distributors that are included in this book.

Mustad
O. Mustad & Son (USA) Inc.
253 Grant Ave.
P.O. Box 838
Auburn, NY 13021

Eagle Claw
Wright & McGill
P.O. Box 16011
Denver, CO 80216

Tiemco
Umpqua Feather Merchants
P.O. Box 700
Glide, OR 97443

Kamasan
World Wide Outfitters
425 College Ave.
Santa Rosa, CA 95401

Partridge of Redditch Ltd.
Partridge (USA)
P.O. Box 585
Wakefield, MA 01880

Daiichi
Angler Sport Group
6619 Oak Orchard Rd.
Elba, NY 14058

VMC
VMC, Inc.
1901 Oakcrest Ave., Suite 10
St. Paul, MN 55113

Gamakatsu
Gamakatsu
P.O. Box 1797
Tacoma, WA 98401

Fly-Tying Hook Descriptions

Hook Parts

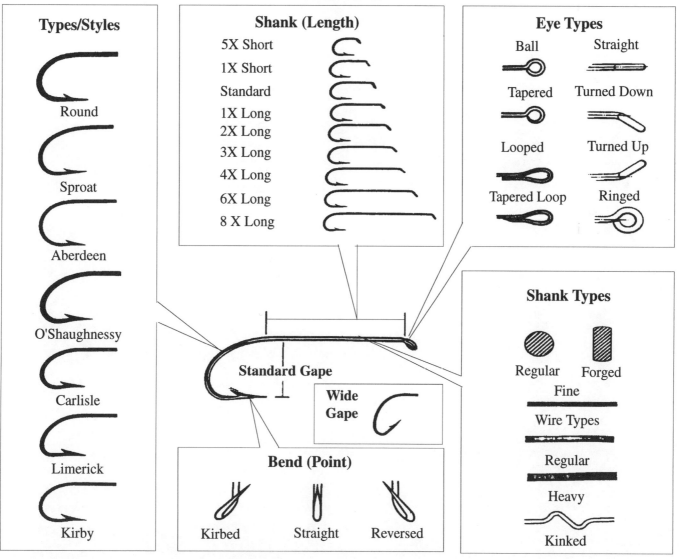

Types/Styles

Round

Sproat

Aberdeen

O'Shaughnessy

Carlisle

Limerick

Kirby

Shank (Length)

5X Short

1X Short

Standard

1X Long

2X Long

3X Long

4X Long

6X Long

8 X Long

Eye Types

Ball

Straight

Tapered

Turned Down

Looped

Turned Up

Tapered Loop

Ringed

Standard Gape

Wide Gape

Bend (Point)

Kirbed

Straight

Reversed

Shank Types

Regular

Forged

Fine

Wire Types

Regular

Heavy

Kinked

Hook Sizes

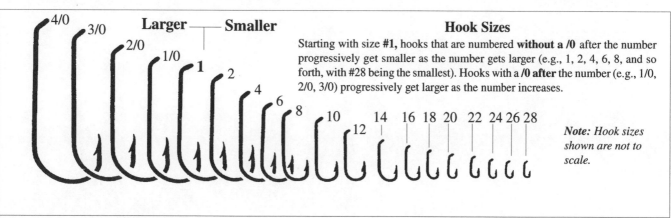

Starting with size **#1,** hooks that are numbered **without a /0** after the number progressively get smaller as the number gets larger (e.g., 1, 2, 4, 6, 8, and so forth, with #28 being the smallest). Hooks with a **/0 after** the number (e.g., 1/0, 2/0, 3/0) progressively get larger as the number increases.

4/0 3/0 2/0 1/0 1 2 4 6 8 10 12 14 16 18 20 22 24 26 28

Larger ── Smaller

Note: Hook sizes shown are not to scale.

Mustad Hooks

O. Mustad and Son is one of the oldest and largest manufacturers of fish hooks in the world. Established in 1832 in Gjovik, Norway, Mustad manufactures more than 30,000 different types of hooks for both sport and commercial fishing.

Mustad hooks can be purchased through most fly shops or catalog houses or directly from O. Mustad & Son (USA) Inc., 253 Grant Ave., P.O. Box 838 Auburn, NY 13021; phone 315-253-2793; fax 315-253-0157.

Mustad Selection and Substitution Chart

Pattern Application

The pattern application lists various types of patterns that can be tied using the specified hooks shown below.

Possible Substitutes

Listed across the page are other manufacturers' hooks that can be used as alternatives. In most cases, the hooks listed are similar or have the same characteristics with minor differences.

Note: Hook illustrations are only examples and are not shown at actual sizes. Also note that an "AC" (Accu-Point) preceding the hook number is a Mustad process used on specific hooks. In addition, after the eye description; **(S)** indicates a straight eye, **(TD)** indicates a turned-down eye, and **(TU)** indicates a turned-up eye.

Mustad	Eagle Claw	Tiemco	Kamasan	Partridge	Daiichi	VMC	Gamakatsu
Pattern Application: Midges and Tiny Dry Flies							
#540L Round Bend, Forged, Ball Eye (TD), Gold Plated, Size #28	None	None	None	**#K1A** Capt. Hamilton, Ball Eye (TD), Offset, Std. Shank. Sizes #28 to 24	None	None	None
Pattern Application: Wet Flies and Nymphs							
#3123 Limerick, Ball Eye (TD), Bronze, Sizes #2 to 16	None	None	None	**#CS11** **#CS11GRS** Redditch, Forged, 4X Long, St. Stl or Gray Shadow, Ball Eye (TD), Sizes #2 to 10	None	None	**#L10-2H** Limerick, 2X Strong, Ball Eye (TD), Bronze, Sizes #6 to 12
Pattern Application: Streamers							
#3190, 90A Carlisle, Ringed Eye (S), Gold Plated, Kirbed, Sizes #5/0-12, 14, 16, 18, 20	None	None	None	**#CS5** Thunder Creek, Heavy Wire, Blued, Ball Eye (S), Sizes #4, 6, 8	None	None	None
Pattern Application: Streamers							
#3191, 91A, 92, 93, 94N Carlisle, Kirbed, Ringed Eye (S), Bronzed, Blued, or Tinned, Sizes #10/0-10, 12, 14, 16, 18, 20	None	None	None	**#CS5** Thunder Creek, Heavy Wire, Blued, Ball Eye (S), Sizes #4, 6, 8	None	None	None
Pattern Application: Streamers							
#3214, 14A, !4E Carlisle, Kirbed, Ball Eye (TD), Sizes #6/0-2, 4 to 10 Tinned, Bronze, or Gold	None	None	None	**#CS5** Thunder Creek, Heavy Wire, Blued, Ball Eye (S), Sizes #4, 6, 8	None	None	None
Pattern Application: Dry Flies							
#3257B Sproat (Barbless), Tapered Eye (TD), Kirbed, Bronze, Sizes #8, 10, 12, 14	None	None	None	None	None	None	None

Mustad Selection and Substitution Chart

Mustad	Eagle Claw	Tiemco	Kamasan	Partridge	Daiichi	VMC	Gamakatsu

Pattern Application: Streamers, Nymphs, Wet Flies, and Baitfish

Mustad	Eagle Claw	Tiemco	Kamasan	Partridge	Daiichi	VMC	Gamakatsu
#3260B, 61, 62 Aberdeen, Ringed Eye (S), Gold, Bronze, Blued, Sizes #7/0 -10, 12, 14, 16	None	None	None	**#CS5** Thunder Creek, Heavy Wire, Blued, Ball Eye (S), Sizes #4, 6, 8	**#2461** Aberdeen, Ball Eye (S), Black, 3X Long, Sizes #6/0 to 1/0, 1, 2, 4, 6	None	None

Pattern Application: Streamers, Nymphs, Wet Flies, and Baitfish

Mustad	Eagle Claw	Tiemco	Kamasan	Partridge	Daiichi	VMC	Gamakatsu
#3263, 63A, 63B Aberdeen, Fine Wire, Ringed Eye (S), Blued, Bronze, Gold Sizes #5/0 -8, 10, 12	None	None	None	**#CS5** Thunder Creek, Heavy Wire, Blued, Ball Eye (S), Sizes #4, 6, 8	**#2461** Aberdeen, Ball Eye (S), Black, 3X Long, Sizes #6/0 to 1/0, 1, 2, 4, 6	None	None

Pattern Application: Wet Flies

Mustad	Eagle Claw	Tiemco	Kamasan	Partridge	Daiichi	VMC	Gamakatsu
#3365A, 65C, 66, 66A, 66F, 66G, 67 Sproat, Ringed Eye (S), Nickl., Brz., Gold, Blued, Sizes #8/0 -2, 4, 6, 8, 10, 12, 14	None	None	None	None	None	**#8410** Special Sproat, Bronze, Ball Eye (S), Forged, Sizes #4 to 12	**#S10S** Sproat, Ball Eye (S), Black, Sizes #2 to 20

Pattern Application: Wet Flies and Nymphs

Mustad	Eagle Claw	Tiemco	Kamasan	Partridge	Daiichi	VMC	Gamakatsu
#3399, 99A, 99D, 99N Sproat, Ball Eye (TD), Brz., Gold, 99D-Fine Wire, Sizes #9/0 -2, 4 to 20	**#57, #L057, #NT057** Sproat, Ball Eye (TD), Bronze, Sizes #4 to 16	**#TMC3769** Sproat, 1X Long, Forged, Ball Eye (TD), 2X Heavy, Bronze, Sizes #2 to 20	**#B-170** Sproat, Ball Eye (TD), Bronze, Sizes #6 to 16	**#A** Improved Sproat, 2X Fine, 1X Short, Bronze, Ball Eye (TD), Sizes #10 to 16	**#1550** Sproat, Ball Eye (TD), Bronze, Sizes #2 to 18	**#8526** Sproat, Bronze, Ball Eye (TD), Forged, Sizes #8 to 16	**#S10** Sproat, Ball Eye (TD), Black, Sizes #2 to 24

Pattern Application: Saltwater Patterns, Crustaceans, Wet Flies, and Baitfish

Mustad	Eagle Claw	Tiemco	Kamasan	Partridge	Daiichi	VMC	Gamakatsu
#3406, 06B O' Shaughnessy, Forged, Ringed Eye (S), Bronze or Nickle, Sizes #14/0 to 8	**#L054SS** O' Shaughnessy, Ringed Eye (S), Stainless Steel, Sizes #1/0 to 4/0	**#TMC811S** O' Shaughnessy, X Strong, Ringed Eye (S), Stainless Steel, Sizes #4/0 to 8	None	None	**#2546** O'Shaughnessy, Forged, Ball Eye (S), Stainless Steel, Sizes #6/0 to1/0, 1 to 6	**#9255** O' Shaughnessy, Ball Eye (S), Bronze, Sizes #5/0 to 6	None

Pattern Application: Saltwater Patterns, Crustaceans, Wet Flies, and Baitfish

Mustad	Eagle Claw	Tiemco	Kamasan	Partridge	Daiichi	VMC	Gamakatsu
#3407, 07A, 07B, 07SS O' Shaughnessy, Forged, X or 2X Strong Ringed Eye (S), Cad. Tinned Sizes #14/0 to 12	**#L054SS** O' Shaughnessy, Ringed Eye (S), Stainless Steel, Sizes #1/0 to 4/0	**#TMC811S** O' Shaughnessy, X Strong, Ringed Eye (S), Stainless Steel, Sizes #4/0 to 8	None	None	**#2451** O' Shaughnessy, Forged, Eye (S), Black, Sizes #1, 2, 4, 6, 8	**#9255** O' Shaughnessy, Ball Eye (S), Bronze, Sizes #5/0 to 6	None

Pattern Application: Saltwater Patterns, Crustaceans, Wet Flies, and Baitfish

Mustad	Eagle Claw	Tiemco	Kamasan	Partridge	Daiichi	VMC	Gamakatsu
#3408B O' Shaughnessy, Forged, Ball Eye (TD), Cad./Tinned, Sizes #7/0-2, 4, 6, 8	**#L054SS** O' Shaughnessy, Ringed Eye (S), Stainless Steel, Sizes #1/0 to 4/0	**#TMC811S** O' Shaughnessy, X Strong, Ringed Eye (S), Stainless Steel, Sizes #4/0 to 8	None	None	**#2451** O' Shaughnessy, Forged, Eye (S), Black, Sizes #1, 2, 4, 6, 8	**#9255** O' Shaughnessy, Ball Eye (S), Bronze, Sizes #5/0 to 6	None

Pattern Application: Salmon and Steelhead Patterns

Mustad	Eagle Claw	Tiemco	Kamasan	Partridge	Daiichi	VMC	Gamakatsu
#3582, 82C, 82F Double, Sizes #2/0 to 12 Ball (TD), Tapered, or Oval Eye (TU) Bronze or Black	None	None	None	**#R1A, R2A, R3HF, P, Q, 02** Double, Looped Eye (S, TU, or TD), Bronze or Black, Sizes #3/0-2 to 18	**#7131** Double Limerick, Looped Eye (TU), Black, Sizes #4 to 12	None	None

Mustad Selection and Substitution Chart

Mustad	Eagle Claw	Tiemco	Kamasan	Partridge	Daiichi	VMC	Gamakatsu

Pattern Application: Streamers and Baitfish

Mustad	Eagle Claw	Tiemco	Kamasan	Partridge	Daiichi	VMC	Gamakatsu
#3665A Limerick, 1/2 longer than regular, Tapered Eye (TD), Bronze, Sizes #2 to 14	#74 Eagle Claw Design, Forged, XX Long, Gold, Ball Eye (TD), Sizes #4/0 to 4	None	None	#CS17 Limerick, 6X Long, Tapered Loop Eye (TD), Black, Sizes #1, 2, 4, 6	#J171 Improved Limerick, 6X Long, 1X Heavy, Tapered Loop Eye (TD), Black, Sizes #1, 2	None	None

Pattern Application: Wet Flies and Nymphs

Mustad	Eagle Claw	Tiemco	Kamasan	Partridge	Daiichi	VMC	Gamakatsu
#3777 Central Draught, Ringed Eye (S), Bronze, Sizes #18 to 30, 32, 34, 36	None	#TMC400T Special, Ball Eye (S), Bronze, Sizes #8 to 14	None	#K6ST Special (Price), Long Curve, Ball Eye (S), Bronze, Sizes #8 to 14	#1770 Sproat, 3X Long, 1X Fine, Forged, Ball Eye (S), Bronze, Sizes #6 to 16	None	None

Pattern Application: Wet Flies, Larvae, Pupae, and Nymphs

Mustad	Eagle Claw	Tiemco	Kamasan	Partridge	Daiichi	VMC	Gamakatsu
#3906, #AC3906 Sproat, Tapered Eye (TD), Bronze, Sizes #2 to 20	#57, #L057, #NT057 Sproat, Ball Eye (TD), Bronze, Sizes #4 to 16	#TMC3761 Sproat, Forged, 1X Long, 2X Heavy, Ball Eye (TD), Bronze, Sizes #8 to 18	#B-170 Sproat, Ball Eye (TD), Bronze, Sizes #6 to 16	#G3A Sproat, Forged, Heavy Wire, Ball Eye (TD), Bronze, Sizes #8 to 16	#1550 Sproat, Ball Eye (TD), Bronze, Sizes #2 to 18	#8526 Sproat, Forged Ball Eye (TD), Bronze, Sizes #8 to 16	#S10-3F Sproat, 1X Fine, Black, Ball Eye (TD), Sizes #4 to 20

Pattern Application: Wet Flies, Larvae, Pupae, Nymphs, and Crustaceans

Mustad	Eagle Claw	Tiemco	Kamasan	Partridge	Daiichi	VMC	Gamakatsu
#3906B, #AC3906B Sproat, 1X Long, Tapered Eye (TD), Bronze, Sizes #4 to 18	#57, #L057, #NT057 Sproat, Ball Eye (TD), Bronze, Sizes #4 to 16	#TMC3761 Sproat, Forged, 1X Long, 2X Heavy, Ball Eye (TD), Bronze, Sizes #8 to 18	#B-170 Sproat, Ball Eye (TD), Bronze, Sizes #6 to 16	#L2A Capt. Hamilton, Forged, Bronze, Ball Eye (TD), Sizes #2 to 14	#1550 Sproat, Ball Eye (TD), Bronze, Sizes #2 to 18	#8527 Sproat, Forged, X Long, Bronze, Ball Eye (TD), Sizes #8 to 16	#S10-3F Sproat, 1X Fine, Black, Ball Eye (TD), Sizes #4 to 20

Pattern Application: Wet Flies, Larvae, Pupae, Nymphs, and Crustaceans

Mustad	Eagle Claw	Tiemco	Kamasan	Partridge	Daiichi	VMC	Gamakatsu
#3908 #3908C Sproat, X Heavy, Tapered Eye (TD), Bronze, Sizes #4 to 8	#57, #L057, #NT057 Sproat, Ball Eye (TD), Bronze, Sizes #4 to 16	#TMC3761 Sproat, Forged, 1X Long, 2X Heavy, Ball Eye (TD), Bronze, Sizes #8 to 18	#B-170 Sproat, Ball Eye (TD), Bronze, Sizes #6 to 16	#L2A Capt. Hamilton, Forged, Bronze, Ball Eye (TD), Sizes #2 to 14	#1550 Sproat, Ball Eye (TD), Bronze, Sizes #2 to 18	#8526 Sproat, Forged Ball Eye (TD), Bronze, Sizes #8 to 16	#S10-3F Sproat, 1X Fine, Black, Ball Eye (TD), Sizes #4 to 20

Pattern Application: Salmon and Steelhead Patterns

Mustad	Eagle Claw	Tiemco	Kamasan	Partridge	Daiichi	VMC	Gamakatsu
#7827 Double, Ringed, Loose Eye (S), Bronze, Sizes #5/0-2 to 16	None	None	None	#R1A, R2A, R3HF, P, Q, 02 Double, Looped Eye (S, TU, or TD), Bronze or Black, Sizes #3/0-2 to 18	#7131 Double Limerick, Looped Eye (TU), Black, Sizes #4 to 12	None	None

Pattern Application: Dry Flies, Wet Flies, Pupae, and Nymphs

Mustad	Eagle Claw	Tiemco	Kamasan	Partridge	Daiichi	VMC	Gamakatsu
#7948A Round Bend, Forged, Bronze, Tapered Eye (TD), Sizes #2 to 20	#59, #L059, #NT059 Round Bend, Fine Wire, Forged, Ball Eye (TD), Brz. & Nkl. Teflon, Sizes #4 to 24	#TMC5210 Round, Forged, 1X Fine, Ball Eye (TD), Bronze, Sizes #10 to 20	#B-400 Round Bend, Forged, Ball Eye (TD), Bronze, Sizes #8 to 16	#L2A Capt. Hamilton, Forged, 2X Fine, Ball Eye (TD), Bronze, Sizes #6 to 18	#1170 Round Bend, Forged, Ball Eye (TD), Bronze, Sizes #8 to 16	#9288 Round Bend, Forged, 2X Fine, Short Shank, Bronze, Forged, Ball Eye (TD), Sizes #6 to 20	#P10 Model Perfect Round, Bronze, Ball Eye (TD), Sizes #4 to 24

Pattern Application: Dry Flies, Wet Flies, Terrestrials, and Nymphs

Mustad	Eagle Claw	Tiemco	Kamasan	Partridge	Daiichi	VMC	Gamakatsu
#7957B, 57BX Round Bend, Bronze, Tapered Eye (TD), Forged, Sizes #2 to 20, 57BX Extra Strong	#59, #L059, #NT059 Round Bend, Fine Wire, Forged, Ball Eye (TD), Brz. & Nkl. Teflon, Sizes #4 to 24	#TMC102 Round Bend, Ball Eye (TD), Bronze, Sizes #11, 13, 15, 17	#B-400 Round Bend, Forged, Ball Eye (TD), Bronze, Sizes #8 to 16	#L2A Capt. Hamilton, Forged, 2X Fine, Ball Eye (TD), Bronze, Sizes #6 to 18	#1170 Round Bend, Forged, Ball Eye (TD), Bronze, Sizes #8 to 16	#9288 Round Bend, Forged, 2X Fine, Short Shank, Bronze, Forged Ball Eye (TD), Sizes #6 to 20	#P10 Model Perfect Round, Bronze, Ball Eye (TD), Sizes #4 to 24

Mustad Selection and Substitution Chart

Mustad	Eagle Claw	Tiemco	Kamasan	Partridge	Daiichi	VMC	Gamakatsu

Pattern Application: Wet Flies and Nymphs

Mustad	Eagle Claw	Tiemco	Kamasan	Partridge	Daiichi	VMC	Gamakatsu
#7958 Round Bend, Offset, Forged, Bronze, Tapered Eye (TD), Sizes #2/0 to 18	#59, #L059, #NT059 Round Bend, Fine Wire, Forged, Ball Eye (TD), Brz. & Nkl. Teflon, Sizes #4 to 24	#TMC102 Round Bend, Ball Eye (TD), Bronze, Sizes #11, 13, 15, 17	#B-400 Round Bend, Forged, Ball Eye (TD), Bronze, Sizes #8 to 16	#L2A Capt. Hamilton, Forged, 2X Fine, Ball Eye (TD), Bronze, Sizes #6 to 18	#1170 Round Bend, Forged, Ball Eye (TD), Bronze, Sizes #8 to 16	#9288 Round Bend, Forged, 2X Fine, Short Shank, Bronze, Forged Ball Eye (TD), Sizes #6 to 20	#P10 Model Perfect Round, Bronze, Ball Eye (TD), Sizes #4 to 24

Pattern Application: Wet Flies and Nymphs

Mustad	Eagle Claw	Tiemco	Kamasan	Partridge	Daiichi	VMC	Gamakatsu
#7970 Limerick, 5X Strong, Bronze, Ball Eye (TD), Sizes #2 to 8	None	None	None	#J1A Limerick, Ball Eye (TD), Bronze, Sizes #4 to 16	None	None	#L10-2H Limerick, 2X Strong, Ball Eye (TD), Bronze, Sizes #6 to 12

Pattern Application: Salmon and Steelhead Patterns

Mustad	Eagle Claw	Tiemco	Kamasan	Partridge	Daiichi	VMC	Gamakatsu
#9049, 49X Limerick, Fine Wire, 5X Strong, Black, Loop Oval Eye (TU), Sizes #2 to 10	None	#TMC7999 Salmon, Forged, Heavy Wire, Tapered Loop Eye (TU), Black, Sizes #2/0 to 12	#B-180 Salmon, Forged, Tapered Loop Eye (TU), Black, Sizes #2/0 to 12	#O1 Salmon (Wilson), Forged, Heavy Wire, Black, Tapered Loop Eye (TU), Sizes #2 to 16	#2441 Salmon, Forged, 1X Strong, Tapered Loop Eye (TU), Black, Sizes #2/0, 1/0, 1 to 8	#8923 Limerick, Forged, 2X Long, Ball Eye (TU), Bronze, Sizes #2 to 12	None

Pattern Application: Saltwater Patterns and Egg or Glo-Bug Patterns

Mustad	Eagle Claw	Tiemco	Kamasan	Partridge	Daiichi	VMC	Gamakatsu
#9174, 75 O'Shaughnessy, 3X Short, X Strong, Bronze & Cad., Ball Eye (S), Sizes #9/0 to 8	None	#TMC105 O'Shaughnessy, Reverse Bend, 5X Short, 2X Strong, Forged, Ball Eye (S), Bronze, Sizes #4 to 10	None	None	None	None	None

Pattern Application: Egg or Glo-Bug Patterns

Mustad	Eagle Claw	Tiemco	Kamasan	Partridge	Daiichi	VMC	Gamakatsu
#9479 Round Bend, Reversed, 5X Short, X Fine, Bronze, Tapered Eye (TD), Sizes #2/0 to 18	#781 Wide Gape, Forged, X Short, Ball Eye (TD), Gold, Sizes #6 to 16	None	None	#K4A Special (Veniard) Offset, Curved Shank, 2X Fine, Ball Eye (TD), Bronze, Sizes #8 to 18	None	None	#C12 Special Curve, Bronze, Ball Eye (TD), Sizes #10 to 20

Pattern Application: Saltwater Patterns

Mustad	Eagle Claw	Tiemco	Kamasan	Partridge	Daiichi	VMC	Gamakatsu
#9510XXXC, XXXT, XXXS, XXXDT Siwash, 3X Strong, Tinned & Stl. Steel, Open Ring Eye (S), Sizes #9/0 to 2	None	None	None	None	None	None	None

Pattern Application: Egg or Midge Patterns

Mustad	Eagle Claw	Tiemco	Kamasan	Partridge	Daiichi	VMC	Gamakatsu
#9523 Round Bend, Offset, Forged, 5X Short, X Fine, Bronze, Tapered Eye (TU), Sizes #3/0 to 16	#182RE Wide Gape, Forged, X Short, Ball Eye (TU), Nickel, Sizes #5/0 to 2	None	None	None	#1140 Continuous Bend, Forged, 1X Fine, 1X Short, Bronze, Ball Eye (TU), Sizes #10 to 16	None	None

Pattern Application: Streamers or Baitfish

Mustad	Eagle Claw	Tiemco	Kamasan	Partridge	Daiichi	VMC	Gamakatsu
#9575 Limerick, Forged, 1/2 Longer Shank, Bronze, Tapered Loop Eye (TD), Sizes #2 to 12	#74 Eagle Claw Design, Forged, XX Long, Gold, Ball Eye (TD), Sizes #4/0 to 4	None	None	#CS17 Limerick, 6X Long, Tapered Loop Eye (TD), Black, Sizes #1, 2, 4, 6	#J171 Improved Limerick, 6X Long, 1X Heavy, Tapered Loop Eye (TD), Black, Sizes #1, 2	None	None

Mustad Selection and Substitution Chart

Mustad	Eagle Claw	Tiemco	Kamasan	Partridge	Daiichi	VMC	Gamakatsu

Pattern Application: Dry Flies, Wet Flies, Terrestrials, Baitfish, Larvae, Pupae, and Nymphs

Mustad	Eagle Claw	Tiemco	Kamasan	Partridge	Daiichi	VMC	Gamakatsu
#9671, #AC9671 Round Bend, Forged, 2X Long, Bronze, Tapered Eye (TD), Sizes #2 to 18	**#63, #L063, #NT063** Round Bend, 2X Long, Brz. & Nkl. Teflon, Ball Eye (TD), Sizes #4 to 18	None	**#B-830** Round Bend, Forged, 2X Long, Ball Eye (TD), Bronze, Sizes #6 to 14	**#H1A** Capt. Hamilton, Forged, 2X Fine, 2-1/2X Long, Bronze, Ball Eye (TD), Sizes #2 to 14	None	None	**#P10-2L1H** Model Perfect Round, 2X Long, 1X Strong, Bronze, Ball Eye (TD), Sizes #4 to 16

Pattern Application: Wet Flies, Baitfish, Larvae, and Nymphs

Mustad	Eagle Claw	Tiemco	Kamasan	Partridge	Daiichi	VMC	Gamakatsu
#9672, #AC9672 Round Bend, Forged, 3X Long, Bronze, Tapered Eye (TD), Sizes #2 to 18	None	**#TMC5263** Round, Forged, 3X Long, Ball Eye (TD), Bronze, Sizes #2 to18	None	**#H1A** Capt. Hamilton, Forged, 2X Fine, 2-1/2X Long, Bronze, Ball Eye (TD), Sizes #2 to 14	**#1720** Round Bend, Forged, 3X Long, 1X Strong, Bronze, Ball Eye (TD), Sizes #6 to 18	None	None

Pattern Application: Wet Flies, Larvae, Pupae, and Nymphs

Mustad	Eagle Claw	Tiemco	Kamasan	Partridge	Daiichi	VMC	Gamakatsu
#9674 Round Bend, Forged, 4X Long, Bronze, Ball Eye (S), Sizes #4 to 12	None	None	None	None	**#1750** Round Bend, 4X Long, 1X Strong, Forged, Ball Eye (S), Mini Barb, Bronze, Sizes #4 to 14	None	None

Pattern Application: Pencil Poppers

Mustad	Eagle Claw	Tiemco	Kamasan	Partridge	Daiichi	VMC	Gamakatsu
#32669CT Aberdeen, Forged, X Long, 3X Strong Ringed Eye (S), Tinned, Sizes #1/0	None	**#TMC511S** Round, Forged, 4X Long, 2X Strong, Ball Eye (S), Stl. Steel, Sizes #2/0, 1/0, 2	None	None	None	None	None

Pattern Application: Wet Flies and Nymphs

Mustad	Eagle Claw	Tiemco	Kamasan	Partridge	Daiichi	VMC	Gamakatsu
#33602 Sproat, Ringed Eye (S), Gold Plated, Sizes #5/0 to 16	None	None	None	None	None	**#8410** Special (Crystal), Forged, Ball Eye (S), Bronze, Sizes #4 to 12	**#S10S** Sproat, Black, Ball Eye (S), Sizes #4 to 14

Pattern Application: Poppers

Mustad	Eagle Claw	Tiemco	Kamasan	Partridge	Daiichi	VMC	Gamakatsu
#33900 Sproat, X Long, Ringed Eye (S), Bronze, Sizes #1/0 to 14	**#L200** Special, Kinked Shank, Ringed Eye (S), Bronze, Sizes #1/0 to 4	None	None	None	None	None	None

Pattern Application: Poppers

Mustad	Eagle Claw	Tiemco	Kamasan	Partridge	Daiichi	VMC	Gamakatsu
#33903 Sproat, Ringed Eye (S), Bronze, Sizes #5/0 to 16	**#L200** Special, Kinked Shank, Ringed Eye (S), Bronze, Sizes #1/0 to 4	None	None	None	None	None	None

Pattern Application: Wet Flies, Baitfish, and Nymphs

Mustad	Eagle Claw	Tiemco	Kamasan	Partridge	Daiichi	VMC	Gamakatsu
#33956, 57 Sproat, Shank Longer than Regular, Bronze, Ball Eye (TD), Sizes #2 to 14	None	None	None	None	None	None	None

Mustad Selection and Substitution Chart

Mustad	Eagle Claw	Tiemco	Kamasan	Partridge	Daiichi	VMC	Gamakatsu

Pattern Application: Streamers and Nymphs

Mustad	Eagle Claw	Tiemco	Kamasan	Partridge	Daiichi	VMC	Gamakatsu
#33960 Sproat, 4X Long, Bronze, Ball Eye (TD), Sizes #2 to 12	#281, #L281, #NT281 Sproat, 4X Long, 1X Heavy, Brz. & Nkl. Teflon, Ball Eye (TD), Sizes #2 to 10	None	None	#D4A Redditch, Forged, 4X Long, Heavy Wire, Ball Eye (TD),Bronze, Sizes #2 to 12	#2340 Limerick, 6X Long, 1X Strong, Ball Eye (TD), Bronze, Sizes #4 to 12	None	#S11-4L2H Sproat, 4X Long, 2X Strong, Black, Ball Eye (TD), Sizes #6 to 12

Pattern Application: Saltwater Patterns

Mustad	Eagle Claw	Tiemco	Kamasan	Partridge	Daiichi	VMC	Gamakatsu
#34007, 09 O' Shaughnessy, Forged, Large Ringed Eye (S), Stainless Steel Sizes #11/0 to 2	#L054SS O' Shaughnessy, Ringed Eye (S), Stainless Steel, Sizes #1/0 to 4/0	#TMC811S O' Shaughnessy, X Strong, Ringed Eye (S), Stainless Steel, Sizes #4/0 to 8	None	None	#2546 O'Shaughnessy, Forged, Ball Eye (S), Stainless Steel, Sizes #6/0 to1/0, 1 to 6	#9255 O'Shaughnessy, Long Shank, Ball Eye (S), Brz., Nkl., Perma Stl., Gold, Sizes #5/0 to 6	None

Pattern Application: Saltwater Patterns

Mustad	Eagle Claw	Tiemco	Kamasan	Partridge	Daiichi	VMC	Gamakatsu
#34081, 82, 91 O' Shaughnessy, Forged, Large Ringed Eye (S), Cad. Tinned or Nickel, Sizes #10/0 to 4	#L054SS O' Shaughnessy, Ringed Eye (S), Stainless Steel, Sizes #1/0 to 4/0	#TMC811S O' Shaughnessy, X Strong, Ringed Eye (S), Stainless Steel, Sizes #4/0 to 8	None	None	#2546 O'Shaughnessy, Forged, Ball Eye (S), Stainless Steel, Sizes #6/0 to 1/0, 1 to 6	#9255 O'Shaughnessy, Long Shank, Ball Eye (S), Brz., Nkl., Perma Stl., Gold, Sizes #5/0 to 6	None

Pattern Application: Baitfish, Streamers, and Thunder Creek Streamers

Mustad	Eagle Claw	Tiemco	Kamasan	Partridge	Daiichi	VMC	Gamakatsu
#36620 Limerick, 1/2" Longer Shank, Bronze, Ball Eye (TD), Sizes #2 to 10	#74 Eagle Claw Design, Forged, XX Long, Gold, Ball Eye (TD), Sizes #4/0 to 4	None	None	#CS17 Limerick, 6X Long, Tapered Loop Eye (TD), Black, Sizes #1, 2, 4, 6	#J171 Improved Limerick, 6X Long, 1X Heavy, Tapered Loop Eye (TD), Black, Sizes #1, 2	None	None

Pattern Application: Baitfish and Streamers

Mustad	Eagle Claw	Tiemco	Kamasan	Partridge	Daiichi	VMC	Gamakatsu
#36680 Limerick, 1/4" Longer Shank, Bronze, Tapered Eye (TD), Sizes #4 to 12	#74 Eagle Claw Design, Forged, XX Long, Gold, Ball Eye (TD), Sizes #4/0 to 4	None	None	#CS17 Limerick, 6X Long, Tapered Loop Eye (TD), Black, Sizes #1, 2, 4, 6	#J171 Improved Limerick, 6X Long, 1X Heavy, Tapered Loop Eye (TD), Black, Sizes #1, 2	None	None

Pattern Application: Baitfish and Streamers

Mustad	Eagle Claw	Tiemco	Kamasan	Partridge	Daiichi	VMC	Gamakatsu
#36717 Russian River, Bronze, 1/2" Longer Shank, 5X Strong, Ball Eye (TD), Sizes #2	None	None	None	None	None	None	#Russian River Modified Limerick, Bronze, Ball Eye (TD), Sizes #2

Pattern Application: Salmon and Steelhead Patterns

Mustad	Eagle Claw	Tiemco	Kamasan	Partridge	Daiichi	VMC	Gamakatsu
#36890, #AC36890 Limerick, Black, Looped Oval Eye (TU), Sizes #6/0 to 12	None	#TMC7999 Salmon, Forged, Heavy Wire, Tapered Loop Eye (TU), Black, Sizes #2/0 to 12	#B-180 Salmon, Forged, Tapered Loop Eye (TU), Black, Sizes #2/0 to 12	#M Salmon, Forged, 2X Heavy,Tapered Loop Eye (TU), Black, Sizes #4/0 to 1/0, 1 to 10	#2441 Salmon, Forged, 1X Strong, Tapered Loop Eye (TU), Black, Sizes #2/0, 1/0, 1 to 8	#8923 Limerick, Forged, 2X Long, Ball Eye (TU), Bronze, Sizes #2 to 12	#T10-3H Salmon, 1X Fine, Tapered Loop Eye (TU), Black, Sizes #2 to 8

Pattern Application: Wet Flies, Crustaceans, Larvae, Pupae, and Nymphs

Mustad	Eagle Claw	Tiemco	Kamasan	Partridge	Daiichi	VMC	Gamakatsu
#37140, 41, 42 Wide Gape, Slightly Reversed, Ringed Eye (S), Brz., Nkl., or Gold Plated, Sizes #8/0 to 14	None	None	None	None	None	None	#SC15 Sproat, Wide Gape, Tinned, Ball Eye (S), Sizes #2/0 to 8

Mustad Selection and Substitution Chart

Mustad	Eagle Claw	Tiemco	Kamasan	Partridge	Daiichi	VMC	Gamakatsu
Pattern Application: Wet Flies, Crustaceans, Larvae, Pupae, and Nymphs							
#37160, 60S Wide Gape, Slightly Reversed, Ball Eye (TU), Brz., or St, Steel, Sizes #7/0 to 26	None	None	None	**#K2B** Special (Yorkshire) Forged, Curved Shank, Ball Eye (TU), Bronze, Sizes #8 to 18	**#4250** Egg, Forged, Reversed, Wide Gape, Short Shank, Ball Eye (TU), Bronze, Red & Gold, Sizes #4 to 14	None	**#C12U** Special Curve, Bronze, Ball Eye (TU), Sizes #6 to 16
Pattern Application: Wet Flies, Crustaceans, Larvae, Pupae, and Nymphs							
#37161, 62, 65 Wide Gape, Slightly Reversed, Ball Eye (TU), Gold or Nickel Plated, Sizes #6/0 to 10	None	None	None	**#K2B** Special (Yorkshire) Forged, Curved Shank, Ball Eye (TU), Bronze, Sizes #8 to 18	**#4250** Egg, Forged, Reversed, Wide Gape, Short Shank, Ball Eye (TU), Bronze, Red & Gold, Sizes #4 to 14	None	**#C13U** Special Curve, Keel Balance, Bronze, Ball Eye (TU), Sizes #10 to 20
Pattern Application: Bass Bugs, Hair Flies, Divers, and Lures							
#37187 Stinger, Ringed Eye (S), Bronze, Sizes #1/0, 2, 6, 10	None	None	None	None	**#2720** Stinger, Wide Gape, Lt. Wire, Ball Eye (S), Bronze., Sizes #5/0, 3/0, 1/0, 2	None	None
Pattern Application: Poppers							
#37190 Round Bend, Kinked, Ball Eye (S), Bronze, Sizes #2, 6, 10	None	None	None	None	None	None	None
Pattern Application: Streamers and Baitfish							
#37350, 53 Aberdeen, X Fine Wire, Ball Eye (TD), Bronze & Gold, Sizes #4/0 to 10	None	None	None	None	None	None	None
Pattern Application: Streamers and Baitfish							
#37360, 61, 63 Aberdeen, X Fine Wire, Ringed Eye (S), Bronze, Blued & Gold, Sizes #4/0, 3/0, 8, 10, 12	None	None	None	None	**#2461** Aberdeen, 3X Long, Ball Eye (S), Black, Sizes #6/0 to1/0, 1 to 6	None	None
Pattern Application: Streamers and Baitfish							
#38941 Sproat, 3X Long, Tapered Eye (TD), Bronze, Sizes #2 to 16	**#58, #L058, #NT058** Round Bend, 3X Long, Forged, Ball Eye (TD), Bronze & Nkl. Teflon, Sizes #4 to 14	**#TMC5263** Round, Forged, 3X Long, Ball Eye (TD), Bronze, Sizes #2 to18	None	None	**#1720** Round Bend, Forged, 3X Long, 1X Strong, Bronze, Ball Eye (TD), Sizes #6 to 18	None	None
Pattern Application: Bass Flies and Keel Flies							
#38972 Keel Sproat, Wide Gape, Ringed Eye (S), Bronze, Sizes #14, 16	None	None	None	None	None	None	None

Mustad Selection and Substitution Chart

Mustad	Eagle Claw	Tiemco	Kamasan	Partridge	Daiichi	VMC	Gamakatsu

Pattern Application: Streamers and Bucktails

| **#79579**
Round Bend, Barbless, Forged, 3X Long, Tapered Eye (TD), Bronze, Sizes #2 to 18 | None | None | None | None | None | None | None |

Pattern Application: Streamers, Baitfish, Bucktails, Muddlers, and Stonefly Nymphs

| **#79580, #AC79580**
Round Bend, Forged, Straight, 4X Long, Tapered Eye (TD), Bronze, Sizes #1 to 18 | None | None | None | **#D4A**
Redditch, Forged, 4X Long, Heavy Wire, Ball Eye (TD), Bronze, Sizes #2 to 12 | None | **#9283**
Round Bend, Forged, 4X Long Forged Ball Eye (TD), Bronze, Sizes #2 to 16 | None |

Pattern Application: Streamers, Bucktails, and Stonefly Nymphs

| **#79582**
Round Bend, Forged, Straight, 5X Long, Tapered Eye (TD), Bronze, Sizes #6 to 12 | None | None | None | None | None | None | None |

Pattern Application: Weedless Bass Flies and Keel Patterns

| **#79666**
Keel (Sproat), Straight, Forged, Bronze, Ringed Eye (S), Sizes #1/0, 1 to 10 | None | None | None | None | None | None | None |

Pattern Application: Dry and Wet Flies

| **#AC80000**
Round Bend, Ball Eye (TD), Bronze, Sizes #10 to 26 | **#59, #L059, #NT059**
Round Bend, Fine Wire, Forged, Ball Eye (TD), Brz. & Nkl. Teflon, Sizes #4 to 24 | **#TMC5210**
Round, Forged, 1X Fine, Ball Eye (TD), Bronze, Sizes #10 to 20 | **#B-400**
Round Bend, Forged, Ball Eye (TD), Bronze, Sizes #8 to 16 | **#L2A**
Capt. Hamilton, Forged, 2X Fine, Ball Eye (TD), Bronze, Sizes #6 to 18 | **#1170**
Round Bend, Forged, Ball Eye (TD), Bronze, Sizes #8 to 16 | **#9288**
Round Bend, Forged, 2X Fine, Short Shank, Bronze, Forged Ball Eye (TD), Sizes #6 to 20 | **#P10**
Model Perfect Round, Bronze, Ball Eye (TD), Sizes #4 to 24 |

Pattern Application: Dry Flies, Wet Flies, and Nymphs

| **#AC80050**
Special, 3X Long, Ball Eye (S), Bronze, Sizes #6 to 22 | **#52, #L052, #NT052**
Special Bend, Light Wire, Ringed Eye (TD), Nkl. Teflon & Bronze, Sizes #6 to 20 | **#TMC200**
Special, Ball Eye (S), Bronze, Sizes #4 to 20 | None | **#K12ST**
Special, Forged, 3X Long, Ball Eye (S), Bronze, Sizes #8 to 22 | **#1270**
Special Bend (York), Curved Shank, 3X Long, Bronze, Ball Eye (S), Sizes #6 to 22 | None | None |

Pattern Application: Nymphs and Leeches

| **#AC80150**
Special, Long Upbent Shank, Fine Wire, Ball Eye (S), Bronze, Sizes #8 to 14 | None | **#TMC400T**
Special, Ball Eye (S), Bronze, Sizes #8 to 14 | None | **#K6ST**
Special (Price), Long Curve, Ball Eye (S), Bronze, Sizes #8 to 14 | **#1770**
Sproat, 3X Long, 1X Fine, Forged, Ball Eye (S), Bronze, Sizes #6 to 16 | None | None |

Pattern Application: Glo-Bugs, Scuds, Shrimp, Pupae, and Nymphs

| **#AC80200**
Special, 2X Short, 2X Wide, Ball Eye (TD), Bronze, Sizes #6 to 18 | **#L055, #NT055**
Special Bend, Short Shank, Bronze & Nkl. Teflon, Ringed Eye (TD), Sizes #10 to 20 | **#TMC2487**
Special, Forged, Offset, Fine Wire, 2X Short, Ball Eye (TD), Bronze, Sizes #10 to 20 | None | **#K4A**
Special (Veniard) Offset, Curved Shank, 2X Fine, Ball Eye (TD), Bronze, Sizes #8 to 18 | **#1130**
Continuous Bend, 1X Fine,1X Short, Ball Eye (TD), Bronze, Sizes #10 to 16 | None | **#C12**
Special Curve, Bronze, Ball Eye (TD), Sizes #10 to 20 |

Mustad Selection and Substitution Chart

Mustad	Eagle Claw	Tiemco	Kamasan	Partridge	Daiichi	VMC	Gamakatsu

Pattern Application: Glo-Bugs, Scuds, Shrimp, Pupae, and Nymphs

Mustad	Eagle Claw	Tiemco	Kamasan	Partridge	Daiichi	VMC	Gamakatsu
#AC80250 — Special, 2X Short, 2X Wide, Ball Eye (TD), Bronze, Sizes #10 to 22	#L055, #NT055 — Special Bend, Short Shank, Bronze & Nkl. Teflon, Ringed Eye (TD), Sizes #10 to 20	#TMC2487 — Special, Forged, Offset, Fine Wire, 2X Short, Ball Eye (TD), Bronze, Sizes #10 to 20	None	#K4A — Special (Veniard) Offset, Curved Shank, 2X Fine, Ball Eye (TD), Bronze, Sizes #8 to 18	#1130 — Continuous Bend, 1X Fine, 1X Short, Ball Eye (TD), Bronze, Sizes #10 to 16	None	#C12 — Special Curve, Bronze, Ball Eye (TD), Sizes #10 to 20

Pattern Application: Salmon and Steelhead Patterns

Mustad	Eagle Claw	Tiemco	Kamasan	Partridge	Daiichi	VMC	Gamakatsu
#90240 — Limerick, 2X Fine Wire, X Long, Black, Loop Oval Eye (TU), Sizes #4, 6, 8, 10	None	#TMC7999 — Salmon, Forged, Heavy Wire, Tapered Loop Eye (TU), Black, Sizes #2/0 to 12	#B-180 — Salmon, Forged, Tapered Loop Eye (TU), Black, Sizes #2/0 to 12	#M — Salmon, Forged, 2X Heavy, Tapered Loop Eye (TU), Black, Sizes #4/0-1/0, 1 to 10	#2441 — Salmon, Forged, 1X Strong, Tapered Loop Eye (TU), Black, Sizes #2/0, 1/0, 1 to 8	#8923 — Limerick, Forged, 2X Long, Ball Eye (TU), Bronze, Sizes #2 to 12	#T10-3H — Salmon, 1X Fine, Tapered Loop Eye (TU), Black, Sizes #2 to 8

Pattern Application: Saltwater Patterns

Mustad	Eagle Claw	Tiemco	Kamasan	Partridge	Daiichi	VMC	Gamakatsu
#AC91742 — O'Shaughnessy, Forged, 3X Short, X Strong, Ringed Eye (S), Bronze, Sizes #7/0 to 6	#L156, #NT156 — O'Shaughnessy, Forged, Offset, 2X Short, Brz. & Nkl. Teflon, Ringed Eye (S), Sizes #4/0 to 4	None	None	None	#2451 — O'Shaughnessy, Forged, Short Shank, Ball Eye (S), Black, Sizes #1 to 8	#8410 — Special (Crystal), Forged, Ball Eye (S), Bronze, Sizes #4 to 12	None

Pattern Application: Saltwater Patterns

Mustad	Eagle Claw	Tiemco	Kamasan	Partridge	Daiichi	VMC	Gamakatsu
#92162 — Beak, Forged, X Short, 3X Strong, Tapered Eye (TU), Nckl., Sizes #3/0 to 2	None	None	None	None	None	None	None

Pattern Application: Saltwater Patterns

Mustad	Eagle Claw	Tiemco	Kamasan	Partridge	Daiichi	VMC	Gamakatsu
#92553, 53S, 54 — Beak, X & 2X Strong, X Short, Tapered & Ball Eye (TU), Forged, Nickel & Stl. Steel Sizes #12/0 to 14	None	None	None	None	None	None	None

Pattern Application: Bass Bugs and Wet Flies

Mustad	Eagle Claw	Tiemco	Kamasan	Partridge	Daiichi	VMC	Gamakatsu
#92625, 27 — Beak, Reversed Special Long, Forged, Ball Eye (TD), Bronze Sizes #8/0-6 to 14	None	None	None	None	None	None	None

Pattern Application: Saltwater Patterns

Mustad	Eagle Claw	Tiemco	Kamasan	Partridge	Daiichi	VMC	Gamakatsu
#92677 — Beak, Reversed Special Short, Forged, Ball Eye (S), Bronze Sizes #8/0-6 to 14	None	None	None	None	None	None	None

Pattern Application: Trolling Streamers, Large Stonefly Nymphs, and Baitfish

Mustad	Eagle Claw	Tiemco	Kamasan	Partridge	Daiichi	VMC	Gamakatsu
#94720 — Round Bend, Forged, Tapered Eye (TD), Bronze, Sizes #2 to 8	None	None	None	#CS15 — Limerick, Heavy Wire, X Long, Tapered Loop Eye (TD), Bronze, Sizes #2/0, 2, 4	None	None	None

Mustad Selection and Substitution Chart

Mustad	Eagle Claw	Tiemco	Kamasan	Partridge	Daiichi	VMC	Gamakatsu

Pattern Application: Large Mayflies and Grasshoppers

Mustad	Eagle Claw	Tiemco	Kamasan	Partridge	Daiichi	VMC	Gamakatsu
#94831 — Round Bend, Forged, 2X Long, 2X Fine Tapered Eye (TD), Bronze, Sizes #4 to 16	#63, #L063, #NT063 — Round Bend, 2X Long, Brz. & Nkl. Teflon, Ball Eye (TD), Sizes #4 to 18	#TMC5263 — Round, Forged, 3X Long, Ball Eye (TD), Bronze, Sizes #2 to 18	#B-830 — Round Bend, Forged, 2X Long, Ball Eye (TD), Bronze, Sizes #6 to 14	#H1A — Capt. Hamilton, Forged, 2X Fine, 2-1/2X Long, Bronze, Ball Eye (TD), Sizes #2 to 14	#1720 — Round Bend, Forged, 3X Long, 1X Strong, Bronze, Ball Eye (TD), Sizes #6 to 18	#9283 — Round Bend, Forged, 4X Long Forged Ball Eye (TD), Bronze, Sizes #2 to 16	#P10-2L1H — Model Perfect Round, 2X Long, 1X Strong, Bronze, Ball Eye (TD), Sizes #4 to 16

Pattern Application: Standard Dry Flies, Floating Nymphs, Ants, No-Hackles, and Sparsely Dressed

Mustad	Eagle Claw	Tiemco	Kamasan	Partridge	Daiichi	VMC	Gamakatsu
#94833 #AC94833 — Round Bend, X Long, 3X Fine, Forged, Tapered Eye (TD), Bronze, Sizes #6 to 22	#63, #L063, #NT063 — Round Bend, 2X Long, Brz. & Nkl. Teflon, Ball Eye (TD), Sizes #4 to 18	#TMC5263 — Round, Forged, 3X Long, Ball Eye (TD), Bronze, Sizes #2 to 18	#B-830 — Round Bend, Forged, 2X Long, Ball Eye (TD), Bronze, Sizes #6 to 14	#H1A — Capt. Hamilton, Forged, 2X Fine, 2-1/2X Long, Bronze, Ball Eye (TD), Sizes #2 to 14	#1720 — Round Bend, Forged, 3X Long, 1X Strong, Bronze, Ball Eye (TD), Sizes #6 to 18	#9283 — Round Bend, Forged, 4X Long Forged Ball Eye (TD), Bronze, Sizes #2 to 16	#P10-2L1H — Model Perfect Round, 2X Long, 1X Strong, Bronze, Ball Eye (TD), Sizes #4 to 16

Pattern Application: Traditional Dry Flies and Variants

Mustad	Eagle Claw	Tiemco	Kamasan	Partridge	Daiichi	VMC	Gamakatsu
#94836 — Round Bend, Short Shank, X Fine, Forged, Tapered Eye (TD), Bronze, Sizes #10 to 20	#59, #L059, #NT059 — Round Bend, Fine Wire, Forged, Ball Eye (TD), Brz. & Nkl. Teflon, Sizes #4 to 24	#TMC5210 — Round, Forged, 1X Fine, Ball Eye (TD), Bronze, Sizes #10 to 20	#B-400 — Round Bend, Forged, Ball Eye (TD), Bronze, Sizes #8 to 16	#L2A — Capt. Hamilton, Forged, 2X Fine, Ball Eye (TD), Bronze, Sizes #6 to 18	#1170 — Round Bend, Forged, Ball Eye (TD), Bronze, Sizes #8 to 16	#9288 — Round Bend, Forged, 2X Fine, Short Shank, Bronze, Forged Ball Eye (TD), Sizes #6 to 20	#P10 — Model Perfect Round, Bronze, Ball Eye (TD), Sizes #4 to 24

Pattern Application: Dry Flies, Extended Bodies, and Beetles

Mustad	Eagle Claw	Tiemco	Kamasan	Partridge	Daiichi	VMC	Gamakatsu
#94838 — Round Bend, X Short, X Fine, Forged, Tapered Eye (TD), Bronze, Sizes #10 to 20	#59, #L059, #NT059 — Round Bend, Fine Wire, Forged, Ball Eye (TD), Brz. & Nkl. Teflon, Sizes #4 to 24	#TMC5210 — Round, Forged, 1X Fine, Ball Eye (TD), Bronze, Sizes #10 to 20	#B-400 — Round Bend, Forged, Ball Eye (TD), Bronze, Sizes #8 to 16	#L2A — Capt. Hamilton, Forged, 2X Fine, Ball Eye (TD), Bronze, Sizes #6 to 18	#1170 — Round Bend, Forged, Ball Eye (TD), Bronze, Sizes #8 to 16	#9288 — Round Bend, Forged, 2X Fine, Short Shank, Bronze, Forged Ball Eye (TD), Sizes #6 to 20	#P10 — Model Perfect Round, Bronze, Ball Eye (TD), Sizes #4 to 24

Pattern Application: Dry Flies and Nymphs

Mustad	Eagle Claw	Tiemco	Kamasan	Partridge	Daiichi	VMC	Gamakatsu
#94840, #AC94840 — Round Bend, X Fine, Forged, Tapered Eye (TD), Bronze, Sizes #2 to 28	#59, #L059, #NT059 — Round Bend, Fine Wire, Forged, Ball Eye (TD), Brz. & Nkl. Teflon, Sizes #4 to 24	#TMC5210 — Round, Forged, 1X Fine, Ball Eye (TD), Bronze, Sizes #10 to 20	#B-400 — Round Bend, Forged, Ball Eye (TD), Bronze, Sizes #8 to 16	#L2A — Capt. Hamilton, Forged, 2X Fine, Ball Eye (TD), Bronze, Sizes #6 to 18	#1170 — Round Bend, Forged, Ball Eye (TD), Bronze, Sizes #8 to 16	#9288 — Round Bend, Forged, 2X Fine, Short Shank, Bronze, Forged Ball Eye (TD), Sizes #6 to 20	#P10 — Model Perfect Round, Bronze, Ball Eye (TD), Sizes #4 to 24

Pattern Application: Dry Flies

Mustad	Eagle Claw	Tiemco	Kamasan	Partridge	Daiichi	VMC	Gamakatsu
#94842 — Round Bend, X Fine, Forged, Tapered Eye (TU), Bronze, Sizes #8 to 28	#159, #L159 — Round Bend, X Fine, Ball Eye (TU), Bronze, Sizes #4 to 18	None	None	#L3B — Capt. Hamilton, Forged, 4X Fine, Ball Eye (TU), Bronze, Sizes #10 to 18	#1330 — Round Bend, 1X Short, Ball Eye (TD), Bronze, Sizes #8 to 24	#9281 — Modified Round Bend, Forged, X Fine, Forged Ball Eye (TU), Bronze, Sizes #8 to 20	None

Pattern Application: Dry Flies and Nymphs

Mustad	Eagle Claw	Tiemco	Kamasan	Partridge	Daiichi	VMC	Gamakatsu
#94845 — Round Bend, Barbless, X Fine, Forged, Tapered Eye (TD), Bronze, Sizes #8 to 22	#61, #L061B, — Round Bend, Barbless, Bronze, Ball Eye (TD), Sizes #4 to 18	#TMC100BL — Round Bend, Barbless, Forged, 1X Fine, Bronze, Ball Eye (TD), Sizes #10 to 22	None	#L3AY — Capt. Hamilton, Barbless, Forged, 4X Fine, Bronze, Ball Eye (TD), Sizes #8 to 22	#1190 — Round Bend, Barbless, Ball Eye (TD), Bronze, Sizes #8 to 18	None	#R10-BN — Retainer Bend Barbless,, Black, Ball Eye (TD), Sizes #10 to 20

Pattern Application: Small Dry Flies, Midges, and Pupae

Mustad	Eagle Claw	Tiemco	Kamasan	Partridge	Daiichi	VMC	Gamakatsu
#94859 — Round Bend, Straight, X Fine, Forged, Ringed Eye (TD), Bronze, Sizes #20 to 28	None	None	None	#K1A — Capt. Hamilton, Ball Eye (TD), Offset, Std. Shank. Sizes #24 to 28	None	None	None

Mustad Selection and Substitution Chart

Mustad	Eagle Claw	Tiemco	Kamasan	Partridge	Daiichi	VMC	Gamakatsu
Pattern Application: Wet Flies, Dry Flies, and Nymphs							
#94863 Round Bend, Forged, Bronze, Loop Oval Eye (TU), Sizes #10 to 20	None	None	None	None	None	None	None
Pattern Application: Saltwater Patterns							
#95141, 60 Siwash, 2X & 3X Strong, Cad. & Stl. Steel Open Ring Eye (S), Sizes #9/0 to 2	None	None	None	None	None	None	None

Eagle Claw Hooks

Eagle Claw hooks are manufactured by the Wright and McGill Company of Denver, Colorado. They are produced in countless shapes, sizes, lengths, strengths, finishes, points, and other variations for every type of fly pattern. They are quality hooks that are ideal for fly tying.

Eagle Claw hooks can be purchased through most fly shops or catalog houses or directly from Eagle Claw at Wright & McGill, P.O. Box 16011, Denver, CO 80216-0011; phone 303-321-1481; fax 303-321-4750.

Eagle Claw Selection and Substitution Chart

Pattern Application
The pattern application lists various types of patterns that can be tied using the specified hooks shown below.

Possible Substitutes
Listed across the page are other manufacturers' hooks that can be used as alternatives. In most cases, the hooks listed are similar or have the same characteristics with minor differences.

Note: Hook illustrations are only examples and are not shown at actual sizes. Also note that an "L" preceding the hook number indicates Lazer Sharp; "NT" preceding the hook number indicates a nickel Teflon finish. Both are Eagle Claw manufacturing processes, as is the "Sea Guard" finish. In addition, after the eye description, **(S)** indicates a straight eye, **(TD)** indicates a turned-down eye, and **(TU)** indicates a turned-up eye.

Eagle Claw	Tiemco	Kamasan	Partridge	Daiichi	VMC	Gamakatsu	Mustad
Pattern Application: Dry Flies, Nymphs, and Larvae							
#52, #L052, #NT052 Special Bend, Light Wire, Ringed Eye (TD), Nkl. Teflon & Bronze, Sizes #6 to 20	**#TMC200** Special, Ball Eye (S), Bronze, Sizes #4 to 20	None	**K12ST** Special, Forged, 3X Long, Ball Eye (S), Bronze, Sizes #8 to 22	**#1270** Special Bend (York), Curved Shank, 3X Long, Bronze, Ball Eye (S), Sizes #6 to 22	None	None	**#AC80050** Special, 3X Long, Ball Eye (S), Bronze, Sizes #6 to 22
Pattern Application: Saltwater, Bass Bugs, and Streamers							
#L054SS O'Shaughnessy, Ringed Eye (S), Stainless Steel, Sizes #1/0 to 4/0	**#TMC811S** O'Shaughnessy, X Strong, Ringed Eye (S), Stainless Steel, Sizes #4/0 to 8	None	None	**#2546** O'Shaughnessy, Forged, Ball Eye (S), Stainless Steel, Sizes #6/0 to1/0, 1 to 6	**#9255** O'Shaughnessy, Long Shank, Ball Eye (S), Brz., Nkl., Perma Stl., Gold, Sizes #5/0 to 6	None	**#3406, 06B** O'Shaughnessy, Forged, Ringed Eye (S), Bronze or Nickel, Sizes #14/0 to 8
Pattern Application: Nymphs, Scuds, and Shrimp							
#L055, #NT055 Special Bend, Short Shank, Bronze & Nkl. Teflon, Ringed Eye (TD), Sizes #10 to 20	**#TMC2487** Special, Forged, Offset, Fine Wire, 2X Short, Ball Eye (TD), Bronze, Sizes #10 to 20	None	**#K4A** Special (Veniard) Offset, Curved Shank, 2X Fine, Ball Eye (TD), Bronze, Sizes #8 to 18	**#1130** Continuous Bend, 1X Fine, 1X Short, Ball Eye (TD), Bronze, Sizes #10 to 16	None	**#C12** Special Curve, Bronze, Ball Eye (TD), Sizes #10 to 20	**#AC80200** Special, 2X Short, 2X Wide, Ball Eye (TD), Bronze, Sizes #6 to 18
Pattern Application: Nymphs, Scuds, and Shrimp							
#L056, #NT056 Special Bend, Hump Shank, Brz. & Nickel Teflon, Ringed Eye (TD), Sizes #2 to14	**#TMC2487** Special, Forged, Offset, Fine Wire, 2X Short, Ball Eye (TD), Bronze, Sizes #10 to 20	None	**#K4A** Special (Veniard) Offset, Curved Shank, 2X Fine, Ball Eye (TD), Bronze, Sizes #8 to 18	**#1130** Continuous Bend, 1X Fine, 1X Short, Ball Eye (TD), Bronze, Sizes #10 to 16	None	**#C12** Special Curve, Bronze, Ball Eye (TD), Sizes #10 to 20	**#AC80200** Special, 2X Short, 2X Wide, Ball Eye (TD), Bronze, Sizes #6 to 18
Pattern Application: Wet Flies, Nymphs, Terrestrials, Larvae, and Pupae							
#57, #L057, #NT057 Sproat, Ball Eye(TD), Bronze & Nkl. Teflon, Sizes #4 to 16	**#TMC3761** Sproat, Forged, 1X Long, 2X Heavy, Ball Eye (TD), Bronze, Sizes #8 to 18	**#B-170** Sproat, Ball Eye (TD), Bronze, Sizes #6 to 16	**#G3A** Sproat, Forged, Heavy Wire, Ball Eye (TD), Bronze, Sizes #8 to 16	**#1550** Sproat, Ball Eye (TD), Bronze, Sizes #2 to 18	**#8526** Sproat, Forged Ball Eye (TD), Bronze, Sizes #8 to 16	**#S10** Sproat, Black, Ball Eye (TD), Sizes #2 to 24	**#3906, #AC3906** Sproat, Tapered Eye (TD), Bronze, Size #2 to 20

Eagle Claw Selection and Substitution Chart

Pattern Application: Wet Flies, Streamers, Nymphs, and Larvae

Eagle Claw	Tiemco	Kamasan	Partridge	Daiichi	VMC	Gamakatsu	Mustad
#58, #L058, #NT058 Round Bend, 3X Long, Forged, Ball Eye (TD), Bronze & Nkl. Teflon, Sizes #4 to 14	**#TMC5263** Round, Forged, 3X Long, Ball Eye (TD), Bronze, Sizes #2 to 18	**#B-830** Round Bend, Forged, 2X Long, Ball Eye (TD), Bronze, Sizes #6 to 14	**#H1A** Capt. Hamilton, Forged, 2X Fine, 2-1/2X Long, Bronze, Ball Eye (TD), Sizes #2 to 14	**#1720** Round Bend, Forged, 3X Long, 1X Strong, Bronze, Ball Eye (TD), Sizes #6 to 18	**#9283** Round Bend, Forged, 4X Long Forged Ball Eye (TD), Bronze, Sizes #2 to 16	**#P10-2L1H** Model Perfect Round, 2X Long, 1X Strong, Bronze, Ball Eye (TD), Sizes #4 to 16	**#9672, #AC9672** Round Bend, Forged, 3X Long, Bronze, Tapered Eye (TD), Sizes #2 to 18

Pattern Application: Dry Flies, Wet Flies, Midges, Nymphs, Larvae, Pupae, and Terrestrials

Eagle Claw	Tiemco	Kamasan	Partridge	Daiichi	VMC	Gamakatsu	Mustad
#59, #L059, #NT059 Round Bend, Fine Wire, Forged, Ball Eye (TD), Brz. & Nkl. Teflon, Sizes #4 to 24	**#TMC5210** Round, Forged, 1X Fine, Ball Eye (TD), Bronze, Sizes #10 to 20	**#B-400** Round Bend, Forged, Ball Eye (TD), Bronze, Sizes #8 to 16	**#L2A** Capt. Hamilton, Forged, 2X Fine, Ball Eye (TD), Bronze, Sizes #6 to 18	**#1170** Round Bend, Forged, Ball Eye (TD), Bronze, Sizes #8 to 16	**#9288** Round Bend, Forged, 2X Fine, Short Shank, Bronze, Forged Ball Eye (TD), Sizes #6 to 20	**#P10** Model Perfect Round, Bronze, Ball Eye (TD), Sizes #4 to 24	**#94840, #AC94840** Round Bend, X Fine, Forged, Tapered Eye (TD), Bronze, Sizes #2 to 28

Pattern Application: Dry Flies, Wet Flies, Nymphs, and Larvae

Eagle Claw	Tiemco	Kamasan	Partridge	Daiichi	VMC	Gamakatsu	Mustad
#60, #L060, #NT060 Sproat, Fine Wire, Ball Eye (TD), Bronze & Nkl. Teflon, Sizes #8 to 16	None	**#B-170** Sproat, Ball Eye (TD), Bronze, Sizes #6 to 16	**#A** Improved Sproat, Offset, 1X Short, 2X Fine, Ball Eye (TD), Bronze, Sizes #10 to 16	**#1550** Sproat, Ball Eye (TD), Bronze, Sizes #2 to 18	**#9282** Sproat, Forged, X Fine, Offset, Forged Ball Eye (TD), Bronze, Sizes #8 to 18	**#S10-3F** Sproat, 1X Fine, Black, Ball Eye (TD), Sizes #4 to 20	**#3399, 99A, 99D, 99N** Sproat, Ball Eye (TD), Brz., Gold, 99D-Fine Wire, Sizes #9/0 to -2, #4 to 20

Pattern Application: Dry Flies, Wet Flies, Midges, Nymphs, Larvae, Pupae, and Terrestrials

Eagle Claw	Tiemco	Kamasan	Partridge	Daiichi	VMC	Gamakatsu	Mustad
#61, #L061B, Round Bend, Barbless, Bronze, Ball Eye (TD), Sizes #4 to 18	**#TMC100BL** Round Bend, Barbless, Forged, 1X Fine, Bronze, Ball Eye (TD), Sizes #10 to 22	None	**#L3AY** Capt. Hamilton, Barbless, Forged, 4X Fine, Bronze, Ball Eye (TD), Sizes #8 to 22	**#1190** Round Bend, Barbless, Ball Eye (TD), Bronze, Sizes #8 to 18	None	**#R10-BN** Retainer Bend Barbless, Black, Ball Eye (TD), Sizes #10 to 20	**#94845** Round Bend, Barbless, X Fine, Forged, Tapered Eye (TD), Bronze, Sizes #8 to 22

Pattern Application: Wet Flies, Nymphs, Larvae, and Pupae

Eagle Claw	Tiemco	Kamasan	Partridge	Daiichi	VMC	Gamakatsu	Mustad
#63, #L063, #NT063 Round Bend, 2X Long, Brz. & Nkl. Teflon, Ball Eye (TD), Sizes #4 to 18	**#TMC5263** Round, Forged, 3X Long, Ball Eye (TD), Bronze, Sizes #2 to 18	**#B-830** Round Bend, Forged, 2X Long, Ball Eye (TD), Bronze, Sizes #6 to 14	**#H1A** Capt. Hamilton, Forged, 2X Fine, 2-1/2X Long, Bronze, Ball Eye (TD), Sizes #2 to 14	**#1720** Round Bend, Forged, 3X Long, 1X Strong, Bronze, Ball Eye (TD), Sizes #6 to 18	**#9283** Round Bend, Forged, 4X Long Forged Ball Eye (TD), Bronze, Sizes #2 to 16	**#P10-2L1H** Model Perfect Round, 2X Long, 1X Strong, Bronze, Ball Eye (TD), Sizes #4 to 16	**#9672, #AC9672** Round Bend, Forged, 3X Long, Bronze, Tapered Eye (TD), Sizes #2 to 18

Pattern Application: Salmon and Steelheads

Eagle Claw	Tiemco	Kamasan	Partridge	Daiichi	VMC	Gamakatsu	Mustad
#64B, #L064B Sproat, Barbless, Long Shank. Ball Eye (TD), Bronze, Sizes #1 to 8	None	None	None	None	None	None	**#3257B** Sproat (Barbless), Tapered Eye (TD), Kirbed, Bronze, Size #8

Pattern Application: Saltwater Patterns

Eagle Claw	Tiemco	Kamasan	Partridge	Daiichi	VMC	Gamakatsu	Mustad
#L067 Special (Billy Pate) Ringed Eye (S), Sea Guard, Sizes #5/0 to 6	None	None	None	None	None	None	None

Pattern Application: Saltwater Patterns, Bass Streamers, and Trolling Streamers

Eagle Claw	Tiemco	Kamasan	Partridge	Daiichi	VMC	Gamakatsu	Mustad
#74 Eagle Claw Design, Forged, XX Long, Gold, Ball Eye (TD), Sizes #4/0 to 4	None	None	**#CS17** Limerick, 6X Long, Tapered Loop Eye (TD), Black, Sizes #1, 2, 4, 6	**#J171** Improved Limerick, 6X Long, 1X Heavy, Tapered Loop Eye (TD), Black, Sizes #1, 2	None	None	**#3665A** Limerick, 1/2 Longer than Regular, Tapered Eye (TD), Bronze, Sizes #2 to 14

Eagle Claw Selection and Substitution Chart

Eagle Claw	Tiemco	Kamasan	Partridge	Daiichi	VMC	Gamakatsu	Mustad

Pattern Application: Nymphs, Larvae, Pupae, San Juan Worm, and Shrimp

Eagle Claw	Tiemco	Kamasan	Partridge	Daiichi	VMC	Gamakatsu	Mustad
#L144 Special (Kahle) Wide Gap, X Short, Ball Eye (TU), Bronze, Sizes #4 to 16	None	None	#K2B Special (Yorkshire) Forged, Curved Shank, Ball Eye (TU), Bronze, Sizes #8 to 18	#1140 Continuous Bend, Forged, 1X Fine, 1X Short, Bronze, Ball Eye (TU), Sizes #10 to 16	None	#C12U Special Curve, Bronze, Ball Eye (TU), Sizes #6 to 16	#37160, 60S Wide Gape, Slightly Reversed, Ball Eye (TU), Brz., or St. Steel, Sizes #7/0 to 26

Pattern Application: Saltwater Patterns

Eagle Claw	Tiemco	Kamasan	Partridge	Daiichi	VMC	Gamakatsu	Mustad
#L156, #NT156 O'Shaughnessy, Forged, Offset, 2X Short, Brz. & Nkl. Teflon, Ringed Eye (S), Sizes #4/0 to 4	None	None	None	#2451 O'Shaughnessy, Forged, Short Shank, Ball Eye (S), Black, Sizes #1 to 8	#8410 Special (Crystal), Forged, Ball Eye (S), Bronze, Sizes #4 to 12	None	#3406, 06B O'Shaughnessy, Forged, Ringed Eye (S), Bronze or Nickel, Sizes #14/0 to 8

Pattern Application: Dry Flies, Wet Flies, Nymphs, and Terrestrials

Eagle Claw	Tiemco	Kamasan	Partridge	Daiichi	VMC	Gamakatsu	Mustad
#159, #L159 Round Bend, X Fine, Ball Eye (TU), Bronze, Sizes #4 to 18	None	None	#L3B Capt. Hamilton, Forged, 4X Fine, Ball Eye (TU), Bronze, Sizes #10 to 18	#1330 Round Bend, 1X Short, Ball Eye (TD), Bronze, Sizes #8 to 24	#9281 Modified Round Bend, Forged, X Fine, Forged Ball Eye (TU), Bronze, Sizes #8 to 20	None	#94842 Round Bend, X Fine, Forged, Tapered Eye (TU), Bronze, Sizes #8 to 28

Pattern Application: Saltwater Patterns and Bass Streamers

Eagle Claw	Tiemco	Kamasan	Partridge	Daiichi	VMC	Gamakatsu	Mustad
#178 Special, Forged, Offset, Ball Eye (TD), Gold, Sizes #1/0 to 4	None	None	None	None	None	None	None

Pattern Application: Poppers

Eagle Claw	Tiemco	Kamasan	Partridge	Daiichi	VMC	Gamakatsu	Mustad
#L200 Special, Kinked Shank, Ringed Eye (S), Bronze, Sizes #1/0 to 4	None	None	None	None	None	None	#33900 Sproat, X Long, Ringed Eye (S), Bronze, Sizes #1/0 to 14

Pattern Application: Saltwater Patterns, Bass Bugs, Hair Flies, and Lures

Eagle Claw	Tiemco	Kamasan	Partridge	Daiichi	VMC	Gamakatsu	Mustad
#250, #L250 O'Shaughnessy, Forged, Offset, Bronze, 1X Long, Ringed Eye (S), Sizes #4/0 to 4	None	None	None	#2451 O'Shaughnessy, Forged, Short Shank, Ball Eye (S), Black, Sizes #1 to 8	#8410 Special (Crystal), Forged, Ball Eye (S), Bronze, Sizes #4 to 12	None	#3406, 06B O'Shaughnessy, Forged, Ringed Eye (S), Bronze or Nickel, Sizes #14/0 to 8

Pattern Application: Saltwater Patterns, Bass Bugs, Hair Flies, and Lures

Eagle Claw	Tiemco	Kamasan	Partridge	Daiichi	VMC	Gamakatsu	Mustad
#254, #254N, #L254N #254SS O'Shaughnessy, Forged, Offset, 2X Short, Nckl., Cad., & Stl. Stl Ball Eye(S), Sizes #14/0 to 6	None	None	None	#2451 O'Shaughnessy, Forged, Short Shank, Ball Eye (S), Black, Sizes #1 to 8	#8410 Special (Crystal), Forged, Ball Eye (S), Bronze, Sizes #4 to 12	None	#3406, 06B O'Shaughnessy, Forged, Ringed Eye (S), Bronze or Nickel, Sizes #14/0 to 8

Pattern Application: Streamers, Bucktails, and Thunder Creeks

Eagle Claw	Tiemco	Kamasan	Partridge	Daiichi	VMC	Gamakatsu	Mustad
#281, #L281, #NT281 Sproat, 4X Long, 1X Heavy, Brz. & Nkl. Teflon, Ball Eye (TD), Sizes #2 to 10	None	None	#D4A Redditch, Forged, 4X Long, Heavy Wire, Ball Eye (TD), Bronze, Sizes #2 to 12	#2340 Limerick, 6X Long, 1X Strong, Ball Eye (TD), Bronze, Sizes #4 to 12	None	#S11-4L2H Sproat, 4X Long, 2X Strong, Black, Ball Eye (TD), Sizes #6 to 12	#33960 Sproat, 4X Long, Bronze, Ball Eye (TD), Sizes #2 to 12

Eagle Claw Selection and Substitution Chart

Eagle Claw	Tiemco	Kamasan	Partridge	Daiichi	VMC	Gamakatsu	Mustad

Pattern Application: Saltwater Shrimp, Freshwater Nymphs, and Larvae

Eagle Claw	Tiemco	Kamasan	Partridge	Daiichi	VMC	Gamakatsu	Mustad
#182RE Wide Gape, Forged, X Short, Ball Eye (TU), Nickel, Sizes #5/0 to 2	None	None	None	None	None	None	**#9523** Round Bend, Offset, Forged, 5X Short, X Fine, Bronze, Tapered Eye (TU), Sizes #3/0 to 16

Pattern Application: Nymphs, Larvae, and Pupae

Eagle Claw	Tiemco	Kamasan	Partridge	Daiichi	VMC	Gamakatsu	Mustad
#479 Wide Gape, Forged, X Short, Ball Eye (TU), Gold, Sizes #4 to 14	None	None	**#K2B** Special (Yorkshire) Forged, Curved Shank, Ball Eye (TU), Bronze, Sizes #8 to 18	**#1150** Continuous Bend, Forged,1X Strong, Reversed, Bronze, Ball Eye (TU), Sizes #18, 20, 22	None	**#C12U** Special Curve, Bronze, Ball Eye (TU), Sizes #6 to 16	**#9523** Round Bend, Offset, Forged, 5X Short, X Fine, Bronze, Tapered Eye (TU), Sizes #3/0 to 16

Pattern Application: Nymphs, Larvae, and Pupae

Eagle Claw	Tiemco	Kamasan	Partridge	Daiichi	VMC	Gamakatsu	Mustad
#781 Wide Gape, Forged, X Short, Ball Eye (TD), Gold, Sizes #6 to 16	None	None	**#K4A** Special (Veniard) Offset, Curved Shank, 2X Fine, Ball Eye (TD), Bronze, Sizes #8 to 18	**#1140** Continuous Bend, Forged, 1X Fine, 1X Short, Bronze, Ball Eye (TU), Sizes #10 to 16	None	**#C12** Special Curve, Bronze, Ball Eye (TD), Sizes #10 to 20	**#9479** Round Bend, Reversed, 5X Short, X Fine, Bronze, Tapered Eye (TD), Sizes #2/0 to 18

Pattern Application: Bass Wet Flies and Salmon and Steelhead Patterns

Eagle Claw	Tiemco	Kamasan	Partridge	Daiichi	VMC	Gamakatsu	Mustad
#1197B, #L1197B Sproat, Long Shank, Bronze, Ball Eye (TD), Sizes #1 to 8	**#TMC3761** Sproat, Forged, 1X Long, 2X Heavy, Ball Eye (TD), Bronze, Sizes #8 to 18	**#B-170** Sproat, Ball Eye (TD), Bronze, Sizes #6 to 16	**#G3A** Sproat, Forged, Ball Eye (TD), Bronze, Sizes #8 to 16	**#1560** Sproat, 1X Long, 1X Strong, Ball Eye (TD), Bronze, Sizes #6 to 18	**#8527** Sproat, 1X Long, Forged Ball Eye (TD), Bronze, Sizes #8 to 16	**#S10-3F** Sproat, 1X Fine, Black, Ball Eye (TD), Sizes #4 to 20	**#3906B, #AC3906B** Sproat, 1X Long, Tapered Eye (TD), Bronze, Size #4 to 18

Pattern Application: Bass Wet Flies and Salmon and Steelhead Patterns

Eagle Claw	Tiemco	Kamasan	Partridge	Daiichi	VMC	Gamakatsu	Mustad
#1197G #L1197G Sproat, Long Shank, Ball Eye (TD), Gold, Sizes #1 to 8	**#TMC3761** Sproat, Forged, 1X Long, 2X Heavy, Ball Eye (TD), Bronze, Sizes #8 to 18	**#B-170** Sproat, Ball Eye (TD), Bronze, Sizes #6 to 16	**#G3A** Sproat, Forged, Ball Eye (TD), Bronze, Sizes #8 to 16	**#1560** Sproat, 1X Long, 1X Strong, Ball Eye (TD), Bronze, Sizes #6 to 18	**#8527** Sproat, 1X Long, Forged Ball Eye (TD), Bronze, Sizes #8 to 16	**#S10-3F** Sproat, 1X Fine, Black, Ball Eye (TD), Sizes #4 to 20	**#3906B, #AC3906B** Sproat, 1X Long, Tapered Eye (TD), Bronze, Sizes #4 to 18

Pattern Application: Bass Wet Flies and Salmon and Steelhead Patterns

Eagle Claw	Tiemco	Kamasan	Partridge	Daiichi	VMC	Gamakatsu	Mustad
#1197N, #L1197N Sproat, Long Shank, Nickel, Ball Eye (TD), Sizes #1 to 8	**#TMC3761** Sproat, Forged, 1X Long, 2X Heavy, Ball Eye (TD), Bronze, Sizes #8 to 18	**#B-170** Sproat, Ball Eye (TD), Bronze, Sizes #6 to 16	**#G3A** Sproat, Forged, Ball Eye (TD), Bronze, Sizes #8 to 16	**#1560** Sproat, 1X Long, 1X Strong, Ball Eye (TD), Bronze, Sizes #6 to 18	**#8527** Sproat, 1X Long, Forged Ball Eye (TD), Bronze, Sizes #8 to 16	**#S10-3F** Sproat, 1X Fine, Black, Ball Eye (TD), Sizes #4 to 20	**#3906B, #AC3906B** Sproat, 1X Long, Tapered Eye (TD), Bronze, Size #4 to 18

Pattern Application: Bass Wet Flies and Salmon and Steelhead Patterns

Eagle Claw	Tiemco	Kamasan	Partridge	Daiichi	VMC	Gamakatsu	Mustad
#NT1197 Sproat, Long Shank, Ball Eye (TD), Nickel Teflon, Sizes #1 to 8	**#TMC3761** Sproat, Forged, 1X Long, 2X Heavy, Ball Eye (TD), Bronze, Sizes #8 to 18	**#B-170** Sproat, Ball Eye (TD), Bronze, Sizes #6 to 16	**#G3A** Sproat, Forged, Ball Eye (TD), Bronze, Sizes #8 to 16	**#1560** Sproat, 1X Long, 1X Strong, Ball Eye (TD), Bronze, Sizes #6 to 18	**#8527** Sproat, 1X Long, Forged Ball Eye (TD), Bronze, Sizes #8 to 16	**#S10-3F** Sproat, 1X Fine, Black, Ball Eye (TD), Sizes #4 to 20	**#3906B, #AC3906B** Sproat, 1X Long, Tapered Eye (TD), Bronze, Size #4 to 18

Pattern Application: Saltwater Patterns, Freshwater Shrimp, and Nymphs

Eagle Claw	Tiemco	Kamasan	Partridge	Daiichi	VMC	Gamakatsu	Mustad
#NT2050, #NT2052 Special (Circle Sea), Long Shank, Ringed Eye (S), Nickel Teflon, Sizes #5/0 to 18	None	None	None	None	None	None	None

Tiemco Hooks

Tiemco produces high-quality hooks for sport fishing that are sold worldwide. Tiemco hooks are favored over those of other manufacturers by many fly tiers in their pattern construction.

Tiemco hooks can be purchased through most fly shops or catalog houses or through its U.S. distributor: Umpqua Feather Merchants, P.O. Box 700, Glide, OR 97443; phone 800-322-3218.

Tiemco Selection and Substitution Chart

Pattern Application
The pattern application lists various types of patterns that can be tied using the specified hooks shown below.

Possible Substitutes
Listed across the page are other manufacturers' hooks that can be used as alternatives. In most cases, the hooks listed are similar or have the same characteristics with minor differences.

Note: Hook illustrations are only examples and are not shown at actual sizes. In addition, "BL" after the number indicates that the hook is barbless. After the eye description, **(S)** indicates a straight eye, **(TD)** indicates a turned-down eye, and **(TU)** indicates a turned-up eye.

Tiemco	Kamasan	Partridge	Daiichi	VMC	Gamakatsu	Mustad	Eagle Claw
Pattern Application: Standard Dry Flies and Floating Nymphs							
#TMC100 TMC100BL Round, Ball Eye (TD), Bronze, Sizes #8 to 26	**#B-400** Round Bend, Forged, Ball Eye (TD), Bronze, Sizes #8 to 16	**#L2A** Capt. Hamilton, Forged, 2X Fine, Ball Eye (TD), Bronze, Sizes #6 to 18	**#1170** Round Bend, Forged, Ball Eye (TD), Bronze, Sizes #8 to 16	**#9288** Round Bend, Forged, 2X Fine, Short Shank, Bronze, Forged Ball Eye (TD), Sizes #6 to 20	**#P10** Model Perfect Round, Bronze, Ball Eye (TD), Sizes #4 to 24	**#94833** **#AC94833** Round Bend, X Long, 3X Fine, Forged, Tapered Eye (TD), Bronze, Sizes #6 to 22	**#59, #L059,** **#NT059** Round Bend, Fine Wire, Forged, Ball Eye (TD), Brz. & Nkl. Teflon, Sizes #4 to 24
Pattern Application: Dry Flies and Floating Nymphs							
#TMC101 Round, Ball Eye (S), Bronze, Sizes #8 to 20	None	None	**#1640** Round Bend, Forged, Reversed, 2X Short, Fine Wire, Ball Eye (S), Bronze, Sizes #2 to 20	None	None	None	None
Pattern Application: Dry Flies and Floating Nymphs							
#TMC102Y Round, Ball Eye (S), Bronze, Sizes #11, 13, 15, 17	None	None	**#1640** Round Bend, Forged, Reversed, 2X Short, Fine Wire, Ball Eye (S), Bronze, Sizes #2 to 20	None	None	None	None
Pattern Application: Barbless Dry Flies							
#TMC103BL Round, Barbless X Fine, Wide Gape, Ball Eye (S), Bronze, Sizes #11 to 19	None	None	**#1190** Round Bend, Barbless, Ball Eye (TD), Bronze, Sizes #8 to 18	None	None	None	None
Pattern Application: Eggs and Glo-Bugs							
#TMC105 O'Shaughnessy, Reverse Bend, 5X Short, 2X Strong, Forged, Ball Eye (S), Bronze, Sizes #4 to 10	None	None	None	None	None	**#9174, 75** O'Shaughnessy, 3X Short, X Strong, Bronze & Cad., Ball Eye (S), Sizes #9/0 to 8	None
Pattern Application: Barbless Dry Flies							
#TMC109BL Round, Barbless, 1X Fine, 1 & 3X Long, Ball Eye (TD), Forged, Black, Sizes #7 to 9, 11 to 19	None	None	**#1190** Round Bend, Barbless, Ball Eye (TD), Bronze, Sizes #8 to 18	None	None	None	None

Tiemco Selection and Substitution Chart

Tiemco	Kamasan	Partridge	Daiichi	VMC	Gamakatsu	Mustad	Eagle Claw

Pattern Application: Dry Flies

Tiemco	Kamasan	Partridge	Daiichi	VMC	Gamakatsu	Mustad	Eagle Claw
#TMC146Z Special (Goetz), Quick Eye (TD), Forged, Black, Sizes #10 to 20	None	None	None	None	None	None	None

Pattern Application: Dry Flies and Nymphs

Tiemco	Kamasan	Partridge	Daiichi	VMC	Gamakatsu	Mustad	Eagle Claw
#TMC200R TMC200RBL Special, Forged, 3X Long, Ball Eye (S), Bronze, Sizes #4 to 22	None	**#K12ST** Special, Forged, 3X Long, Ball Eye (S), Bronze, Sizes #8 to 22	**#1270** Special Bend (York), Curved Shank, 3X Long, Bronze, Ball Eye (S), Sizes #6 to 22	None	None	**#AC80050** Special, 3X Long, Ball Eye (S), Bronze, Sizes #6 to 22	**#52, #L052, #NT052** Special Bend, Light Wire, Ringed Eye (TD), Nkl. Teflon & Bronze, Sizes #6 to 20

Pattern Application: Barbless Caddis Flies and Nymphs

Tiemco	Kamasan	Partridge	Daiichi	VMC	Gamakatsu	Mustad	Eagle Claw
#TMC205BL Special Curve, Barbless, Ball Eye (TU), Bronze, Sizes #8 to 20	None	None	None	None	None	None	None

Pattern Application: Barbless Caddis Flies and Nymphs

Tiemco	Kamasan	Partridge	Daiichi	VMC	Gamakatsu	Mustad	Eagle Claw
#TMC206BL Special Curve, Forged 2X Short, Barbless, Fine Wire, Ball Eye (TU), Black Sizes #6 to 20	None	None	None	None	None	None	None

Pattern Application: Nymphs

Tiemco	Kamasan	Partridge	Daiichi	VMC	Gamakatsu	Mustad	Eagle Claw
#TMC246Z Special (Goetz), Quick Eye (TD), Forged, Black, Sizes #10 to 20	None	None	None	None	None	None	None

Pattern Application: Streamers, Bucktails, and Stonefly Nymphs

Tiemco	Kamasan	Partridge	Daiichi	VMC	Gamakatsu	Mustad	Eagle Claw
#TMC300 Round, Ball Eye (TD), Bronze, Sizes #2 to 14	**#B-800** Round Bend, Forged, 4X Long, Ball Eye (TD), Bronze, Sizes #1 to 14	None	**#2220** Round Bend, 4X Long, 1X Strong, Forged, Ball Eye (TD), Bronze, Sizes #1 to 14	None	None	None	None

Pattern Application: Streamers

Tiemco	Kamasan	Partridge	Daiichi	VMC	Gamakatsu	Mustad	Eagle Claw
#TMC346Z Special (Goetz), Quick Eye (TD), Forged, Black, Sizes #10 to 16	None	None	None	None	None	None	None

Pattern Application: Swimming Nymphs, Large Mayfly Nymphs, Leech Patterns, Larvae, and Pupae

Tiemco	Kamasan	Partridge	Daiichi	VMC	Gamakatsu	Mustad	Eagle Claw
#TMC400T Special, Ball Eye (S), Bronze, Sizes #8 to 14	None	**#K6ST** Special (Price), Long Curve, Ball Eye (S), Bronze, Sizes #8 to 14	**#1770** Sproat, 3X Long, 1X Fine, Forged, Ball Eye (S), Bronze, Sizes #6 to 16	None	None	**#3777** Central Draught, Ringed Eye (S), Bronze, Sizes #18-30, 32, 34, 36	None

121

Tiemco Selection and Substitution Chart

Tiemco	Kamasan	Partridge	Daiichi	VMC	Gamakatsu	Mustad	Eagle Claw
Pattern Application: Saltwater Flies							
#TMC411S Special Bend Back, Forged, Ball Eye (S), Stainless Steel, Sizes #3/0, 1/0, 4, 6, 8	None	None	None	None	None	None	None
Pattern Application: Dry Flies and Midges							
#TMC500U Round, 2X Short, Ball Eye (TU), Bronze, Sizes #16 to 22	None	**#L3B** Capt. Hamilton, Forged, 4X Fine, Ball Eye (TU), Bronze, Sizes #10 to 18	**#1330** Round Bend, 1X Short, Ball Eye (TD), Bronze, Sizes #8 to 24	**#9281** Modified Round Bend, Forged, X Fine, Forged Ball Eye (TU), Bronze, Sizes #8 to 20	None	**#94842** Round Bend, X Fine, Forged, Tapered Eye (TU), Bronze, Sizes #8 to 28	**#159, #L159** Round Bend, X Fine, Ball Eye (TU), Bronze, Sizes #4 to 18
Pattern Application: Dry Flies							
#TMC501 Round, 1X Short, Ball Eye (S), Bronze, Sizes #20 to 24	None	None	**#1110** Model Perfect Bend, Wide Gape, 1X Fine, Oversize Ball Eye (S), Mini Barb, Bronze, Sizes #16 to 24	None	None	None	None
Pattern Application: Pencil Poppers and Saltwater Poppers							
#TMC511S Round, Forged, 4X Long, 2X Strong, Ball Eye (S), Stl. Steel, Sizes #2/0, 1/0, 2	None	None	None	None	None	**#32669CT** Aberdeen, Forged, X Long, 3X Strong, Ringed Eye (S), Tinned, Size #1/0	None
Pattern Application: Dry Flies							
#TMC531 Perfect Bend, 2X Fine, 2X Short, Ball Eye (TD), Black, Sizes #10 to 20	**#B-400** Round Bend, Forged, Ball Eye (TD), Bronze, Sizes #8 to 16	None	None	None	**#P10** Model Perfect Round, Bronze, Ball Eye (TD), Sizes #4 to 24	**#94836** Round Bend, Short Shank, X Fine, Forged, Tapered Eye (TD), Bronze, Sizes #10 to 20	None
Pattern Application: Streamers							
#TMC700 Limerick, Forged, Heavy Wire, Ball Eye (TD), Black, Size #1/0	None	None	**#J1A** Limerick, Ball Eye (TD), Bronze, Sizes #4 to 16	None	**#L10-2H** Limerick, 2X Strong, Ball Eye (TD), Bronze, Sizes #6 to 12	**#7970** Limerick, 5X Strong, Bronze, Ball Eye (TD), Sizes #2 to 8	None
Pattern Application: Saltwater Flies							
#TMC800S O'Shaughnessy, Heavy Wire, Ball Eye (S), Stainless, Sizes #4/0 to 8	None	None	None	**#9255** O'Shaughnessy, Long Shank, Ball Eye (S), Brz., Nkl., Perma Stl., Gold, Sizes #5/0 to 6	None	None	**#L054SS** O'Shaughnessy, Ringed Eye (S), Stainless Steel, Sizes #1/0 to 4/0
Pattern Application: Saltwater Flies							
#TMC811S O'Shaughnessy, X Strong, Ringed Eye (S), Stainless Steel, Sizes #4/0 to 8	None	None	**#2546** O'Shaughnessy, Forged, Ball Eye (S), Stainless Steel, Sizes #6/0 to1/0, 1 to 6	**#9255** O'Shaughnessy, Ball Eye (S), Bronze, Sizes #5/0 to 6	None	**#3406, 06B** O'Shaughnessy, Forged, Ringed Eye (S), Bronze or Nickel, Sizes #14/0 to 8	**#L054SS** O'Shaughnessy, Ringed Eye (S), Stainless Steel, Sizes #1/0 to 4/0

Tiemco Selection and Substitution Chart

Tiemco	Kamasan	Partridge	Daiichi	VMC	Gamakatsu	Mustad	Eagle Claw

Pattern Application: Barbless Dry Flies

| **#TMC900BL** Perfect Bend, Barbless, 1X Fine, 1X Wide, Ball Eye (TD), Black, Sizes #8 to 24 | None | None | None | None | None | None | **#61, #L061B,** Round Bend, Barbless, Bronze, Ball Eye (TD), Sizes #4 to 18 |

Pattern Application: Barbless Dry Flies

| **#TMC902BL** Perfect Bend, Barbless, 2X Fine, 1X Wide, Ball Eye (TD), Black Sizes #12 to 20 | None | None | None | None | None | None | **#61, #L061B,** Round Bend, Barbless, Bronze, Ball Eye (TD), Sizes #4 to 18 |

Pattern Application: Barbless Salmon and Steelhead Flies

| **#TMC905BL** Round, Barbless, 1X Fine, Ball Eye (TD), Black, Sizes #2 to 10 | None | None | None | None | None | None | **#61, #L061B,** Round Bend, Barbless, Bronze, Ball Eye (TD), Sizes #4 to 18 |

Pattern Application: Saltwater Flies

| **#TMC911S** O'Shaughnessy, 3X Strong, 4X Long Ball Eye (S), Forged, Stainless Steel, Sizes #4/0 to 4 | None | None | None | None | None | None | None |

Pattern Application: Dry Flies

| **#TMC921** Perfect Bend, 1X Fine, 2X Short, Ball Eye (TD), Forged, Bronze, Sizes #8 to 20 | None | None | None | None | None | None | None |

Pattern Application: Barbless Nymphs and Leeches

| **#TMC947BL** Perfect Bend, Barbless, 2X or 3X Long Shank, Ball Eye (TD), Forged, Bronze, Sizes #4 to 20 | None | None | None | None | None | None | None |

Pattern Application: Dry Flies, Terrestrials, Caddis, Stoneflies, Nymphs, Larvae, and Pupae

| **#TMC2302** Special, Forged, 2X Long, Ball Eye (TD), Bronze, Sizes #8 to 20 | None | None | None | None | None | None | None |

Pattern Application: Dry Flies, Terrestrials, Caddis, and Stoneflies

| **#TMC2312** Special, Forged, 2X Long, 1X Fine, Ball Eye (S), Bronze, Sizes #6 to 16 | None | **K12ST** Special, Forged, 3X Long, Ball Eye (S), Bronze, Sizes #8 to 22 | **#1270** Special Bend (York), Curved Shank, 3X Long, Bronze, Ball Eye (S), Sizes #6 to 22 | None | None | **#AC80050** Special, 3X Long, Ball Eye (S), Bronze, Sizes #6 to 22 | **#52, #L052, #NT052** Special Bend, Light Wire, Ringed Eye (TD), Nkl. Teflon & Bronze, Sizes #6 to 20 |

123

Tiemco Selection and Substitution Chart

Tiemco	Kamasan	Partridge	Daiichi	VMC	Gamakatsu	Mustad	Eagle Claw

Pattern Application: Nymphs, Larvae, and Pupae

Tiemco	Kamasan	Partridge	Daiichi	VMC	Gamakatsu	Mustad	Eagle Claw
#TMC2457 — Special, Forged, 2X Heavy, 2X Wide, 2X Short, Bronze, Ball Eye (TD), Sizes #6 to 18	None	#K4A — Special (Veniard) Offset, Curved Shank, 2X Fine, Ball Eye (TD), Bronze, Sizes #8 to 18	#1130 — Continuous Bend, 1X Fine, 1X Short, Ball Eye (TD), Bronze, Sizes #10 to 16	None	#C12 — Special Curve, Bronze, Ball Eye (TD), Sizes #10 to 20	#AC80200 — Special, 2X Short, 2X Wide, Ball Eye (TD), Bronze, Sizes #6 to 18	#L056, #NT056 — Special Bend, Hump Shank, Brz. & Nickel Teflon, Ringed Eye (TD), Sizes #2 to 14

Pattern Application: Nymphs, Larvae, and Pupae

Tiemco	Kamasan	Partridge	Daiichi	VMC	Gamakatsu	Mustad	Eagle Claw
#TMC2487 — Special, Forged, Offset, Fine Wire, 2X Short, Bronze, Ball Eye (TD), Sizes #10 to 20	None	#K4A — Special (Veniard) Offset, Curved Shank, 2X Fine, Ball Eye (TD), Bronze, Sizes #8 to 18	#1130 — Continuous Bend, 1X Fine, 1X Short, Ball Eye (TD), Bronze, Sizes #10 to 16	None	#C12 — Special Curve, Bronze, Ball Eye (TD), Sizes #10 to 20	#AC80200 — Special, 2X Short, 2X Wide, Ball Eye (TD), Bronze, Sizes #6 to 18	#L056, #NT056 — Special Bend, Hump Shank, Brz. & Nickel Teflon, Ringed Eye (TD), Sizes #2 to 14

Pattern Application: Nymphs, Larvae, and Pupae

Tiemco	Kamasan	Partridge	Daiichi	VMC	Gamakatsu	Mustad	Eagle Claw
#TMC2487G — Special, Forged, Offset, Fine Wire, 2X Short, Gold, Ball Eye (TD), Sizes #10 to 20	None	#K4A — Special (Veniard) Offset, Curved Shank, 2X Fine, Ball Eye (TD), Bronze, Sizes #8 to 18	#1130 — Continuous Bend, 1X Fine, 1X Short, Ball Eye (TD), Bronze, Sizes #10 to 16	None	#C12 — Special Curve, Bronze, Ball Eye (TD), Sizes #10 to 20	#AC80200 — Special, 2X Short, 2X Wide, Ball Eye (TD), Bronze, Sizes #6 to 18	#L056, #NT056 — Special Bend, Hump Shank, Brz. & Nickel Teflon, Ringed Eye (TD), Sizes #2 to 14

Pattern Application: Barbless Nymphs, Larvae, Caddis Pupae, Emergers, and Shrimp

Tiemco	Kamasan	Partridge	Daiichi	VMC	Gamakatsu	Mustad	Eagle Claw
#TMC2487BL — Special, Barbless, Forged, Offset, Fine Wire, 2X Short, Bronze, Ball Eye (TD), Sizes #12 to 22	None	#K4A — Special (Veniard) Offset, Curved Shank, 2X Fine, Ball Eye (TD), Bronze, Sizes #8 to 18	#1130 — Continuous Bend, 1X Fine, 1X Short, Ball Eye (TD), Bronze, Sizes #10 to 16	None	#C12 — Special Curve, Bronze, Ball Eye (TD), Sizes #10 to 20	#AC80200 — Special, 2X Short, 2X Wide, Ball Eye (TD), Bronze, Sizes #6 to 18	#L056, #NT056 — Special Bend, Hump Shank, Brz. & Nickel Teflon, Ringed Eye (TD), Sizes #2 to 14

Pattern Application: Nymphs, Larvae, and Pupae

Tiemco	Kamasan	Partridge	Daiichi	VMC	Gamakatsu	Mustad	Eagle Claw
#TMC3761 — Sproat, Forged, 1X Long, 2X Heavy, Ball Eye (TD), Bronze, Sizes #8 to 18	#B-170 — Sproat, Ball Eye (TD), Bronze, Sizes #6 to 16	#G3A — Sproat, Forged, Heavy Wire, Ball Eye (TD), Bronze, Sizes #8 to 16	#1550 — Sproat, Ball Eye (TD), Bronze, Sizes #2 to 18	#8526 — Sproat, Forged, Ball Eye (TD), Bronze, Sizes #8 to 16	#S10-3F — Sproat, 1X Fine, Black, Ball Eye (TD), Sizes #4 to 20	#3906, #AC3906 — Sproat, Tapered Eye (TD), Bronze, Size #2 to 20	#57, #L057, #NT057 — Sproat, Ball Eye (TD), Bronze, Sizes #4 to 16

Pattern Application: Barbless Nymphs, Larvae, and Pupae

Tiemco	Kamasan	Partridge	Daiichi	VMC	Gamakatsu	Mustad	Eagle Claw
#TMC3761BL — Sproat, Barbless, 1X Long, 2X Heavy, Forged, Ball Eye (TD), Brz., Sizes #8 to 18	None	None	None	None	None	None	None

Pattern Application: Nymphs, Larvae, and Pupae

Tiemco	Kamasan	Partridge	Daiichi	VMC	Gamakatsu	Mustad	Eagle Claw
#TMC3769 — Sproat, Forged, 2X Heavy, Ball Eye (TD), Bronze, Sizes #10 to 16	#B-170 — Sproat, Ball Eye (TD), Bronze, Sizes #6 to 16	#A — Improved Sproat, 2X Fine, 1X Short, Bronze, Ball Eye (TD), Sizes #10 to 16	#1550 — Sproat, Ball Eye (TD), Bronze, Sizes #2 to 18	#8526 — Sproat, Bronze, Ball Eye (TD), Forged, Sizes #8 to 16	#S10 — Sproat, Ball Eye (TD), Black, Sizes #2 to 24	#3399, 99A, 99D, 99N — Sproat, Ball Eye (TD), Brz., Gold, 99D-Fine Wire, Sizes #9/0 -2, 4 to 20	#57, #L057, #NT057 — Sproat, Ball Eye (TD), Bronze, Sizes #4 to 16

Pattern Application: Nymphs, Larvae, and Pupae

Tiemco	Kamasan	Partridge	Daiichi	VMC	Gamakatsu	Mustad	Eagle Claw
#TMC5210 — Round, Forged, 1X Fine, Ball Eye (TD), Bronze, Sizes #10 to 20	#B-400 — Round Bend, Forged, Ball Eye (TD), Bronze, Sizes #8 to 16	#L2A — Capt. Hamilton, Forged, 2X Fine, Ball Eye (TD), Bronze, Sizes #6 to 18	#1170 — Round Bend, Forged, Ball Eye (TD), Bronze, Sizes #8 to 16	#9288 — Round Bend, Forged, 2X Fine, Short Shank, Bronze, Forged Ball Eye (TD), Sizes #6 to 20	#P10 — Model Perfect Round, Bronze, Ball Eye (TD), Sizes #4 to 24	#94840, #AC94840 — Round Bend, X Fine, Forged, Tapered Eye (TD), Bronze, Sizes #2 to 28	#59, #L059, #NT059 — Round Bend, Fine Wire, Forged, Ball Eye (TD), Brz. & Nkl. Teflon, Sizes #4 to 24

Tiemco Selection and Substitution Chart

Tiemco	Kamasan	Partridge	Daiichi	VMC	Gamakatsu	Mustad	Eagle Claw

Pattern Application: Nymphs, Larvae, and Pupae

#TMC5212	#B-400	#L2A	#1170	#9288	#P10	#94840, #AC94840	#59, #L059, #NT059
Round, Forged, 1X Fine, 2X Long Ball Eye (TD), Bronze, Sizes #8 to 14	Round Bend, Forged, Ball Eye (TD), Bronze, Sizes #8 to 16	Capt. Hamilton, Forged, 2X Fine, Ball Eye (TD), Bronze, Sizes #6 to 18	Round Bend, Forged, Ball Eye (TD), Bronze, Sizes #8 to 16	Round Bend, Forged, 2X Fine, Short Shank, Bronze, Forged Ball Eye (TD), Sizes #6 to 20	Model Perfect Round, Bronze, Ball Eye (TD), Sizes #4 to 24	Round Bend, X Fine, Forged, Tapered Eye (TD), Bronze, Sizes #2 to 28	Round Bend, Fine Wire, Forged, Ball Eye (TD), Brz. & Nkl. Teflon, Sizes #4 to 24

Pattern Application: Nymphs, Larvae, and Pupae

#TMC5230	#B-400	#L4A	#1170	#9288	#P10	#94840, #AC94840	#59, #L059, #NT059
Modified Round, Forged, 3X Fine, Ball Eye (TD), Bronze, Sizes #10 to 18	Round Bend, Forged, Ball Eye (TD), Bronze, Sizes #8 to 16	Capt. Hamilton, Forged, 6X Fine, Ball Eye (TD), Bronze, Sizes #10 to 20	Round Bend, Forged, Ball Eye (TD), Bronze, Sizes #8 to 16	Round Bend, Forged, 2X Fine, Short Shank, Bronze, Forged Ball Eye (TD), Sizes #6 to 20	Model Perfect Round, Bronze, Ball Eye (TD), Sizes #4 to 24	Round Bend, X Fine, Forged, Tapered Eye (TD), Bronze, Sizes #2 to 28	Round Bend, Fine Wire, Forged, Ball Eye (TD), Brz. & Nkl. Teflon, Sizes #4 to 24

Pattern Application: Nymphs, Larvae, and Pupae

#TMC5262	#B-830	#H1A	#1720	#9283	#P10-2L1H	#94833 #AC94833	#63, #L063, #NT063
Round, Forged, 2X Long Ball Eye (TD), Bronze, Sizes #2 to 18	Round Bend, Forged, 2X Long, Ball Eye (TD), Bronze, Sizes #6 to 14	Capt. Hamilton, Forged, 2X Fine, 2-1/2X Long, Bronze, Ball Eye (TD), Sizes #2 to 14	Round Bend, Forged, 3X Long, 1X Strong, Bronze, Ball Eye (TD), Sizes #6 to 18	Round Bend, Forged, 4X Long Forged Ball Eye (TD), Bronze, Sizes #2 to 16	Model Perfect Round, 2X Long, 1X Strong, Bronze, Ball Eye (TD), Sizes #4 to 16	Round Bend, X Long, 3X Fine, Forged, Tapered Eye (TD), Bronze, Sizes #6 to 22	Round Bend, 2X Long, Brz. & Nkl. Teflon, Ball Eye (TD), Sizes #4 to 18

Pattern Application: Nymphs, Larvae, and Pupae

#TMC5263	#B-830	#H1A	#1720	#9283	#P10-2L1H	#94833 #AC94833	#63, #L063, #NT063
Round, Forged, 3X Long, Ball Eye (TD), Bronze, Sizes #2 to 18	Round Bend, Forged, 2X Long, Ball Eye (TD), Bronze, Sizes #6 to 14	Capt. Hamilton, Forged, 2X Fine, 2-1/2X Long, Bronze, Ball Eye (TD), Sizes #2 to 14	Round Bend, Forged, 3X Long, 1X Strong, Bronze, Ball Eye (TD), Sizes #6 to 18	Round Bend, Forged, 4X Long, Forged Ball Eye (TD), Bronze, Sizes #2 to 16	Model Perfect Round, 2X Long, 1X Strong, Bronze, Ball Eye (TD), Sizes #4 to 16	Round Bend, X Long, 3X Fine, Forged, Tapered Eye (TD), Bronze, Sizes #6 to 22	Round Bend, 2X Long, Brz. & Nkl. Teflon, Ball Eye (TD), Sizes #4 to 18

Pattern Application: Barbless Streamers, Nymphs, Larvae, and Pupae

#TMC5263BL							
Perfect Bend, Barbless, Forged, 3X Long, 2X Heavy, Ball Eye (TD), Brz., Sizes #2 to 18	None	None	None	None	None	None	None

Pattern Application: Salmon and Steelhead Patterns

#TMC7989	#B-180	#M	#2441	#8923	#T10-3H	#90240	None
Salmon, Forged, Light Wire, Tapered Loop Eye (TU), Black, Sizes #2 to 8	Salmon, Forged, Tapered Loop Eye (TU), Black, Sizes #2/0 to 12	Salmon, Forged, 2X Heavy, Tapered Loop Eye (TU), Black, Sizes #4/0-1/0, 1 to 10	Salmon, Forged, 1X Strong, Tapered Loop Eye (TU), Black, Sizes #2/0, 1/0, 1 to 8	Limerick, Forged, 2X Long, Ball Eye (TU), Bronze, Sizes #2 to 12	Salmon, 1X Fine, Tapered Loop Eye (TU), Black, Sizes #2 to 8	Limerick, 2XFine Wire, X Long, Black, Loop Oval Eye (TU), Sizes #4, 6, 8, 10	None

Pattern Application: Salmon and Steelhead Patterns

#TMC7999	#B-180	#M	#2441	#8923	#T10-3H	#90240	None
Salmon, Forged, Heavy Wire, Tapered Loop Eye (TU), Black, Sizes #2/0 to 12	Salmon, Forged, Tapered Loop Eye (TU), Black, Sizes #2/0 to 12	Salmon, Forged, 2X Heavy, Tapered Loop Eye (TU), Black, Sizes #4/0-1/0, 1 to 10	Salmon, Forged, 1X Strong, Tapered Loop Eye (TU), Black, Sizes #2/0, 1/0, 1 to 8	Limerick, Forged, 2X Long, Ball Eye (TU), Bronze, Sizes #2 to 12	Salmon, 1X Fine, Tapered Loop Eye (TU), Black, Sizes #2 to 8	Limerick, 2XFine Wire, X Long, Black, Loop Oval Eye (TU), Sizes #4, 6, 8, 10	None

Pattern Application: Bass Bugs

#TMC8089	None	None	None	#8410	#S10S	#33602	None
Sproat, Forged, Wide Gape, Fine Wire, Bronze, Ball Eye (S), Sizes #2, 6, 10	None	None	None	Special (Crystal), Forged, Ball Eye (S), Bronze, Sizes #4 to 12	Sproat, Black, Ball Eye (S), Sizes #4 to 14	Sproat, Ringed Eye (S), Gold Plated, Sizes #5/0 to 16	None

Tiemco Selection and Substitution Chart

Tiemco	Kamasan	Partridge	Daiichi	VMC	Gamakatsu	Mustad	Eagle Claw
Pattern Application: Bass Bugs							
#TMC8089NP Sproat, Forged, Wide Gape, Fine Wire, Nkl. Plt., Ball Eye (S), Sizes #2, 6, 10	None	None	None	**#8410** Special (Crystal), Forged, Ball Eye (S), Bronze, Sizes #4 to 12	**#S10S** Sproat, Black, Ball Eye (S), Sizes #4 to 14	**#33602** Sproat, Ringed Eye (S), Gold Plated, Sizes #5/0 to 16	None
Pattern Application: Dry Flies and Wet Flies							
#TMC9300 Round, Forged, 1X Heavy, Wide Gape, Ball Eye (TD), Bronze, Sizes #10 to 20	**#B-400** Round Bend, Forged, Ball Eye (TD), Bronze, Sizes #8 to 16	**#L2A** Capt. Hamilton, Forged, 2X Fine, Ball Eye (TD), Bronze, Sizes #6 to 18	**#1170** Round Bend, Forged, Ball Eye (TD), Bronze, Sizes #8 to 16	**#9288** Round Bend, Forged, 2X Fine, Short Shank, Bronze, Forged Ball Eye (TD), Sizes #6 to 20	**#P10** Model Perfect Round, Bronze, Ball Eye (TD), Sizes #4 to 24	**#94840, #AC94840** Round Bend, X Fine, Forged, Tapered Eye (TD), Bronze, Sizes #2 to 28	**#59, #L059, #NT059** Round Bend, Fine Wire, Forged, Ball Eye (TD), Brz. & Nkl. Teflon, Sizes #4 to 24
Pattern Application: Dry Flies and Wet Flies							
#TMC9394 Sproat, Forged, 3X Heavy, 4X Long, Ball Eye (S), Nkl. Pltd., Sizes #2 to 10	None	None	None	None	None	None	None
Pattern Application: Dry Flies and Wet Flies							
#TMC9395 Sproat, Forged, 3X Heavy, 4X Long, Ball Eye (S), Bronze., Sizes #2 to 10	None	None	None	None	None	None	None

Kamasan Hooks

Kamasan hooks are manufactured in Japan from high-carbon steel and are chemically sharpened to a needle point, allowing quick penetration with superior hooking and holding power.

Kamasan hooks can be obtained through World Wide Outfitters, 425 College Ave., Santa Rosa, CA 95401; phone 707-545-4656.

Kamasan Selection and Substitution Chart

Pattern Application
The pattern application lists various types of patterns that can be tied using the specified hooks shown below.

Possible Substitutes
Listed across the page are other manufacturers' hooks that can be used as alternatives. In most cases, the hooks listed are similar or have the same characteristics with minor differences.

Note: Hook illustrations are only examples and are not shown at actual sizes. Also note that after the eye description, **(S)** indicates a straight eye, **(TD)** indicates a turned-down eye, and **(TU)** indicates a turned-up eye.

Kamasan	Partridge	Daiichi	VMC	Gamakatsu	Mustad	Eagle Claw	Tiemco
Pattern Application: Wet Flies, Nymphs, and Heavy-Hackled Dry Flies							
#B-170 — Sproat, Ball Eye (TD), Bronze, Sizes #6 to 16	#G3A — Sproat, Forged, Heavy Wire, Ball Eye (TD), Bronze, Sizes #8 to 16	#1550 — Sproat, Ball Eye (TD), Bronze, Sizes #2 to 18	#8526 — Sproat, Forged Ball Eye (TD), Bronze, Sizes #8 to 16	#S10-3F — Sproat, 1X Fine, Black, Ball Eye (TD), Sizes #4 to 20	#3906, #AC3906 — Sproat, Tapered Eye (TD), Bronze, Size #2 to 20	#57, #L057, #NT057 — Sproat, Ball Eye (TD), Bronze, Sizes #4 to 16	#TMC3761 — Sproat, Forged, 1X Long, 2X Heavy, Ball Eye (TD), Bronze, Sizes #8 to 18
Pattern Application: Salmon and Steelhead Patterns							
#B-180 — Salmon, Forged, Tapered Loop Eye (TU), Black, Sizes #2/0 to 12	#M — Salmon, Forged, 2X Heavy, Tapered Loop Eye (TU), Black, Sizes #4/0-1/0, 1 to 10	#2441 — Salmon, Forged, 1X Strong, Tapered Loop Eye (TU), Black, Sizes #2/0, 1/0, 1 to 8	#8923 — Limerick, Forged, 2X Long, Ball Eye (TU), Bronze, Sizes #2 to 12	#T10-3H — Salmon, 1X Fine, Tapered Loop Eye (TU), Black, Sizes #2 to 8	#90240 — Limerick, 2X Fine Wire, X Long, Black, Loop Oval Eye (TU), Sizes #4, 6, 8, 10	None	#TMC7989 — Salmon, Forged, Light Wire, Tapered Loop Eye (TU), Black, Sizes #2 to 8
Pattern Application: Traditional and Full-Hackled Dry Flies, Wulffs, Humpys, and Nymphs							
#B-400 — Round Bend, Forged, Ball Eye (TD), Bronze, Sizes #8 to 16	#L2A — Capt. Hamilton, Forged, 2X Fine, Ball Eye (TD), Bronze, Sizes #6 to 18	#1170 — Round Bend, Forged, Ball Eye (TD), Bronze, Sizes #8 to 16	#9288 — Round Bend, Forged, 2X Fine, Short Shank, Bronze, Forged Ball Eye (TD), Sizes #6 to 20	#P10 — Model Perfect Round, Bronze, Ball Eye (TD), Sizes #4 to 24	#94840, #AC94840 — Round Bend, X Fine, Forged, Tapered Eye (TD), Bronze, Sizes #2 to 28	#59, #L059, #NT059 — Round Bend, Fine Wire, Forged, Ball Eye (TD), Brz. & Nkl. Teflon, Sizes #4 to 24	#TMC5210 — Round, Forged, 1X Fine, Ball Eye (TD), Bronze, Sizes #10 to 20
Pattern Application: Streamers, Bucktails, Stonefly Nymphs, Muddlers, and Hoppers							
#B-800 — Round Bend, Forged, 4X Long, Ball Eye (TD), Bronze, Sizes #1 to 14	#D4A — Redditch, Forged, 4X Long, Heavy Wire, Ball Eye (TD), Bronze, Sizes #2 to 12	#2220 — Round Bend, 4X Long, 1X Strong, Forged, Ball Eye (TD), Bronze, Sizes #1 to 14	#9283 — Round Bend, Forged, 4X Long, Forged Ball Eye (TD), Bronze, Sizes #2 to 16	#S11-4L2H — Sproat, 4X Long, 2X Strong, Black, Ball Eye (TD), Sizes #6 to 12	#79580, #AC79580 — Round Bend, Forged, Straight, 4X Long, Tapered Eye (TD), Bronze, Sizes #1 to 18	#281, #L281, #NT281 — Sproat, 4X Long, 1X Heavy, Brz. & Nkl. Teflon, Ball Eye (TD), Sizes #2 to 10	#TMC300 — Round, Ball Eye (TD), Bronze, Sizes #2 to 14
Pattern Application: Stonefly and Larger Mayfly Nymphs							
#B-810 — Round Bend, Forged, 4X Long, Special Bend, Ball Eye (TD), Bronze, Sizes #6 to 12	None	#1730 — Round Bend, 3X Long, 1X Strong, Forged, Ball Eye (TD), Bronze, Sizes #6 to 14	None	#C11-5L2H — Special Curve, 5X Long, 2X Strong, Bronze, Ball Eye (TD), Sizes #6 to 12	None	None	None
Pattern Application: Nymphs, Larvae, and Pupae							
#B-830 — Round Bend, Forged, 2X Long, Ball Eye (TD), Bronze, Sizes #6 to 14	#D4A — Redditch, Forged, 4X Long, Heavy Wire, Ball Eye (TD), Bronze, Sizes #2 to 12	#1720 — Round Bend, Forged, 4X Long, 1X Strong, Bronze, Ball Eye (TD), Sizes #6 to 18	#9283 — Round Bend, Forged, 4X Long, Forged Ball Eye (TD), Bronze, Sizes #2 to 16	#P10-2L1H — Model Perfect Round, 2X Long, 1X Strong, Bronze, Ball Eye (TD), Sizes #4 to 16	#94833, #AC94833 — Round Bend, X Long, 3X Fine, Forged, Tapered Eye (TD), Bronze, Sizes #6 to 22	#63, #L063, #NT063 — Round Bend, 2X Long, Brz. & Nkl. Teflon, Ball Eye (TD), Sizes #4 to 18	#TMC5262 — Round, Forged, 2X Long, Ball Eye (TD), Bronze, Sizes #2 to 18

Partridge Hooks

Partridge of Redditch Ltd. is located in Mount Pleasant, Redditch, Worcestershire, England. For over a century, Partridge has provided fly fishermen with some of the best handmade fly hooks in the world.

Partridge hooks can be obtained from most fly shops or catalog houses or from Partridge USA Inc., P.O. Box 585, Wakefield, MA 01880; phone 617-245-0755.

Partridge Selection and Substitution Chart

Pattern Application
The pattern application lists various types of patterns that can be tied using the specified hooks shown below.

Possible Substitutes
Listed across the page are other manufacturers' hooks that can be used as alternatives. In most cases, the hooks listed are similar or have the same characteristics with minor differences.

Note: Hook illustrations are only examples and are not shown at actual sizes. In addition, after the eye description, **(S)** indicates a straight eye, **(TD)** indicates a turned-down eye, and **(TU)** indicates a turned-up eye.

Partridge	Daiichi	VMC	Gamakatsu	Mustad	Eagle Claw	Tiemco	Kamasan
Pattern Application: Standard and Soft-Hackle Wet Flies and Short-Bodied Nymphs							
#A Improved Sproat, Offset, 1X Short, 2X Fine, Ball Eye (TD), Bronze, Sizes #10 to 16	**#1550** Sproat, Ball Eye (TD), Bronze, Sizes #2 to 18	**#8526** Sproat, Bronze, Ball Eye (TD), Forged, Sizes #8 to 16	**#S10** Sproat, Ball Eye (TD), Black, Sizes #2 to 24	**#3399, 99A, 99D, 99N** Sproat, Ball Eye (TD), Brz., Gold, 99D-Fine Wire, Sizes #9/0 -2, #4 to 20	**#57, #L057, #NT057** Sproat, Ball Eye (TD), Bronze, Sizes #4 to 16	**#TMC3769** Sproat, 1X Long, Forged, Ball Eye (TD), 2X Heavy, Bronze, Sizes #2 to 20	**#B-170** Sproat, Ball Eye (TD), Bronze, Sizes #6 to 16
Pattern Application: Salmon and Steelhead Patterns, Streamers, and Bucktails							
#CS2, #CS2SH Salmon, Forged, Black, Tapered Loop Eye (TD), Sizes #2, 4, 6, 8	None	None	None	None	None	None	None
Pattern Application: Thundercreek Streamers							
#CS5 Round Bend, 2X Long, Heavy Wire, Blued, Ball Eye (S), Sizes #4, 6, 8	None	None	None	**#3191, 91A, 92, 93, 94N** Carlisle, Kirbed, Ringed Eye (S), Bronzed, Blued, or Tinned, Sizes #10/0-10, 12, 14, 16, 18, 20	None	None	None
Pattern Application: Classic Salmon Flies							
#CS6 Dublin Salmon, Eyeless Hook, Black, Size #4/0	None	None	None	None	None	None	None
Pattern Application: Wet Flies							
#CS7MW Capt. Hamilton, X Wide Gape, Black, Ball Eye (TD), Sizes #10, 12, 14	**#1170** Round Bend, Forged, Ball Eye (TD), Bronze, Sizes #8 to 16	**#9288** Round Bend, Forged, 2X Fine, Short Shank, Bronze, Forged Ball Eye (TD), Sizes #6 to 20	**#P10** Model Perfect Round, Bronze, Ball Eye (TD), Sizes #4 to 24	**#7948A** Round Bend, Forged, Bronze, Tapered Eye (TD), Sizes #2 to 20	**#59, #L059, #NT059** Round Bend, Fine Wire, Forged, Ball Eye (TD), Brz. & Nkl. Teflon, Sizes #4 to 24	**#TMC5210** Round, Forged, 1X Fine, Ball Eye (TD), Bronze, Sizes #10 to 20	**#B-400** Round Bend, Forged, Ball Eye (TD), Bronze, Sizes #8 to 16
Pattern Application: Classic and Traditional Salmon Flies, Steelhead Patterns, and Sea Trout Flies							
#CS10 Bartleet Salmon, Forged, 2X Long, Tapered Loop Eye (TU), Black, Sizes #1/0, 1, 2, 4, 6	None	None	None	None	None	None	None

Partridge Selection and Substitution Chart

Partridge	Daiichi	VMC	Gamakatsu	Mustad	Eagle Claw	Tiemco	Kamasan

Pattern Application: Saltwater Patterns, Baitfish, and Streamers

Partridge	Daiichi	VMC	Gamakatsu	Mustad	Eagle Claw	Tiemco	Kamasan
#CS11 **#CS11GRS** Redditch, Forged, 4X Long, St. Stl or Gray Shadow, Ball Eye (TD), Sizes #2 to 10	None	**#9148** Aberdeen, Light Wire, Ball Eye (TD), Bronze, Sizes #4/0 to 12	None	None	None	None	None

Pattern Application: Trolling Streamers

Partridge	Daiichi	VMC	Gamakatsu	Mustad	Eagle Claw	Tiemco	Kamasan
#CS15 Limerick, Heavy Wire, X Long, Tapered Loop Eye (TD), Bronze, Sizes #2/0, 2, 4	None	None	None	**#94720** Round Bend, Forged, Tapered Eye (TD), Bronze, Sizes #2 to 8	None	None	None

Pattern Application: Streamers and Bucktails

Partridge	Daiichi	VMC	Gamakatsu	Mustad	Eagle Claw	Tiemco	Kamasan
#CS17 Limerick, Heavy Wire, 6X Long, Tapered Loop Eye (TD), Black, Sizes #1, 2, 4, 6	**#J171** Improved Limerick, 6X Long, 1X Heavy, Tapered Loop Eye (TD), Black, Sizes #1, 2	None	None	**#36680** Limerick, 1/4" Longer Shank, Bronze, Tapered Eye (TD), Sizes #4 to 12	**#74** Eagle Claw Design, Forged, XX Long, Gold, Ball Eye (TD), Sizes #4/0 to 4	None	None

Pattern Application: Barbless Dry Flies

Partridge	Daiichi	VMC	Gamakatsu	Mustad	Eagle Claw	Tiemco	Kamasan
#CS20 Special (Barbless) "Arrowpoint," Gray Shadow, Ball Eye (TD), Sizes #10 to 18	None	None	None	None	None	None	None

Pattern Application: Midges and Small Dry Flies

Partridge	Daiichi	VMC	Gamakatsu	Mustad	Eagle Claw	Tiemco	Kamasan
#CS21 Special (Sneck), Ball Eye (TD), Black, Sizes #16, 18	None	None	None	None	None	None	None

Pattern Application: Barbless Dry Flies and Emergers

Partridge	Daiichi	VMC	Gamakatsu	Mustad	Eagle Claw	Tiemco	Kamasan
#CS27GRS Special (Moser Barbless), Ball Eye (TD), Gray Shadow, Sizes #10 to 18	None	None	None	**#3257B** Sproat (Barbless), Tapered Eye (TD), Kirbed, Bronze, Sizes #8, 10, 12, 14	None	None	None

Pattern Application: Barbless Nymphs and Large Dry Flies

Partridge	Daiichi	VMC	Gamakatsu	Mustad	Eagle Claw	Tiemco	Kamasan
#CS28GRS Special Med. Shank (Moser Barbless), Ball Eye (TD), Gray Shadow, Sizes #8 to 14	None	None	None	**#3257B** Sproat (Barbless), Tapered Eye (TD), Kirbed, Bronze, Sizes #8, 10, 12, 14	None	None	None

Pattern Application: Barbless Streamer and Attractor Patterns

Partridge	Daiichi	VMC	Gamakatsu	Mustad	Eagle Claw	Tiemco	Kamasan
#CS29GRS Special Long Shank (Moser Barbless), Ball Eye (TD), Gray Shadow, Sizes #2, 4, 6, 8	None	None	None	None	None	None	None

Partridge Selection and Substitution Chart

Partridge	Daiichi	VMC	Gamakatsu	Mustad	Eagle Claw	Tiemco	Kamasan

Pattern Application: Salmon and Steelhead Dry and Streamer Flies

| #CS42
Salmon (MW Bomber),
Fine Wire, X Strong,
Looped Eye (TD),
Bronze,
Sizes #2, 4, 6 | None | None | None | None | None | None | None |

Pattern Application: Streamers, Attractor Patterns, and Long-Bodied Nymphs

| #D3ST
Salmon, Forged,
4X Long, Heavy Wire,
Ball Eye (S),
Bronze,
Sizes #4 to 12 | None | None | None | None | None | None | None |

Pattern Application: Traditional Streamers, Bucktails, Attractors, and Nymphs

| #D4A
Redditch, Forged,
4X Long, Heavy Wire,
Ball Eye (TD),
Bronze,
Sizes #2 to 12 | None | None | #P10-2L1H
Model Perfect Round,
2X Long, 1X Strong,
Bronze, Ball Eye (TD),
Sizes #4 to 16 | #9671,
#AC9671
Round Bend, Forged,
2X Long, Bronze,
Tapered Eye (TD),
Sizes #2 to 18 | #63, #L063,
#NT063
Round Bend, 2X Long,
Brz. & Nkl. Teflon,
Ball Eye (TD),
Sizes #4 to 18 | None | #B-830
Round Bend, Forged,
2X Long,
Ball Eye (TD), Bronze,
Sizes #6 to 14 |

Pattern Application: Small Streamers and Nymphs

| #D5B
Redditch, Forged,
Offset, 2X Long,
2X Fine, Bronze,
Ball Eye (TU),
Sizes #8 to 12 | None | None | None | None | None | None | None |

Pattern Application: Streamers

| #D7A
Special (Finnish),
Long Shank,
2X Fine, Bronze,
Ball Eye (TD),
Sizes #2 to 8 | None | None | None | None | None | None | None |

Pattern Application: Dry Flies, Nymphs, and Emergers

| #E1A
Redditch, Forged,
1/2X Long, 4X Fine,
Bronze,
Ball Eye (TD),
Sizes #10 to 18 | #1170
Round Bend,
Forged,
Ball Eye (TD),
Bronze,
Sizes #8 to 16 | #9288
Round Bend,
Forged, 2X Fine,
Short Shank, Bronze,
Forged Ball Eye (TD),
Sizes #6 to 20 | #P10
Model Perfect Round,
Bronze,
Ball Eye (TD),
Sizes #4 to 24 | #94840,
#AC94840
Round Bend, X Fine,
Forged,
Tapered Eye (TD),
Bronze, Sizes #2 to 28 | #59, #L059,
#NT059
Round Bend, Fine Wire,
Forged, Ball Eye (TD),
Brz. & Nkl. Teflon,
Sizes #4 to 24 | #TMC5210
Round, Forged,
1X Fine,
Ball Eye (TD), Bronze,
Sizes #10 to 20 | #B-400
Round Bend, Forged,
Ball Eye (TD),
Bronze,
Sizes #8 to 16 |

Pattern Application: Barbless Traditional Dry Flies and Floating Nymphs

| #E3AY
Redditch (Barbless),
Forged, 1/2X Long,
4X Fine, Bronze,
Ball Eye (TD),
Sizes #10 to 18 | None | None | None | None | None | None | None |

Pattern Application: Dry Flies

| #E4A
Redditch, Offset,
Forged, 1/2X Long,
4X Fine, Bronze,
Ball Eye (TD),
Sizes #10 to 18 | #1170
Round Bend,
Forged,
Ball Eye (TD),
Bronze,
Sizes #8 to 16 | #9288
Round Bend,
Forged, 2X Fine,
Short Shank, Bronze,
Forged Ball Eye (TD),
Sizes #6 to 20 | #P10
Model Perfect Round,
Bronze,
Ball Eye (TD),
Sizes #4 to 24 | #94838
Round Bend, X Short,
X Fine, Forged,
Tapered Eye (TD),
Bronze, Sizes #10 to 20 | #59, #L059,
#NT059
Round Bend, Fine Wire,
Forged, Ball Eye (TD),
Brz. & Nkl. Teflon,
Sizes #4 to 24 | #TMC5210
Round, Forged,
1X Fine,
Ball Eye (TD), Bronze,
Sizes #10 to 20 | #B-400
Round Bend, Forged,
Ball Eye (TD),
Bronze,
Sizes #8 to 16 |

Partridge Selection and Substitution Chart

Partridge	Daiichi	VMC	Gamakatsu	Mustad	Eagle Claw	Tiemco	Kamasan

Pattern Application: Barb and Barbless, Dry Flies, Variants, Extended Bodies, No-Hackles, and Short-Bodied Nymphs

Partridge	Daiichi	VMC	Gamakatsu	Mustad	Eagle Claw	Tiemco	Kamasan
#E6A, #E6AY (Barbless) Redditch, Forged, 1X Short, 4X Fine, Bronze, Ball Eye (TD), Sizes #10 to 18	**#1170** Round Bend, Forged, Ball Eye (TD), Bronze, Sizes #8 to 16	**#9288** Round Bend, Forged, 2X Fine, Short Shank, Bronze, Forged Ball Eye (TD), Sizes #6 to 20	**#P10** Model Perfect Round, Bronze, Ball Eye (TD), Sizes #4 to 24	**#94840, #AC94840** Round Bend, X Fine, Forged, Tapered Eye (TD), Bronze, Sizes #2 to 28	**#59, #L059, #NT059** Round Bend, Fine Wire, Forged, Ball Eye (TD), Brz. & Nkl. Teflon, Sizes #4 to 24	**#TMC5210** Round, Forged, 1X Fine, Ball Eye (TD), Bronze, Sizes #10 to 20	**#B-400** Round Bend, Forged, Ball Eye (TD), Bronze, Sizes #8 to 16

Pattern Application: Wet Flies and Nymphs

Partridge	Daiichi	VMC	Gamakatsu	Mustad	Eagle Claw	Tiemco	Kamasan
#G3A Sproat, Forged, Ball Eye (TD), Bronze, Sizes #8 to 16	**#1550** Sproat, Ball Eye (TD), Bronze, Sizes #2 to 18	**#8526** Sproat, Forged Ball Eye (TD), Bronze, Sizes #8 to 16	**#S10-3F** Sproat, 1X Fine, Black, Ball Eye (TD), Sizes #4 to 20	**#3906, #AC3906** Sproat, Tapered Eye (TD), Bronze, Size #2 to 20	**#57, #L057, #NT057** Sproat, Ball Eye(TD), Bronze, Sizes #4 to 16	**#TMC3761** Sproat, Forged, 1X Long, 2X Heavy, Ball Eye (TD), Bronze, Sizes #8 to 18	**#B-170** Sproat, Ball Eye (TD), Bronze, Sizes #6 to 16

Pattern Application: Wet Flies and Nymphs

Partridge	Daiichi	VMC	Gamakatsu	Mustad	Eagle Claw	Tiemco	Kamasan
#GRS2A Capt. Hamilton, Ball Eye (TD), Gray Shadow, Sizes #10 to 16	**#1170** Round Bend, Forged, Ball Eye (TD), Bronze, Sizes #8 to 16	**#9288** Round Bend, Forged, 2X Fine, Short Shank, Bronze, Forged Ball Eye (TD), Sizes #6 to 20	**#P10** Model Perfect Round, Bronze, Ball Eye (TD), Sizes #4 to 24	**#94838** Round Bend, X Short, X Fine, Forged, Tapered Eye (TD), Bronze, Sizes #10 to 20	**#59, #L059, #NT059** Round Bend, Fine Wire, Forged, Ball Eye (TD), Brz. & Nkl. Teflon, Sizes #4 to 24	**#TMC5210** Round, Forged, 1X Fine, Ball Eye (TD), Bronze, Sizes #10 to 20	**#B-400** Round Bend, Forged, Ball Eye (TD), Bronze, Sizes #8 to 16

Pattern Application: Dry Flies and Nymphs

Partridge	Daiichi	VMC	Gamakatsu	Mustad	Eagle Claw	Tiemco	Kamasan
#GRS3A Capt. Hamilton, Forged, Ball Eye (TD), Gray Shadow, Sizes #12 to 18	**#1170** Round Bend, Forged, Ball Eye (TD), Bronze, Sizes #8 to 16	**#9288** Round Bend, Forged, 2X Fine, Short Shank, Bronze, Forged Ball Eye (TD), Sizes #6 to 20	**#P10** Model Perfect Round, Bronze, Ball Eye (TD), Sizes #4 to 24	**#94838** Round Bend, X Short, X Fine, Forged, Tapered Eye (TD), Bronze, Sizes #10 to 20	**#59, #L059, #NT059** Round Bend, Fine Wire, Forged, Ball Eye (TD), Brz. & Nkl. Teflon, Sizes #4 to 24	**#TMC5210** Round, Forged, 1X Fine, Ball Eye (TD), Bronze, Sizes #10 to 20	**#B-400** Round Bend, Forged, Ball Eye (TD), Bronze, Sizes #8 to 16

Pattern Application: Streamers and Bucktails

Partridge	Daiichi	VMC	Gamakatsu	Mustad	Eagle Claw	Tiemco	Kamasan
#GRS4A Redditch, Long Shank, Ball Eye (TD), Gray Shadow, Sizes #12 to 18	**#1170** Round Bend, Forged, Ball Eye (TD), Bronze, Sizes #8 to 16	**#9288** Round Bend, Forged, 2X Fine, Short Shank, Bronze, Forged Ball Eye (TD), Sizes #6 to 20	**#P10** Model Perfect Round, Bronze, Ball Eye (TD), Sizes #4 to 24	**#94838** Round Bend, X Short, X Fine, Forged, Tapered Eye (TD), Bronze, Sizes #10 to 20	**#59, #L059, #NT059** Round Bend, Fine Wire, Forged, Ball Eye (TD), Brz. & Nkl. Teflon, Sizes #4 to 24	**#TMC5210** Round, Forged, 1X Fine, Ball Eye (TD), Bronze, Sizes #10 to 20	**#B-400** Round Bend, Forged, Ball Eye (TD), Bronze, Sizes #8 to 16

Pattern Application: Nymphs

Partridge	Daiichi	VMC	Gamakatsu	Mustad	Eagle Claw	Tiemco	Kamasan
#GRS7MMB Special (Jardine), Ball Eye (TU), Gray Shadow, Sizes #10 to 20	None	None	None	None	None	None	None

Pattern Application: Nymphs, Sedges, and Caddis

Partridge	Daiichi	VMC	Gamakatsu	Mustad	Eagle Claw	Tiemco	Kamasan
#GRS12ST Special (Sweeping Bend), Long Shank, Ball Eye (S), Gray Shadow, Sizes #8 to 14	None	None	None	None	None	None	None

Pattern Application: Short-Bodied Streamers and Attractors

Partridge	Daiichi	VMC	Gamakatsu	Mustad	Eagle Claw	Tiemco	Kamasan
#H1A Capt. Hamilton, Forged, 2X Fine, 2-1/2X Long, Bronze, Ball Eye (TD), Sizes #2 to 14	**#1720** Round Bend, Forged, 3X Long, 1X Strong, Bronze, Ball Eye (TD), Sizes #6 to 18	None	**#P10-2L1H** Model Perfect Round, 2X Long, 1X Strong, Bronze, Ball Eye (TD), Sizes #4 to 16	**#9672, #AC9672** Round Bend, Forged, 3X Long, Bronze, Tapered Eye (TD), Sizes #2 to 18	**#63, #L063, #NT063** Round Bend, Forged, 3X Long, Brz. & Nkl. Teflon, Ball Eye (TD), Sizes #4 to 18	**#TMC5263** Round, Forged, 3X Long, Ball Eye (TD), Bronze, Sizes #2 to 18	**#B-830** Round Bend, Forged, 2X Long, Ball Eye (TD), Bronze, Sizes #6 to 14

Partridge Selection and Substitution Chart

Partridge	Daiichi	VMC	Gamakatsu	Mustad	Eagle Claw	Tiemco	Kamasan

Pattern Application: Flat-Bodied Nymphs

#H3ST Special (Draper), Double Shank, Ball Eye (S), Bronze, Sizes #6 to 16	None	None	None	None	None	None	None

Pattern Application: Wet Flies

#J1A Limerick, Ball Eye (TD), Bronze, Sizes #4 to 16	None	None	**#L10-2H** Limerick, 2X Strong, Ball Eye (TD), Bronze, Sizes #6 to 12	**#7970** Limerick, 5X Strong, Bronze, Ball Eye (TD), Sizes #2 to 8	None	None	None

Pattern Application: Tiny Dry Flies and Midges

#K1A Special (Marinaro) Offset, 4X Fine, Ball Eye (TD), Bronze, Sizes #20 to 28	None	None	None	**#540L** Round Bend, Forged, Ball Eye (TD), Gold Plated, Size #28	None	None	None

Pattern Application: Sedges, Caddis, and Nymphs

#K2B Special (Yorkshire) Forged, Curved Shank, Ball Eye (TU), Bronze, Sizes #8 to 18	**#4250** Egg, Forged, Reversed, Wide Gape, Short Shank, Ball Eye (TU), Bronze, Red & Gold, Sizes #4 to 14	None	**#C12U** Special Curve, Bronze, Ball Eye (TU), Sizes #6 to 16	**#37160, 60S** Wide Gape, Slightly Reversed, Ball Eye (TU), Brz., or St, Steel, Sizes #7/0 to 26	None	None	None

Pattern Application: Dry Flies and Caddis

#K3A Special (Swedish) Forged, 2X Long, Kinked Shank, 4X Fine, Ball Eye (TD), Bronze, Sizes #10 to 18	None	None	None	None	None	None	None

Pattern Application: Nymphs, Grubs, and Shrimp

#K4A Special (Veniard) Offset, Curved Shank, 2X Fine, Ball Eye (TD), Bronze, Sizes #8 to 18	**#1130** Continuous Bend, 1X Fine, 1X Short, Ball Eye (TD), Bronze, Sizes #10 to 16	None	**#C12** Special Curve, Bronze, Ball Eye (TD), Sizes #10 to 20	**#AC80250** Special, 2X Short, 2X Wide, Ball Eye (TD), Bronze, Sizes #10 to 22	**#L055, #NT055** Special Bend, Short Shank, Bronze & Nkl. Teflon, Ringed Eye (TD), Sizes #10 to 20	**#TMC2487** Special, Forged, Offset, Fine Wire, 2X Short, Ball Eye (TD), Bronze, Sizes #10 to 20	None

Pattern Application: Nymphs, Grubs, and Shrimp

#K5ST Special, Offset, 2X Fine, Ball Eye (S), Bronze, Sizes #12 to 18	None	None	None	None	None	None	None

Pattern Application: Dry Flies, Wet Flies, Nymphs, Larvae, Pupae, Terrestrials, and Leeches

#K6ST Special (Price), Long Curve, Ball Eye (S), Bronze, Sizes #8 to 14	**#1770** Sproat, 3X Long, 1X Fine, Forged, Ball Eye (S), Bronze, Sizes #6 to 16	None	None	**#AC80150** Special, Long Upbent Shank, Fine Wire, Ball Eye (S), Bronze, Sizes #8 to 14	None	**#TMC400T** Special, Ball Eye (S), Bronze, Sizes #8 to 14	None

Partridge Selection and Substitution Chart

Partridge	Daiichi	VMC	Gamakatsu	Mustad	Eagle Claw	Tiemco	Kamasan

Pattern Application: Dry Flies and Extended Bodies

Partridge	Daiichi	VMC	Gamakatsu	Mustad	Eagle Claw	Tiemco	Kamasan
#K10 Special (Yorkshire), Special Shank, Open Loop Ringed Eye (S), Bronze, Sizes #10 to 16	None	None	None	None	None	None	None

Pattern Application: Caddis, Emergers, Larvae, Pupae, Nymphs, and Wet Flies

Partridge	Daiichi	VMC	Gamakatsu	Mustad	Eagle Claw	Tiemco	Kamasan
#K12ST Special, Forged, 3X Long, Ball Eye (S), Bronze, Sizes #8 to 22	**#1270** Special Bend (York), Curved Shank, 3X Long, Bronze, Ball Eye (S), Sizes #6 to 22	None	None	**#AC80050** Special, 3X Long, Ball Eye (S), Bronze, Sizes #6 to 22	**#52, #L052, #NT052** Special Bend, Light Wire, Ringed Eye (TD), Nkl. Teflon & Bronze, Sizes #6 to 20	**#TMC200** Special, Ball Eye (S), Bronze, Sizes #4 to 20	None

Pattern Application: Small Nymphs and Emergers

Partridge	Daiichi	VMC	Gamakatsu	Mustad	Eagle Claw	Tiemco	Kamasan
#K14ST Special (Edwards), 3X Long, Curve, Ball Eye (S), Silver, Sizes #16, 18, 20	**#1270** Special Bend (York), Curved Shank, 3X Long, Bronze, Ball Eye (S), Sizes #6 to 22	None	None	**#AC80050** Special, 3X Long, Ball Eye (S), Bronze, Sizes #6 to 22	**#52, #L052, #NT052** Special Bend, Light Wire, Ringed Eye (TD), Nkl. Teflon & Bronze, Sizes #6 to 20	**#TMC200** Special, Ball Eye (S), Bronze, Sizes #4 to 20	None

Pattern Application: Wet Flies and Crayfish

Partridge	Daiichi	VMC	Gamakatsu	Mustad	Eagle Claw	Tiemco	Kamasan
#L1A Capt. Hamilton, Forged, Ball Eye (TD), Bronze, Sizes #2 to 14	**#1170** Round Bend, Forged, Ball Eye (TD), Bronze, Sizes #8 to 16	**#9288** Round Bend, Forged, 2X Fine, Short Shank, Bronze, Forged Ball Eye (TD), Sizes #6 to 20	**#P10** Model Perfect Round, Bronze, Ball Eye (TD), Sizes #4 to 24	**#94840, #AC94840** Round Bend, X Fine, Forged, Tapered Eye (TD), Bronze, Sizes #2 to 28	**#59, #L059, #NT059** Round Bend, Fine Wire, Forged, Ball Eye (TD), Brz. & Nkl. Teflon, Sizes #4 to 24	**#TMC5210** Round, Forged, 1X Fine, Ball Eye (TD), Bronze, Sizes #10 to 20	**#B-400** Round Bend, Forged, Ball Eye (TD), Bronze, Sizes #8 to 16

Pattern Application: Wet Flies

Partridge	Daiichi	VMC	Gamakatsu	Mustad	Eagle Claw	Tiemco	Kamasan
#L2A Capt. Hamilton, Forged, 2X Fine, Ball Eye (TD), Bronze, Sizes #6 to 18	**#1170** Round Bend, Forged, Ball Eye (TD), Bronze, Sizes #8 to 16	**#9288** Round Bend, Forged, 2X Fine, Short Shank, Bronze, Forged Ball Eye (TD), Sizes #6 to 20	**#P10** Model Perfect Round, Bronze, Ball Eye (TD), Sizes #4 to 24	**#94840, #AC94840** Round Bend, X Fine, Forged, Tapered Eye (TD), Bronze, Sizes #2 to 28	**#59, #L059, #NT059** Round Bend, Fine Wire, Forged, Ball Eye (TD), Brz. & Nkl. Teflon, Sizes #4 to 24	**#TMC5210** Round, Forged, 1X Fine, Ball Eye (TD), Bronze, Sizes #10 to 20	**#B-400** Round Bend, Forged, Ball Eye (TD), Bronze, Sizes #8 to 16

Pattern Application: Dry Flies

Partridge	Daiichi	VMC	Gamakatsu	Mustad	Eagle Claw	Tiemco	Kamasan
#L3A Capt. Hamilton, Forged, 4X Fine, Ball Eye (TD), Bronze, Sizes #8 to 22	**#1170** Round Bend, Forged, Ball Eye (TD), Bronze, Sizes #8 to 16	**#9288** Round Bend, Forged, 2X Fine, Short Shank, Bronze, Forged Ball Eye (TD), Sizes #6 to 20	**#P10** Model Perfect Round, Bronze, Ball Eye (TD), Sizes #4 to 24	**#94840, #AC94840** Round Bend, X Fine, Forged, Tapered Eye (TD), Bronze, Sizes #2 to 28	**#59, #L059, #NT059** Round Bend, Fine Wire, Forged, Ball Eye (TD), Brz. & Nkl. Teflon, Sizes #4 to 24	**#TMC5210** Round, Forged, 1X Fine, Ball Eye (TD), Bronze, Sizes #10 to 20	**#B-400** Round Bend, Forged, Ball Eye (TD), Bronze, Sizes #8 to 16

Pattern Application: Barbless Dry Flies

Partridge	Daiichi	VMC	Gamakatsu	Mustad	Eagle Claw	Tiemco	Kamasan
#L3AY Capt. Hamilton, Barbless, Forged, 4X Fine, Bronze, Ball Eye (TD), Sizes #8 to 22	None	None	None	None	None	None	None

Pattern Application: Dry Flies

Partridge	Daiichi	VMC	Gamakatsu	Mustad	Eagle Claw	Tiemco	Kamasan
#L3B Capt. Hamilton, Forged, 4X Fine, Ball Eye (TU), Bronze, Sizes #10 to 18	**#1330** Round Bend, 1X Short, Ball Eye (TD), Bronze, Sizes #8 to 24	**#9281** Modified Round Bend, Forged, X Fine, Forged Ball Eye (TU), Bronze, Sizes #8 to 20	None	**#94842** Round Bend, X Fine, Forged, Tapered Eye (TU), Bronze, Sizes #8 to 28	**#159, #L159** Round Bend, X Fine, Ball Eye (TU), Bronze, Sizes #4 to 18	None	None

Partridge Selection and Substitution Chart

Partridge	Daiichi	VMC	Gamakatsu	Mustad	Eagle Claw	Tiemco	Kamasan
Pattern Application: Dry Flies and No-Hackles							
#L4A Capt. Hamilton, Forged, 6X Fine, Ball Eye (TD), Bronze, Sizes #10 to 20	**#1170** Round Bend, Forged, Ball Eye (TD), Bronze, Sizes #8 to 16	**#9288** Round Bend, Forged, 2X Fine, Short Shank, Bronze, Forged Ball Eye (TD), Sizes #6 to 20	**#P10** Model Perfect Round, Bronze, Ball Eye (TD), Sizes #4 to 24	**#94840, #AC94840** Round Bend, X Fine, Forged, Tapered Eye (TD), Bronze, Sizes #2 to 28	**#59, #L059, #NT059** Round Bend, Fine Wire, Forged, Ball Eye (TD), Brz. & Nkl. Teflon, Sizes #4 to 24	**#TMC5210** Round, Forged, 1X Fine, Ball Eye (TD), Bronze, Sizes #10 to 20	**#B-400** Round Bend, Forged, Ball Eye (TD), Bronze, Sizes #8 to 16
Pattern Application: Salmon and Steelhead Patterns							
#R1A Limerick Double, Loop Eye (TD), Bronze, Sizes #2 to 12	**#7131** Double Limerick, Looped Eye (TU), Black, Size #4 to 12	None	None	**#3582, 82C, 82F** Double, Ball (TD), Tapered, or Oval Eye (TU), Bronze or Black, Sizes #2/0 to 12	None	None	None
Pattern Application: Salmon and Steelhead Patterns							
#R2A Outpoint Double, Loop Eye (TD), Bronze, Sizes #10 to 18	**#7131** Double Limerick, Looped Eye (TU), Black, Size #4 to 12	None	None	**#3582, 82C, 82F** Double, Ball (TD), Tapered, or Oval Eye (TU), Bronze or Black, Sizes #2/0 to 12	None	None	None
Pattern Application: Salmon and Steelhead Patterns							
#R3HF Outbarb Double, Loop Eye (S), Black, Sizes #6 to 14	**#7131** Double Limerick, Looped Eye (TU), Black, Size #4 to 12	None	None	**#3582, 82C, 82F** Double, Ball (TD), Tapered, or Oval Eye (TU), Bronze or Black, Sizes #2/0 to 12	None	None	None
Pattern Application: Wet Flies							
#SH1 Special (Stronghold), Heavy Wire,, Ball Eye (TD), Gray Shadow, Sizes #8 to 16	**#1550** Sproat, Ball Eye (TD), Bronze, Sizes #2 to 18	**#8526** Sproat, Forged Ball Eye (TD), Bronze, Sizes #8 to 16	**#S10-3F** Sproat, 1X Fine, Black, Ball Eye (TD), Sizes #4 to 20	**#3906, #AC3906** Sproat, Tapered Eye (TD), Bronze, Size #2 to 20	**#57, #L057, #NT057** Sproat, Ball Eye (TD), Bronze, Sizes #4 to 16	**#TMC3761** Sproat, Forged, 1X Long, 2X Heavy, Ball Eye (TD), Bronze, Sizes #8 to 18	**#B-170** Sproat, Ball Eye (TD), Bronze, Sizes #6 to 16
Pattern Application: Wet Flies and Nymphs							
#SH2 Special (Stronghold), 1X Long, Ball Eye (TD), Gray Shadow, Sizes #8 to 16	**#1550** Sproat, Ball Eye (TD), Bronze, Sizes #2 to 18	**#8526** Sproat, Forged Ball Eye (TD), Bronze, Sizes #8 to 16	**#S10-3F** Sproat, 1X Fine, Black, Ball Eye (TD), Sizes #4 to 20	**#3906, #AC3906** Sproat, 1X Long, Tapered Eye (TD), Bronze, Size #4 to 18	**#57, #L057, #NT057** Sproat, Ball Eye (TD), Bronze, Sizes #4 to 16	**#TMC3761** Sproat, Forged, 1X Long, 2X Heavy, Ball Eye (TD), Bronze, Sizes #8 to 18	**#B-170** Sproat, Ball Eye (TD), Bronze, Sizes #6 to 16
Pattern Application: Wet Flies, Nymphs, and Streamers							
#SH3 Special (Stronghold), Long Shank, Ball Eye (TD), Gray Shadow, Sizes #8 to 16	None	None	**#S11-4L2H** Sproat, 4X Long, 2X Strong, Black, Ball Eye (TD), Sizes #6 to 12	**#38941** Sproat, 3X Long, Tapered Eye (TD), Bronze, Sizes #2 to 16	**#281, #L281, #NT281** Sproat, 4X Long, 1X Heavy, Brz. & Nkl. Teflon, Ball Eye (TD), Sizes #2 to 10	None	None
Pattern Application: Salmon and Steelhead Patterns							
#M Salmon, Forged, 2X Heavy, Tapered Loop Eye (TU), Black, Sizes #4/0-1/0, 1 to 10	**#2441** Salmon, Forged, 1X Strong, Tapered Loop Eye (TU), Black, Sizes #2/0, 1/0, 1 to 8	**#8923** Limerick, Forged, 2X Long, Ball Eye (TU), Bronze, Sizes #2 to 12	**#T10-3H** Salmon, 1X Fine, Tapered Loop Eye (TU), Black, Sizes #2 to 8	**#90240** Limerick, 2X Fine Wire, X Long, Black, Loop Oval Eye (TU), Sizes #4, 6, 8, 10	None	**#TMC7999** Salmon, Forged, Heavy Wire, Tapered Loop Eye (TU), Black, Sizes #2/0 to 12	**#B-180** Salmon, Forged, Tapered Loop Eye (TU), Black, Sizes #2/0 to 12

136

Partridge Selection and Substitution Chart

Partridge	Daiichi	VMC	Gamakatsu	Mustad	Eagle Claw	Tiemco	Kamasan

Pattern Application: Wet Flies

Partridge	Daiichi	VMC	Gamakatsu	Mustad	Eagle Claw	Tiemco	Kamasan
#MM1B Special (McHaffie Dublin), Curved, Ball Eye (TU), Black, Sizes #2 to 12	None	None	None	None	None	None	None

Pattern Application: Wet Flies

Partridge	Daiichi	VMC	Gamakatsu	Mustad	Eagle Claw	Tiemco	Kamasan
#MM2A Special (Church), Forged, Wide Gape, Ball Eye (TD), Bronze, Sizes #1/0, 2, 6, 10	None	None	None	None	None	None	None

Pattern Application: Salmon and Steelhead Patterns

Partridge	Daiichi	VMC	Gamakatsu	Mustad	Eagle Claw	Tiemco	Kamasan
#N Salmon, Forged, 1X Heavy, 2X Long, Tapered Loop Eye (TU), Black, Sizes #4/0-1/0, 1 to 10	**#2441** Salmon, Forged, 1X Strong, Tapered Loop Eye (TU), Black, Sizes #2/0, 1/0, 1 to 8	**#8923** Limerick, Forged, 2X Long, Ball Eye (TU), Bronze, Sizes #2 to 12	**#T10-3H** Salmon, 1X Fine, Tapered Loop Eye (TU), Black, Sizes #2 to 8	**#36890, #AC36890** Limerick, Black, Looped Oval Eye (TU), Sizes #6/0 to 12	None	**#TMC7999** Salmon, Forged, Heavy Wire, Tapered Loop Eye (TU), Black, Sizes #2/0 to 12	**#B-180** Salmon, Forged, Tapered Loop Eye (TU), Black, Sizes #2/0 to 12

Pattern Application: Salmon and Steelhead Patterns

Partridge	Daiichi	VMC	Gamakatsu	Mustad	Eagle Claw	Tiemco	Kamasan
#P Salmon Double, 2X Heavy, Black, Loop Eye (TU), Sizes #2 to 10	**#7131** Double Limerick, Looped Eye (TU), Black, Sizes #4 to 12	None	None	**#3582, 82C, 82F** Double, Ball (TD), Tapered, or Oval Eye (TU), Bronze or Black, Sizes #2/0 to 12	None	None	None

Pattern Application: Salmon and Steelhead Patterns

Partridge	Daiichi	VMC	Gamakatsu	Mustad	Eagle Claw	Tiemco	Kamasan
#Q Salmon Double, 1X Heavy, 2X Long, Black, Loop Eye (TU), Sizes #2 to 10	**#7131** Double Limerick, Looped Eye (TU), Black, Sizes #4 to 12	None	None	**#3582, 82C, 82F** Double, Ball (TD), Tapered, or Oval Eye (TU), Bronze or Black, Sizes #2/0 to 12	None	None	None

Pattern Application: Salmon and Steelhead Patterns

Partridge	Daiichi	VMC	Gamakatsu	Mustad	Eagle Claw	Tiemco	Kamasan
#O1 Salmon (Wilson), Forged, Heavy Wire, Black, Tapered Loop Eye (TU), Sizes #2 to 16	**#2441** Salmon, Forged, 1X Strong, Tapered Loop Eye (TU), Black, Sizes #2/0, 1/0, 1 to 8	**#8923** Limerick, Forged, 2X Long, Ball Eye (TU), Bronze, Sizes #2 to 12	**#T10-3H** Salmon, 1X Fine, Tapered Loop Eye (TU), Black, Sizes #2 to 8	**#36890, #AC36890** Limerick, Black, Looped Oval Eye (TU), Sizes #6/0 to 12	None	**#TMC7999** Salmon, Forged, Heavy Wire, Tapered Loop Eye (TU), Black, Sizes #2/0 to 12	**#B-180** Salmon, Forged, Tapered Loop Eye (TU), Black, Sizes #2/0 to 12

Pattern Application: Salmon and Steelhead Patterns

Partridge	Daiichi	VMC	Gamakatsu	Mustad	Eagle Claw	Tiemco	Kamasan
#O2 Salmon Double (Wilson), Forged, Heavy Wire, 6X Long, Black, Tapered Loop Eye (TU), Sizes #2 to 14	**#7131** Double Limerick, Looped Eye (TU), Black, Sizes #4 to 12	None	None	**#3582, 82C, 82F** Double, Ball (TD), Tapered, or Oval Eye (TU), Bronze or Black, Sizes #2/0 to 12	None	None	None

Pattern Application: Salmon and Steelhead Patterns and Spey Flies

Partridge	Daiichi	VMC	Gamakatsu	Mustad	Eagle Claw	Tiemco	Kamasan
#CUSTOM Salmon (Spey), Forged, Tapered Loop Eye (TU), Blk., Brz., Blued, Gold & Silver, Sizes #1-1/2 , 3, 5, 7	**#2441** Salmon, Forged, 1X Strong, Tapered Loop Eye (TU), Black, Sizes #2/0, 1/0, 1 to 8	**#8923** Limerick, Forged, 2X Long, Ball Eye (TU), Bronze, Sizes #2 to 12	**#T10-3H** Salmon, 1X Fine, Tapered Loop Eye (TU), Black, Sizes #2 to 8	**#36890, #AC36890** Limerick, Black, Looped Oval Eye (TU), Sizes #6/0 to 12	None	**#TMC7999** Salmon, Forged, Heavy Wire, Tapered Loop Eye (TU), Black, Sizes #2/0 to 12	**#B-180** Salmon, Forged, Tapered Loop Eye (TU), Black, Sizes #2/0 to 12

Daiichi Hooks

Daiichi hooks are manufactured from high-carbon steel and are chemically sharpened, delivering superb strength and long point life.

Daiichi hooks can be obtained through local fly shops and catalog houses or through Angler Sport Group, 6619 Oak Orchard Rd., Elba, NY 14058; phone 716-757-9958.

Daiichi Selection and Substitution Chart

Pattern Application
The pattern application lists various types of patterns that can be tied using the specified hooks shown below.

Possible Substitutes
Listed across the page are other manufacturers' hooks that can be used as alternatives. In most cases, the hooks listed are similar or have the same characteristics with minor differences.

Note: Hook illustrations are only examples and are not shown at actual sizes. Also note that after the eye description, **(S)** indicates a straight eye, **(TD)** indicates a turned-down eye, and **(TU)** indicates a turned-up eye.

Daiichi	VMC	Gamakatsu	Mustad	Eagle Claw	Tiemco	Kamasan	Partridge

Pattern Application: Standard Dry Flies

Daiichi	VMC	Gamakatsu	Mustad	Eagle Claw	Tiemco	Kamasan	Partridge
#1100 Model Perfect Bend, Wide Gape, 1X Fine, Oversize Ball Eye (TD), Mini Barb, Bronze, Sizes #16 to 24	**#9288** Round Bend, Forged, 2X Fine, Short Shank, Bronze, Forged Ball Eye (TD), Sizes #6 to 20	**#P10** Model Perfect Round, Bronze, Ball Eye (TD), Sizes #4 to 24	**#94840, #AC94840** Round Bend, X Fine, Forged, Tapered Eye (TD), Bronze, Sizes #2 to 28	**#59, #L059, #NT059** Round Bend, Fine Wire, Forged, Ball Eye (TD), Brz. & Nkl. Teflon, Sizes #4 to 24	**#TMC5210** Round, Forged, 1X Fine, Ball Eye (TD), Bronze, Sizes #10 to 20	**#B-400** Round Bend, Forged, Ball Eye (TD), Bronze, Sizes #8 to 16	**#L4A** Capt. Hamilton, Forged, 6X Fine, Ball Eye (TD), Bronze, Sizes #10 to 20

Pattern Application: Dry Flies

Daiichi	VMC	Gamakatsu	Mustad	Eagle Claw	Tiemco	Kamasan	Partridge
#1110 Model Perfect Bend, Wide Gape, 1X Fine, Oversize Ball Eye (S), Mini Barb, Bronze, Sizes #16 to 24	None	None	None	None	**#TMC101** Round, Ball Eye (S), Bronze, Sizes #8 to 20	None	None

Pattern Application: Scuds, Shrimp, Grubs, Pupae, and San Juan Worm

Daiichi	VMC	Gamakatsu	Mustad	Eagle Claw	Tiemco	Kamasan	Partridge
#1130 Continuous Bend, 1X Fine, 1X Short, Ball Eye (TD), Bronze, Sizes #10 to 16	None	**#C12** Special Curve, Bronze, Ball Eye (TD), Sizes #10 to 20	**#AC80200** Special, 2X Short, 2X Wide, Ball Eye (TD), Bronze, Sizes #6 to 18	**#L056, #NT056** Special Bend, Hump Shank, Brz. & Nickel Teflon, Ringed Eye (TD), Sizes #2 to 14	**#TMC2457** Special, Forged, 2X Heavy, 2X Wide, 2X Short, Bronze, Ball Eye (TD), Sizes #6 to 18	None	**#K4A** Special (Veniard) Offset, Curved Shank, 2X Fine, Ball Eye (TD), Bronze, Sizes #8 to 18

Pattern Application: Midges, Pupae, and Micro-Caddis

Daiichi	VMC	Gamakatsu	Mustad	Eagle Claw	Tiemco	Kamasan	Partridge
#1140 Continuous Bend, Forged, 1X Fine, 1X Short, Bronze, Ball Eye (TU), Sizes #10 to 16	None	**#C12U** Special Curve, Bronze, Ball Eye (TU), Sizes #6 to 16	**#9523** Round Bend, Offset, Forged, 5X Short, X Fine, Bronze, Tapered Eye (TU), Sizes #3/0 to 16	**#479** Wide Gape, Forged, X Short, Ball Eye (TU), Gold, Sizes #4 to 14	None	None	**#K2B** Special (Yorkshire) Forged, Curved Shank, Ball Eye (TU), Bronze, Sizes #8 to 18

Pattern Application: Scuds, Shrimp, Grubs, Pupae, and San Juan Worm

Daiichi	VMC	Gamakatsu	Mustad	Eagle Claw	Tiemco	Kamasan	Partridge
#1150 Continuous Bend, Forged, 1X Strong, Reversed, Bronze, Ball Eye (TU), Sizes #18, 20, 22	None	**#C12U** Special Curve, Bronze, Ball Eye (TU), Sizes #6 to 16	**#9523** Round Bend, Offset, Forged, 5X Short, X Fine, Bronze, Tapered Eye (TU), Sizes #3/0 to 16	**#479** Wide Gape, Forged, X Short, Ball Eye (TU), Gold, Sizes #4 to 14	None	None	**#K2B** Special (Yorkshire) Forged, Curved Shank, Ball Eye (TU), Bronze, Sizes #8 to 18

Pattern Application: Traditional Dry Flies

Daiichi	VMC	Gamakatsu	Mustad	Eagle Claw	Tiemco	Kamasan	Partridge
#1170 Round Bend, Forged, Ball Eye (TD), Bronze, Sizes #8 to 16	**#9288** Round Bend, Forged, 2X Fine, Short Shank, Bronze, Forged Ball Eye (TD), Sizes #6 to 20	**#P10** Model Perfect Round, Bronze, Ball Eye (TD), Sizes #4 to 24	**#94840, #AC94840** Round Bend, X Fine, Forged, Tapered Eye (TD), Bronze, Sizes #2 to 28	**#59, #L059, #NT059** Round Bend, Fine Wire, Forged, Ball Eye (TD), Brz. & Nkl. Teflon, Sizes #4 to 24	**#TMC5210** Round, Forged, 1X Fine, Ball Eye (TD), Bronze, Sizes #10 to 20	**#B-400** Round Bend, Forged, Ball Eye (TD), Bronze, Sizes #8 to 16	**#L4A** Capt. Hamilton, Forged, 6X Fine, Ball Eye (TD), Bronze, Sizes #10 to 20

Daiichi Selection and Substitution Chart

Daiichi	VMC	Gamakatsu	Mustad	Eagle Claw	Tiemco	Kamasan	Partridge

Pattern Application: Traditional Dry Flies

Daiichi	VMC	Gamakatsu	Mustad	Eagle Claw	Tiemco	Kamasan	Partridge
#1180 Round Bend, Forged, Mini Barb Ball Eye (TD), Bronze, Sizes #8 to 24	#9288 Round Bend, Forged, 2X Fine, Short Shank, Bronze, Forged Ball Eye (TD), Sizes #6 to 20	#P10 Model Perfect Round, Bronze, Ball Eye (TD), Sizes #4 to 24	#94840, #AC94840 Round Bend, X Fine, Forged, Tapered Eye (TD), Bronze, Sizes #2 to 28	#59, #L059, #NT059 Round Bend, Fine Wire, Forged, Ball Eye (TD), Brz. & Nkl. Teflon, Sizes #4 to 24	#TMC5210 Round, Forged, 1X Fine, Ball Eye (TD), Bronze, Sizes #10 to 20	#B-400 Round Bend, Forged, Ball Eye (TD), Bronze, Sizes #8 to 16	#L4A Capt. Hamilton, Forged, 6X Fine, Ball Eye (TD), Bronze, Sizes #10 to 20

Pattern Application: Barbless Traditional Dry Flies

Daiichi	VMC	Gamakatsu	Mustad	Eagle Claw	Tiemco	Kamasan	Partridge
#1190 Round Bend, Barbless, Ball Eye (TD), Bronze, Sizes #8 to 18	None	None	None	None	#TMC103BL Round, Barbless X Fine, Wide Gape, Ball Eye (S), Bronze, Sizes #11 to 19	None	None

Pattern Application: Hoppers and Terrestrials and Stonefly Nymphs

Daiichi	VMC	Gamakatsu	Mustad	Eagle Claw	Tiemco	Kamasan	Partridge
#1270 Special Bend (York), Curved Shank, 3X Long, Bronze, Ball Eye (S), Sizes #6 to 22	None	None	#AC80050 Special, 3X Long, Ball Eye (S), Bronze, Sizes #6 to 22	#52, #L052, #NT052 Special Bend, Light Wire, Ringed Eye (TD), Nkl. Teflon & Bronze, Sizes #6 to 20	#TMC200R TMC200RBL Special, Forged, 3X Long, Ball Eye (S), Bronze, Sizes #4 to 22	None	K12ST Special, Forged, 3X Long, Ball Eye (S), Bronze, Sizes #8 to 22

Pattern Application: Nymphs

Daiichi	VMC	Gamakatsu	Mustad	Eagle Claw	Tiemco	Kamasan	Partridge
#1273 Special Bend (York), Curved Shank, 3X Long, 1X Strong, Bronze, Ball Eye (S), Sizes #16 to 22	None	None	#AC80050 Special, 3X Long, Ball Eye (S), Bronze, Sizes #6 to 22	#52, #L052, #NT052 Special Bend, Light Wire, Ringed Eye (TD), Nkl. Teflon & Bronze, Sizes #6 to 20	#TMC200R TMC200RBL Special, Forged, 3X Long, Ball Eye (S), Bronze, Sizes #4 to 22	None	K12ST Special, Forged, 3X Long, Ball Eye (S), Bronze, Sizes #8 to 22

Pattern Application: Dry Flies

Daiichi	VMC	Gamakatsu	Mustad	Eagle Claw	Tiemco	Kamasan	Partridge
#1280 Round Bend, 2X Long, Fine Wire, Ball Eye (TD), Mini Barb, Bronze, Sizes #6 to 16	#9288 Round Bend, Forged, 2X Fine, Short Shank, Bronze, Forged Ball Eye (TD), Sizes #6 to 20	#P10 Model Perfect Round, Bronze, Ball Eye (TD), Sizes #4 to 24	#94840, #AC94840 Round Bend, X Fine, Forged, Tapered Eye (TD), Bronze, Sizes #2 to 28	#59, #L059, #NT059 Round Bend, Fine Wire, Forged, Ball Eye (TD), Brz. & Nkl. Teflon, Sizes #4 to 24	#TMC5210 Round, Forged, 1X Fine, Ball Eye (TD), Bronze, Sizes #10 to 20	#B-400 Round Bend, Forged, Ball Eye (TD), Bronze, Sizes #8 to 16	#L4A Capt. Hamilton, Forged, 6X Fine, Ball Eye (TD), Bronze, Sizes #10 to 20

Pattern Application: Short-Bodied Dry Flies

Daiichi	VMC	Gamakatsu	Mustad	Eagle Claw	Tiemco	Kamasan	Partridge
#1310 Round Bend, 1X Short, Ball Eye (TD), Bronze, Sizes #8 to 22	#9288 Round Bend, Forged, 2X Fine, Short Shank, Bronze, Forged Ball Eye (TD), Sizes #6 to 20	#P10 Model Perfect Round, Bronze, Ball Eye (TD), Sizes #4 to 24	#94840, #AC94840 Round Bend, X Fine, Forged, Tapered Eye (TD), Bronze, Sizes #2 to 28	#59, #L059, #NT059 Round Bend, Fine Wire, Forged, Ball Eye (TD), Brz. & Nkl. Teflon, Sizes #4 to 24	#TMC5210 Round, Forged, 1X Fine, Ball Eye (TD), Bronze, Sizes #10 to 20	#B-400 Round Bend, Forged, Ball Eye (TD), Bronze, Sizes #8 to 16	#L4A Capt. Hamilton, Forged, 6X Fine, Ball Eye (TD), Bronze, Sizes #10 to 20

Pattern Application: Dry Flies, Tricos, and Midges

Daiichi	VMC	Gamakatsu	Mustad	Eagle Claw	Tiemco	Kamasan	Partridge
#1330 Round Bend, 1X Short, Ball Eye (TD), Bronze, Sizes #8 to 24	#9281 Modified Round Bend, Forged, X Fine, Forged Ball Eye (TU), Bronze, Sizes #8 to 20	None	#94842 Round Bend, X Fine, Forged, Tapered Eye (TU), Bronze, Sizes #8 to 28	#159, #L159 Round Bend, X Fine, Ball Eye (TU), Bronze, Sizes #4 to 18	#TMC500U Round, 2X Short, Ball Eye (TU), Bronze, Sizes #16 to 22	None	#L3B Capt. Hamilton, Forged, 4X Fine, Ball Eye (TU), Bronze, Sizes #10 to 18

Pattern Application: Dry Flies, Midges, Spiders, and Variants

Daiichi	VMC	Gamakatsu	Mustad	Eagle Claw	Tiemco	Kamasan	Partridge
#1480 Limerick, 2X Short, 1X Fine, Ball Eye (S), Mini Barb, Bronze, Sizes #12 to 24	None	None	None	None	None	None	None

Daiichi Selection and Substitution Chart

Daiichi	VMC	Gamakatsu	Mustad	Eagle Claw	Tiemco	Kamasan	Partridge

Pattern Application: Wet Flies, Egg Patterns, Ants, and Spiders

Daiichi	VMC	Gamakatsu	Mustad	Eagle Claw	Tiemco	Kamasan	Partridge
#1510 Sproat, 3X Short, Ball Eye (TD), Bronze, Sizes #6 to 18	#8526 Sproat, Forged Ball Eye (TD), Bronze, Sizes #8 to 16	#S10 Sproat, Black, Ball Eye (TD), Sizes #2 to 24	#3906, #AC3906 Sproat, Tapered Eye (TD), Bronze, Sizes #2 to 20	#57, #L057, #NT057 Sproat, Ball Eye (TD), Bronze & Nkl. Teflon, Sizes #4 to 16	#TMC3761 Sproat, Forged, 1X Long, 2X Heavy, Ball Eye (TD), Bronze, Sizes #8 to 18	#B-170 Sproat, Ball Eye (TD), Bronze, Sizes #6 to 16	#G3A Sproat, Forged, Heavy Wire, Ball Eye (TD), Bronze, Sizes #8 to 16

Pattern Application: Wet Flies, Nymphs, and Salmon and Steelhead Flies

Daiichi	VMC	Gamakatsu	Mustad	Eagle Claw	Tiemco	Kamasan	Partridge
#1530 Sproat, 1X Short, 2X Strong, Ball Eye (TD), Bronze, Sizes #4 to 16	#8526 Sproat, Forged Ball Eye (TD), Bronze, Sizes #8 to 16	#S10 Sproat, Black, Ball Eye (TD), Sizes #2 to 24	#3906, #AC3906 Sproat, Tapered Eye (TD), Bronze, Sizes #2 to 20	#57, #L057, #NT057 Sproat, Ball Eye (TD), Bronze & Nkl. Teflon, Sizes #4 to 16	#TMC3761 Sproat, Forged, 1X Long, 2X Heavy, Ball Eye (TD), Bronze, Sizes #8 to 18	#B-170 Sproat, Ball Eye (TD), Bronze, Sizes #6 to 16	None

Pattern Application: Traditional Wet Flies

Daiichi	VMC	Gamakatsu	Mustad	Eagle Claw	Tiemco	Kamasan	Partridge
#1550 Sproat, Ball Eye (TD), Bronze, Sizes #2 to 18	#8526 Sproat, Bronze, Ball Eye (TD), Forged, Sizes #8 to 16	#S10 Sproat, Ball Eye (TD), Black, Sizes #2 to 24	#3399, 99A, 99D, 99N Sproat, Ball Eye (TD), Brz., Gold, 99D-Fine Wire, Sizes #9/0 -2, 4 to 20	#57, #L057, #NT057 Sproat, Ball Eye (TD), Bronze, Sizes #4 to 16	#TMC3769 Sproat, 1X Long, Forged, Ball Eye (TD), 2X Heavy, Bronze, Sizes #2 to 20	#B-170 Sproat, Ball Eye (TD), Bronze, Sizes #6 to 16	#A Improved Sproat, Offset, 1X Short, 2X Fine, Ball Eye (TD), Bronze, Sizes #10 to 16

Pattern Application: Wet Flies and Traditional Nymphs

Daiichi	VMC	Gamakatsu	Mustad	Eagle Claw	Tiemco	Kamasan	Partridge
#1560 Sproat, 1X Long, 1X Strong, Ball Eye (TD), Bronze, Sizes #6 to 18	#8527 Sproat, 1X Long, Forged Ball Eye (TD), Bronze, Sizes #8 to 16	#S10-3F Sproat, 1X Fine, Black, Ball Eye (TD), Sizes #4 to 20	#3906B, #AC3906B Sproat, 1X Long, Tapered Eye (TD), Bronze, Size #4 to 18	#1197N, #L1197N Sproat, Long Shank, Nickel, Ball Eye (TD), Sizes #1 to 8	#TMC3761 Sproat, Forged, 1X Long, 2X Heavy, Ball Eye (TD), Bronze, Sizes #8 to 18	#B-170 Sproat, Ball Eye (TD), Bronze, Sizes #6 to 16	#G3A Sproat, Forged, Ball Eye (TD), Bronze, Sizes #8 to 16

Pattern Application: Caddisflies, Spiders, Egg Patterns, Tricos, and Extended-Body Dry Flies

Daiichi	VMC	Gamakatsu	Mustad	Eagle Claw	Tiemco	Kamasan	Partridge
#1640 Round Bend, Forged, Reversed, 2X Short, Fine Wire, Ball Eye (S), Bronze, Sizes #2 to 20	None	None	None	None	#TMC101 Round, Ball Eye (S), Bronze, Sizes #8 to 20	None	None

Pattern Application: Wet Flies, Nymphs, and Muddlers

Daiichi	VMC	Gamakatsu	Mustad	Eagle Claw	Tiemco	Kamasan	Partridge
#1710 Round Bend, 1X Strong, 2X Long. Forged, Bronze, Ball Eye (TD), Sizes #2 to 18	None	#P10-2L1H Model Perfect Round, 2X Long, 1X Strong, Bronze, Ball Eye (TD), Sizes #4 to 16	None	None	None	#B-830 Round Bend, Forged, 2X Long, Ball Eye (TD), Bronze, Sizes #6 to 14	None

Pattern Application: Streamers, Long-Body Nymphs, Woolly Buggers, and Small Streamers

Daiichi	VMC	Gamakatsu	Mustad	Eagle Claw	Tiemco	Kamasan	Partridge
#1720 Round Bend, Forged, 3X Long, 1X Strong, Bronze, Ball Eye (TD), Sizes #6 to 18	#9283 Round Bend, Forged, 4X Long Forged Ball Eye (TD), Bronze, Sizes #2 to 16	#P10-2L1H Model Perfect Round, 2X Long, 1X Strong, Bronze, Ball Eye (TD), Sizes #4 to 16	#9672, #AC9672 Round Bend, Forged, 3X Long, Bronze, Tapered Eye (TD), Sizes #2 to 18	#58, #L058, #NT058 Round Bend, 3X Long, Forged, Ball Eye (TD), Bronze & Nkl. Teflon, Sizes #4 to 14	#TMC5263 Round, Forged, 3X Long, Ball Eye (TD), Bronze, Sizes #2 to 18	#B-830 Round Bend, Forged, 2X Long, Ball Eye (TD), Bronze, Sizes #6 to 14	#H1A Capt. Hamilton, Forged, 2X Fine, 2-1/2X Long, Bronze, Ball Eye (TD), Sizes #2 to 14

Pattern Application: Stonefly Nymphs and Crab Patterns

Daiichi	VMC	Gamakatsu	Mustad	Eagle Claw	Tiemco	Kamasan	Partridge
#1730 Round Bend, 3X Long, 1X Strong, Forged, Ball Eye (TD), Bronze, Sizes #6 to 14	None	None	None	None	None	#B-810 Round Bend, Forged, 4X Long, Special Bend, Ball Eye (TD), Bronze, Sizes #6 to 12	None

Daiichi Selection and Substitution Chart

Daiichi	VMC	Gamakatsu	Mustad	Eagle Claw	Tiemco	Kamasan	Partridge

Pattern Application: Streamers, Zonkers, Bucktails, and Muddlers

Daiichi	VMC	Gamakatsu	Mustad	Eagle Claw	Tiemco	Kamasan	Partridge
#1750 Round Bend, 4X Long, 1X Strong, Forged, Ball Eye (S), Mini Barb, Bronze, Sizes #4 to 14	None	None	**#9674** Round Bend, Forged, 4X Long, Bronze, Ball Eye (S), Sizes #4 to 12	None	None	None	None

Pattern Application: Leeches, Nymphs, and San Juan Worm

Daiichi	VMC	Gamakatsu	Mustad	Eagle Claw	Tiemco	Kamasan	Partridge
#1770 Sproat, 3X Long, 1X Fine, Forged, Ball Eye (S), Bronze, Sizes #6 to 16	None	None	**#3777** Central Draught, Ringed Eye (S), Bronze, Size #18-30, 32, 34, 36	None	**#TMC400T** Special, Ball Eye (S), Bronze, Sizes #8 to 14	None	**#K6ST** Special (Price), Long Curve, Ball Eye (S), Bronze, Sizes #8 to 14

Pattern Application: Free Swimming Patterns

Daiichi	VMC	Gamakatsu	Mustad	Eagle Claw	Tiemco	Kamasan	Partridge
#1850 Round Bend, 4X Long, 1X Strong, Forged, Flat Eye (S), Bronze, Sizes #6 to 12	None	None	None	None	None	None	None

Pattern Application: Salmon and Steelhead Patterns

Daiichi	VMC	Gamakatsu	Mustad	Eagle Claw	Tiemco	Kamasan	Partridge
#2151 Salmon, Forged, Curved Shank, Tapered Loop Eye (S), Black, Sizes #1 to 10	None	None	**#AC80050** Special, 3X Long, Ball Eye (S), Bronze, Sizes #6 to 22	**#52, #L052, #NT052** Special Bend, Light Wire, Ringed Eye (S), Nkl. Teflon & Bronze, Sizes #6 to 20	**#TMC200** Special, Ball Eye (S), Bronze, Sizes #4 to 20	None	**#K12ST** Special, Forged, 3X Long, Ball Eye (S), Bronze, Sizes #8 to 22

Pattern Application: Salmon and Steelhead Patterns

Daiichi	VMC	Gamakatsu	Mustad	Eagle Claw	Tiemco	Kamasan	Partridge
#2161 Salmon, Forged, Curved Shank, Tapered Loop Eye (TU), Black, Sizes #1, 2	None	None	None	None	None	None	None

Pattern Application: Egg Patterns, Emergers, and San Juan Worm

Daiichi	VMC	Gamakatsu	Mustad	Eagle Claw	Tiemco	Kamasan	Partridge
#2170 Round Bend, Forged, Reversed, 1X Short, Shank Bent Up, Brz., Grn., or Blk., Ball Eye (S), Sizes #2 to 12	None	None	None	None	None	None	None

Pattern Application: Streamers, Muddlers, Zonkers, and Woolly Buggers

Daiichi	VMC	Gamakatsu	Mustad	Eagle Claw	Tiemco	Kamasan	Partridge
#2220 Round Bend, 4X Long, 1X Strong, Forged, Ball Eye (TD), Bronze, Sizes #1 to 14	None	None	**#94720** Round Bend, Forged, Tapered Eye (TD), Bronze, Sizes #2 to 8	None	None	None	**#CS15** Limerick, Heavy Wire, X Long, Tapered Loop Eye (TD), Bronze, Sizes #2/0, 2, 4

Pattern Application: Streamers and Bucktails

Daiichi	VMC	Gamakatsu	Mustad	Eagle Claw	Tiemco	Kamasan	Partridge
#2340 Limerick, 6X Long, 1X Strong, Ball Eye (TD), Bronze, Sizes #4 to 12	None	None	**#9575** Limerick, Forged, 1/2 Longer Shank, Bronze, Tapered Loop Eye (TD), Sizes #2 to 12	**#74** Eagle Claw Design, Forged, XX Long, Gold, Ball Eye (TD), Sizes #4/0 to 4	None	None	**#CS17** Limerick, 6X Long, Tapered Loop Eye (TD), Black, Sizes #1, 2, 4, 6

Daiichi Selection and Substitution Chart

Daiichi	VMC	Gamakatsu	Mustad	Eagle Claw	Tiemco	Kamasan	Partridge

Pattern Application: Salmon and Steelhead Patterns

Daiichi	VMC	Gamakatsu	Mustad	Eagle Claw	Tiemco	Kamasan	Partridge
#2421 Salmon, Forged, Tapered Loop Eye (TU), Black, Sizes #2 to 12	#8923 Limerick, Forged, 2X Long, Ball Eye (TU), Bronze, Sizes #2 to 12	#T10-3H Salmon, 1X Fine, Tapered Loop Eye (TU), Black, Sizes #2 to 8	#90240 Limerick, 2X Fine Wire, X Long, Black, Loop Oval Eye (TU), Sizes #4, 6, 8, 10	None	#TMC7999 Salmon, Forged, Heavy Wire, Tapered Loop Eye (TU), Black, Sizes #2/0 to 12	#B-180 Salmon, Forged, Tapered Loop Eye (TU), Black, Sizes #2/0 to 12	#M Salmon, Forged, 2X Heavy, Tapered Loop Eye (TU), Black, Sizes #4/0-1/0, 1 to 10

Pattern Application: Salmon and Steelhead Patterns

Daiichi	VMC	Gamakatsu	Mustad	Eagle Claw	Tiemco	Kamasan	Partridge
#2441 Salmon, Forged, 1X Strong, Tapered Loop Eye (TU), Black, Sizes #2/0, 1/0, 1 to 8	#8923 Limerick, Forged, 2X Long, Ball Eye (TU), Bronze, Sizes #2 to 12	#T10-3H Salmon, 1X Fine, Tapered Loop Eye (TU), Black, Sizes #2 to 8	#90240 Limerick, 2X Fine Wire, X Long, Black, Loop Oval Eye (TU), Sizes #4, 6, 8, 10	None	#TMC7999 Salmon, Forged, Heavy Wire, Tapered Loop Eye (TU), Black, Sizes #2/0 to 12	#B-180 Salmon, Forged, Tapered Loop Eye (TU), Black, Sizes #2/0 to 12	#M Salmon, Forged, 2X Heavy, Tapered Loop Eye (TU), Black, Sizes #4/0-1/0, 1 to 10

Pattern Application: Saltwater Patterns, Tube Flies, Bass Flies, and Salmon and Steelhead Patterns

Daiichi	VMC	Gamakatsu	Mustad	Eagle Claw	Tiemco	Kamasan	Partridge
#2451 O'Shaughnessy, Forged, Short Shank, Ball Eye (S), Black, Sizes #1 to 8	#9255 O'Shaughnessy, Ball Eye (S), Bronze, Sizes #5/0 to 6	None	#3407, 07A, 07B, 07SS O'Shaughnessy, Forged, X or 2X Strong, Ringed Eye (S), Cad. Tinned, Sizes #14/0 to 12	#L054SS O'Shaughnessy, Ringed Eye (S), Stainless Steel, Sizes #1/0 to 4/0	#TMC811S O'Shaughnessy, X Strong, Ringed Eye (S), Stainless Steel, Sizes #4/0 to 8	None	None

Pattern Application: Bass Flies, Muddlers, Matukas, Zonkers, Bucktails, and Woolly Buggers

Daiichi	VMC	Gamakatsu	Mustad	Eagle Claw	Tiemco	Kamasan	Partridge
#2461 Aberdeen, 3X Long, Ball Eye (S), Black, Sizes #6/0 to 1/0, 1 to 6	None	None	#37360, 61, 63 Aberdeen, X Fine Wire, Ringed Eye (S), Bronze, Blued & Gold, Sizes #4/0, 3/0, 8, 10, 12	None	None	None	None

Pattern Application: Saltwater Patterns

Daiichi	VMC	Gamakatsu	Mustad	Eagle Claw	Tiemco	Kamasan	Partridge
#2546 O'Shaughnessy, Forged, Ball Eye (S), Stainless Steel, Sizes #6/0 to 1/0, 1 to 6	#9255 O'Shaughnessy, Long Shank, Ball Eye (S), Brz., Nkl., Perma Stl., Gold, Sizes #5/0 to 6	None	#34007, 09 O'Shaughnessy, Forged, Large Ringed Eye (S), Stainless Steel, Sizes #11/0 to 2	#L054SS O'Shaughnessy, Ringed Eye (S), Stainless Steel, Sizes #1/0 to 4/0	#TMC811S O'Shaughnessy, X Strong, Ringed Eye (S), Stainless Steel, Sizes #4/0 to 8	None	None

Pattern Application: Saltwater Patterns

Daiichi	VMC	Gamakatsu	Mustad	Eagle Claw	Tiemco	Kamasan	Partridge
#2550 Beak, Reversed, Ball Eye (TU), Stl. Steel, Brz., Nckl., Sizes #2, 4, 6	None	None	None	None	None	None	None

Pattern Application: Deer-Hair Bass Bugs, Divers, Frogs, Mice, and Lures

Daiichi	VMC	Gamakatsu	Mustad	Eagle Claw	Tiemco	Kamasan	Partridge
#2720 Stinger, Wide Gape, Lt. Wire, Ball Eye (S), Bronze., Sizes #5/0, 3/0, 1/0, 2	None	None	#37187 Stinger, Ringed Eye (S), Bronze, Sizes #1/0, 2, 6, 10	None	None	None	None

Pattern Application: Egg Patterns

Daiichi	VMC	Gamakatsu	Mustad	Eagle Claw	Tiemco	Kamasan	Partridge
#4250 Egg, Forged, Reversed, Wide Gape, Short Shank, Ball Eye (TU), Bronze, Red & Gold, Sizes #4 to 14	None	#C12U Special Curve, Bronze, Ball Eye (TU), Sizes #6 to 16	#37160, 60S Wide Gape, Slightly Reversed, Ball Eye (TU), Brz. or St Steel, Sizes #7/0 to 26	None	None	None	#K2B Special (Yorkshire) Forged, Curved Shank, Ball Eye (TU), Bronze, Sizes #8 to 18

Daiichi Selection and Substitution Chart

Daiichi	VMC	Gamakatsu	Mustad	Eagle Claw	Tiemco	Kamasan	Partridge

Pattern Application: Double-Hook Salmon and Steelhead Patterns

Daiichi	VMC	Gamakatsu	Mustad	Eagle Claw	Tiemco	Kamasan	Partridge
#7131 Limerick Double, Forged, Black, Loop Eye (TU), Sizes #4 to 12	None	None	#7827 Double, Ringed, Loose Eye (S), Bronze, Size #5/0-2 to 16	None	None	None	#R1A, R2A, R3HF, Double, P, Q, 02 Looped Eye (S, TU, or TD), Bronze or Black, Sizes #3/0-2 to 18

Pattern Application: Streamers, Bucktails, and Zonkers

Daiichi	VMC	Gamakatsu	Mustad	Eagle Claw	Tiemco	Kamasan	Partridge
#J101 Improved Limerick, 4X Heavy, Black, Tapered Loop Eye (S), Size #6	None	None	None	None	None	None	None

Pattern Application: Streamers, Bucktails, and Baitfish Patterns

Daiichi	VMC	Gamakatsu	Mustad	Eagle Claw	Tiemco	Kamasan	Partridge
#J141 Improved Limerick, Tapered Loop Eye (S), Black, Sizes #1 to 6	None	None	None	None	None	None	None

Pattern Application: Trolling Streamers and Baitfish

Daiichi	VMC	Gamakatsu	Mustad	Eagle Claw	Tiemco	Kamasan	Partridge
#J171 Improved Limerick, 6X Long, Tapered Loop Eye (TD), Black, Sizes #1, 2	None	None	#36680 Limerick, 1/4" Longer Shank, Bronze, Tapered Eye (TD), Sizes #4 to 12	#74 Eagle Claw Design, Forged, XX Long, Gold, Ball Eye (TD), Sizes #4/0 to 4	None	None	#CS17 Limerick, Heavy Wire, 6X Long, Tapered Loop Eye (TD), Black, Sizes #1, 2, 4, 6

Pattern Application: Emergers, Scuds, Shrimp, and Nymphs

Daiichi	VMC	Gamakatsu	Mustad	Eagle Claw	Tiemco	Kamasan	Partridge
#J220 Egg, Wide Gape, Offset. Short Shank, Contoured Eye (TD), Bronze, Sizes #20, 22, 24	None	None	None	None	None	None	None

VMC Hooks

V MC hooks are manufactured in France and sold worldwide through various distributors and catalog houses. VMC produces excellent high-quality hooks for both commercial and sport fishing.

VMC hooks can be obtained through most fly shops or catalog houses or VMC's stateside distributor: VMC, Inc., 1901 Oakcrest Ave. Suite #10, St. Paul, MN 55113; phone 612-636-9649; fax 612-636-7053.

VMC Selection and Substitution Chart

Pattern Application
The pattern application lists various types of patterns that can be tied using the specified hooks shown below.

Possible Substitutes
Listed across the page are other manufacturers' hooks that can be used as alternatives. In most cases, the hooks listed are similar or have the same characteristics with minor differences.

Note: Hook illustrations are only examples and are not shown at actual sizes. In addition, after the eye description, **(S)** indicates a straight eye, **(TD)** indicates a turned-down eye, and **(TU)** indicates a turned-up eye.

VMC	Gamakatsu	Mustad	Eagle Claw	Tiemco	Kamasan	Partridge	Daiichi

Pattern Application: Saltwater Streamers and Bass Flies

| **#8410** Special (Crystal), Forged, Ball Eye (S), Bronze, Sizes #4 to 12 | **#S10S** Sproat, Ball Eye (S), Black, Sizes #2 to 20 | **#3365A, 65C, 66, 66A, 66F, 66G, 67** Sproat, Ringed Eye (S), Nickl., Brz., Gold, Blued, Sizes #8/0 -2, 4, 6, 8, 10, 12, 14 | None | None | None | None | None |

Pattern Application: Wet Flies and Nymphs

| **#8526** Sproat, Forged Ball Eye (TD), Bronze, Sizes #8 to 16 | **#S10** Sproat, Ball Eye (TD), Black, Sizes #2 to 24 | **#3399, 99A, 99D, 99N** Sproat, Ball Eye (TD), Brz., Gold, 99D-Fine Wire, Sizes #9/0 -2, 4 to 20 | **#57, #L057, #NT057** Sproat, Ball Eye (TD), Bronze, Sizes #4 to 16 | **#TMC3769** Sproat, 1X Long, Forged, Ball Eye (TD), 2X Heavy, Bronze, Sizes #2 to 20 | **#B-170** Sproat, Ball Eye (TD), Bronze, Sizes #6 to 16 | **#A** Improved Sproat, 2X Fine, 1X Short, Bronze, Ball Eye (TD), Sizes #10 to 16 | **#1550** Sproat, Ball Eye (TD), Bronze, Sizes #2 to 18 |

Pattern Application: Nymphs and Small Bucktails

| **#8527** Sproat, 1X Long, Forged Ball Eye (TD), Bronze, Sizes #8 to 16 | **#S10-3F** Sproat, 1X Fine, Black, Ball Eye (TD), Sizes #4 to 20 | **#3906B, #AC3906B** Sproat, 1X Long, Tapered Eye (TD), Bronze, Size #4 to 18 | **#57, #L057, #NT057** Sproat, Ball Eye (TD), Bronze, Sizes #4 to 16 | **#TMC3761** Sproat, Forged, 1X Long, 2X Heavy, Ball Eye (TD), Bronze, Sizes #8 to 18 | **#B-170** Sproat, Ball Eye (TD), Bronze, Sizes #6 to 16 | **#L2A** Capt. Hamilton, Forged, Bronze, Ball Eye (TD), Sizes #2 to 14 | **#1550** Sproat, Ball Eye (TD), Bronze, Sizes #2 to 18 |

Pattern Application: Salmon and Steelhead Patterns, Streamers, and Baitfish

| **#8923** Limerick, Forged, 2X Long, Ball Eye (TU), Bronze, Sizes #2 to 12 | None | **#9049, 49X** Limerick, Fine Wire, 5X Strong, Black, Loop Oval Eye (TU), Sizes #2 to 10 | None | **#TMC7999** Salmon, Forged, Heavy Wire, Tapered Loop Eye (TU), Black, Sizes #2/0 to 12 | **#B-180** Salmon, Forged, Tapered Loop Eye (TU), Black, Sizes #2/0 to 12 | **#O1** Salmon (Wilson), Forged, Heavy Wire, Black, Tapered Loop Eye (TU), Sizes #2 to 16 | **#2441** Salmon, Forged, 1X Strong, Tapered Loop Eye (TU), Black, Sizes #2/0, 1/0, 1 to 8 |

Pattern Application: Bass and Shad Flies

| **#9145** Round Bend, 3X Fine, Ball Eye (S), Bronze, Sizes #1/0 to 10 | None | None | None | None | None | None | None |

Pattern Application: Salmon and Steelhead Patterns, Streamers, and Baitfish

| **#9146** Aberdeen, Forged, 3X Long, Ball Eye (TU), Bronze, Sizes #2 to 10 | None | None | None | None | None | None | |

VMC Selection and Substitution Chart

VMC	Gamakatsu	Mustad	Eagle Claw	Tiemco	Kamasan	Partridge	Daiichi

Pattern Application: Small Streamers, Bass Flies, Shad Flies, and Saltwater Patterns

VMC	Gamakatsu	Mustad	Eagle Claw	Tiemco	Kamasan	Partridge	Daiichi
#9148 Aberdeen, Light Wire, Ball Eye (TD), Bronze, Sizes #4/0 to 12	None	None	None	None	None	#CS11 #CS11GRS Redditch, Forged, 4X Long, St. Stl or Gray Shadow, Ball Eye (TD), Sizes #2 to 10	None

Pattern Application: Saltwater Streamers, Bass Flies, and Shad Flies

VMC	Gamakatsu	Mustad	Eagle Claw	Tiemco	Kamasan	Partridge	Daiichi
#9255 O'Shaughnessy, Long Shank, Ball Eye (S), Brz., Nkl., Perma Stl., Gold, Sizes #5/0 to 6	None	#34007, 09 O'Shaughnessy, Forged, Large Ringed Eye (S), Stainless Steel, Sizes #11/0 to 2	#L054SS O'Shaughnessy, Ringed Eye (S), Stainless Steel, Sizes #1/0 to 4/0	#TMC811S O'Shaughnessy, X Strong, Ringed Eye (S), Stainless Steel, Sizes #4/0 to 8	None	None	#2451 O'Shaughnessy, Forged, Eye (S), Black, Sizes #1, 2, 4, 6, 8

Pattern Application: Streamers, Bucktails, Muddlers, Hairwings, and Large Dry Flies

VMC	Gamakatsu	Mustad	Eagle Claw	Tiemco	Kamasan	Partridge	Daiichi
#9279 Modified Round Bend, Forged, 2X Long, Ball Eye (TD), Bronze, Sizes #2 to 16	#P10-2L1H Model Perfect Round, 2X Long, 1X Strong, Bronze, Ball Eye (TD), Sizes #4 to 16	#9671, #AC9671 Round Bend, Forged, 2X Long, Bronze, Tapered Eye (TD), Sizes #2 to 18	#63, #L063, #NT063 Round Bend, 2X Long, Brz. & Nkl. Teflon, Ball Eye (TD), Sizes #4 to 18	#TMC5263 Round, Forged, 3X Long, Ball Eye (TD), Bronze, Sizes #2 to 18	#B-830 Round Bend, Forged, 2X Long, Ball Eye (TD), Bronze, Sizes #6 to 14	#H1A Capt. Hamilton, Forged, 2X Fine, 2-1/2X Long, Bronze, Ball Eye (TD), Sizes #2 to 14	#1720 Round Bend, Forged, 3X Long, 1X Strong, Bronze, Ball Eye (TD), Sizes #6 to 18

Pattern Application: Standard and Hairwing Dry Flies

VMC	Gamakatsu	Mustad	Eagle Claw	Tiemco	Kamasan	Partridge	Daiichi
#9280 Modified Round Bend, Forged, X Fine, Ball Eye (TD), Bronze, Sizes #6 to 20	#P10 Model Perfect Round, Bronze, Ball Eye (TD), Sizes #4 to 24	#94840, #AC94840 Round Bend, X Fine, Forged, Tapered Eye (TD), Bronze, Sizes #2 to 28	#59, #L059, #NT059 Round Bend, Fine Wire, Forged, Ball Eye (TD), Brz. & Nkl. Teflon, Sizes #4 to 24	#TMC5210 Round, Forged, 1X Fine, Ball Eye (TD), Bronze, Sizes #10 to 20	#B-400 Round Bend, Forged, Ball Eye (TD), Bronze, Sizes #8 to 16	#L2A Capt. Hamilton, Forged, 2X Fine, Ball Eye (TD), Bronze, Sizes #6 to 18	#1170 Round Bend, Forged, Ball Eye (TD), Bronze, Sizes #8 to 16

Pattern Application: Traditional Dry Flies and Nymphs

VMC	Gamakatsu	Mustad	Eagle Claw	Tiemco	Kamasan	Partridge	Daiichi
#9281 Modified Round Bend, Forged, X Fine, Forged Ball Eye (TU), Bronze, Sizes #8 to 20	None	#94842 Round Bend, X Fine, Forged, Tapered Eye (TU), Bronze, Sizes #8 to 28	#159, #L159 Round Bend, X Fine, Ball Eye (TU), Bronze, Sizes #4 to 18	None	None	#L3B Capt. Hamilton, Forged, 4X Fine, Ball Eye (TU), Bronze, Sizes #10 to 18	#1330 Round Bend, 1X Short, Ball Eye (TD), Bronze, Sizes #8 to 24

Pattern Application: Dry Flies, Wet Flies, Nymphs, Scuds, Terrestrials, Beetles, and Ants

VMC	Gamakatsu	Mustad	Eagle Claw	Tiemco	Kamasan	Partridge	Daiichi
#9282 Sproat, Forged, X Fine, Offset, Forged Ball Eye (TD), Bronze, Sizes #8 to 18	#S10-3F Sproat, 1X Fine, Black, Ball Eye (TD), Sizes #4 to 20	#3906, #AC3906 Sproat, Tapered Eye (TD), Bronze, Size #2 to 20	#57, #L057, #NT057 Sproat, Ball Eye(TD), Bronze, Sizes #4 to 16	#TMC3761 Sproat, Forged, 1X Long, 2X Heavy, Ball Eye (TD), Bronze, Sizes #8 to 18	#B-170 Sproat, Ball Eye (TD), Bronze, Sizes #6 to 16	#G3A Sproat, Forged, Heavy Wire, Ball Eye (TD), Bronze, Sizes #8 to 16	#1550 Sproat, Ball Eye (TD), Bronze, Sizes #2 to 18

Pattern Application: Streamers, Baitfish, Bucktails, and Mayfly and Large Stonefly Nymphs

VMC	Gamakatsu	Mustad	Eagle Claw	Tiemco	Kamasan	Partridge	Daiichi
#9283 Round Bend, Forged, 4X Long Forged Ball Eye (TD), Bronze, Sizes #2 to 16	#P10-2L1H Model Perfect Round, 2X Long, 1X Strong, Bronze, Ball Eye (TD), Sizes #4 to 16	#94833 #AC94833 Round Bend, X Long, 3X Fine, Forged, Tapered Eye (TD), Bronze, Sizes #6 to 22	#63, #L063, #NT063 Round Bend, 2X Long, Brz. & Nkl. Teflon, Ball Eye (TD), Sizes #4 to 18	#TMC5263 Round, Forged, 3X Long, Ball Eye (TD), Bronze, Sizes #2 to 18	#B-830 Round Bend, Forged, 2X Long, Ball Eye (TD), Bronze, Sizes #6 to 14	#H1A Capt. Hamilton, Forged, 2X Fine, 2-1/2X Long, Bronze, Ball Eye (TD), Sizes #2 to 14	#1720 Round Bend, Forged, 3X Long, 1X Strong, Bronze, Ball Eye (TD), Sizes #6 to 18

Pattern Application: Traditional Dry Flies and Variants

VMC	Gamakatsu	Mustad	Eagle Claw	Tiemco	Kamasan	Partridge	Daiichi
#9288 Round Bend, Forged, 2X Fine, Short Shank, Bronze, Forged Ball Eye (TD), Sizes #6 to 20	#P10 Model Perfect Round, Bronze, Ball Eye (TD), Sizes #4 to 24	#94836 Round Bend, Short Shank, X Fine, Forged, Tapered Eye (TD), Bronze, Sizes #10 to 20	#59, #L059, #NT059 Round Bend, Fine Wire, Forged, Ball Eye (TD), Brz. & Nkl. Teflon, Sizes #4 to 24	#TMC5210 Round, Forged, 1X Fine, Ball Eye (TD), Bronze, Sizes #10 to 20	#B-400 Round Bend, Forged, Ball Eye (TD), Bronze, Sizes #8 to 16	#L2A Capt. Hamilton, Forged, 2X Fine, Ball Eye (TD), Bronze, Sizes #6 to 18	#1170 Round Bend, Forged, Ball Eye (TD), Bronze, Sizes #8 to 16

VMC Selection and Substitution Chart

VMC	Gamakatsu	Mustad	Eagle Claw	Tiemco	Kamasan	Partridge	Daiichi

Pattern Application: Traditional Dry Flies and Nymphs

VMC	Gamakatsu	Mustad	Eagle Claw	Tiemco	Kamasan	Partridge	Daiichi
#9289 Round Bend, Forged, 2X Fine, Short Shank, Bronze, Forged Ball Eye (TU), Sizes #6 to 20	None	**#94842** Round Bend, X Fine, Forged, Tapered Eye (TU), Bronze, Sizes #8 to 28	**#159, #L159** Round Bend, X Fine, Ball Eye (TU), Bronze, Sizes #4 to 18	None	None	**#L3B** Capt. Hamilton, Forged, 4X Fine, Ball Eye (TU), Bronze, Sizes #10 to 18	**#1330** Round Bend, 1X Short, Ball Eye (TD), Bronze, Sizes #8 to 24

Gamakatsu Hooks

Gamakatsu's dedication to producing the highest-quality fish hooks has kept the company at the forefront of the premium hook market. Gamakatsu manufactures a variety of hooks used for both fly tying and general fishing.

Gamakatsu hooks can be purchased through local dealers or by contacting Gamakatsu at P.O. Box 1797, Tacoma, WA 98401; fax 206-922-8447.

Gamakatsu Selection and Substitution Chart

Pattern Application

The pattern application lists various types of patterns that can be tied using the specified hooks shown below.

Possible Substitutes

Listed across the page are other manufacturers' hooks that can be used as alternatives. In most cases, the hooks listed are similar or have the same characteristics with minor differences.

Note: Hook illustrations are only examples and are not shown at actual size. Also note that after the eye description, **(S)** indicates a straight eye, **(TD)** indicates a turned-down eye, and **(TU)** indicates a turned-up eye.

Gamakatsu	Mustad	Eagle Claw	Tiemco	Kamasan	Partridge	Daiichi	VMC
Pattern Application: Stoneflies, Nymphs, and Crabs							
#C11-5L2H Special Curve, 5X Long, 2X Strong, Bronze, Ball Eye (TD), Sizes #6 to 12	None	None	None	**#B-810** Round Bend, Forged, 4X Long, Special Bend, Ball Eye (TD), Bronze, Sizes #6 to 12	None	**#1730** Round Bend, 3X Long, 1X Strong, Forged, Ball Eye (TD), Bronze, Sizes #6 to 14	None
Pattern Application: Shrimp and Scuds							
#C12 Special Curve, Bronze, Ball Eye (TD), Sizes #10 to 20	**#AC80250** Special, 2X Short, 2X Wide, Ball Eye (TD), Bronze, Sizes #10 to 22	**#L055, #NT055** Special Bend, Short Shank, Bronze & Nkl. Teflon, Ringed Eye (TD), Sizes #10 to 20	**#TMC2487** Special, Forged, Offset, Fine Wire, 2X Short, Ball Eye (TD), Bronze, Sizes #10 to 20	None	**#K4A** Special (Veniard) Offset, Curved Shank, 2X Fine, Ball Eye (TD), Bronze, Sizes #8 to 18	**#1130** Continuous Bend, 1X Fine, 1X Short, Ball Eye (TD), Bronze, Sizes #10 to 16	None
Pattern Application: Caddis and Pupae							
#C12U Special Curve, Bronze, Ball Eye (TU), Sizes #6 to 16	**#37160, 60S** Wide Gape, Slightly Reversed, Ball Eye (TU), Brz. or St. Steel, Sizes #7/0 to 26	None	None	None	**#K2B** Special (Yorkshire) Forged, Curved Shank, Ball Eye (TU), Bronze, Sizes #8 to 18	**#4250** Egg, Forged, Reversed, Wide Gape, Short Shank, Ball Eye (TU), Bronze, Red & Gold, Sizes #4 to 14	None
Pattern Application: Dry Flies							
#C13U Special Curve, Keel Balance, Bronze, Ball Eye (TU), Sizes #10 to 20	**#37160, 60S** Wide Gape, Slightly Reversed, Ball Eye (TU), Brz. or St. Steel, Sizes #7/0 to 26	None	None	None	**#K2B** Special (Yorkshire) Forged, Curved Shank, Ball Eye (TU), Bronze, Sizes #8 to 18	**#4250** Egg, Forged, Reversed, Wide Gape, Short Shank, Ball Eye (TU), Bronze, Red & Gold, Sizes #4 to 14	None
Pattern Application: Egg Patterns and Glo-Bugs							
#C14S Special Curve (Beak), Black, Ball Eye (S), Sizes #2 to 12	None	None	None	None	None	None	None
Pattern Application: Large Dry Flies, Wet Flies, and Nymphs							
#L10-2H Limerick, 2X Strong, Bronze, Ball Eye (TD), Sizes #6 to 12	**#3123** Limerick, Ball Eye (TD), Bronze, Size #2 to 16	None	None	None	**#CS11 #CS11GRS** Redditch, Forged, 4X Long, St. Stl. or Gray Shadow, Ball Eye (TD), Sizes #2 to 10	None	None

Gamakatsu Selection and Substitution Chart

Gamakatsu	Mustad	Eagle Claw	Tiemco	Kamasan	Partridge	Daiichi	VMC

Pattern Application: Salmon and Steelhead Patterns

Gamakatsu	Mustad	Eagle Claw	Tiemco	Kamasan	Partridge	Daiichi	VMC
#L11S-3H Salmon Limerick, 3X Strong, Bronze, Ball Eye (S), Sizes #8 to 12	None	None	None	None	None	None	None

Pattern Application: Dry Flies

Gamakatsu	Mustad	Eagle Claw	Tiemco	Kamasan	Partridge	Daiichi	VMC
#P10 Model Perfect Round, Bronze, Ball Eye (TD), Sizes #4 to 24	**#7957B, 57BX** Round Bend, Bronze, Tapered Eye (TD), Forged, 57BX Extra Strong, Sizes #2 to 20	**#59, #L059, #NT059** Round Bend, Fine Wire, Forged, Ball Eye (TD), Brz. & Nkl. Teflon, Sizes #4 to 24	**#TMC102** Round Bend, Ball Eye (TD), Bronze, Sizes #11, 13, 15, 17	**#B-400** Round Bend, Forged, Ball Eye (TD), Bronze, Sizes #8 to 16	**#L2A** Capt. Hamilton, Forged, 2X Fine, Ball Eye (TD), Bronze, Sizes #6 to 18	**#1170** Round Bend, Forged, Ball Eye (TD), Bronze, Sizes #8 to 16	**#9288** Round Bend, Forged, 2X Fine, Short Shank, Bronze, Forged Ball Eye (TD), Sizes #6 to 20

Pattern Application: Large Dry Flies, Wet Flies, and Nymphs

Gamakatsu	Mustad	Eagle Claw	Tiemco	Kamasan	Partridge	Daiichi	VMC
#P10-2L1H Model Perfect Round, 2X Long, 1X Strong, Bronze, Ball Eye (TD), Sizes #4 to 16	**#9671, #AC9671** Round Bend, Forged, 2X Long, Bronze, Tapered Eye (TD), Sizes #2 to 18	**#63, #L063, #NT063** Round Bend, 2X Long, Brz. & Nkl. Teflon, Ball Eye (TD), Sizes #4 to 18	**#TMC5263** Round, Forged, 3X Long, Ball Eye (TD), Bronze, Sizes #2 to 18	**#B-830** Round Bend, Forged, 2X Long, Ball Eye (TD), Bronze, Sizes #6 to 14	**#H1A** Capt. Hamilton, Forged, 2X Fine, 2-1/2X Long, Bronze, Ball Eye (TD), Sizes #2 to 14	**#1720** Round Bend, Forged, 3X Long, 1X Strong, Bronze, Ball Eye (TD), Sizes #6 to 18	**#9283** Round Bend, Forged, 4X Long, Forged Ball Eye (TD), Bronze, Sizes #2 to 16

Pattern Application: Barbless Dry Flies, Wet Flies, and Nymphs

Gamakatsu	Mustad	Eagle Claw	Tiemco	Kamasan	Partridge	Daiichi	VMC
#R10-BN Retainer Bend, Barbless, Black, Ball Eye (TD), Sizes #10 to 20	None	None	None	None	None	None	None

Pattern Application: Dry Flies, Wet Flies, Nymphs, Crayfish, and Terrestrials

Gamakatsu	Mustad	Eagle Claw	Tiemco	Kamasan	Partridge	Daiichi	VMC
#S10 Sproat, Black, Ball Eye (TD), Sizes #2 to 24	**#3399, 99A, 99D, 99N** Sproat, Ball Eye (TD), Brz., Gold, 99D-Fine Wire, Sizes #9/0 -2, 4 to 20	**#57, #L057, #NT057** Sproat, Ball Eye (TD), Bronze, Sizes #4 to 16	**#TMC3769** Sproat, 1X Long, Forged, Ball Eye (TD), 2X Heavy, Bronze, Sizes #2 to 20	**#B-170** Sproat, Ball Eye (TD), Bronze, Sizes #6 to 16	**#A** Improved Sproat, 2X Fine, 1X Short, Bronze, Ball Eye (TD), Sizes #10 to 16	**#1550** Sproat, Ball Eye (TD), Bronze, Sizes #2 to 18	**#8526** Sproat, Bronze, Ball Eye (TD), Forged, Sizes #8 to 16

Pattern Application: Barbless Dry Flies, Wet Flies, Nymphs, Crayfish, and Terrestrials

Gamakatsu	Mustad	Eagle Claw	Tiemco	Kamasan	Partridge	Daiichi	VMC
#S10-B Sproat, Barbless, Black, Ball Eye (TD), Sizes #6 to 16	None	None	None	None	None	None	None

Pattern Application: Nymphs and Emergers

Gamakatsu	Mustad	Eagle Claw	Tiemco	Kamasan	Partridge	Daiichi	VMC
#S10-2S Sproat, 2X Short, Black, Ball Eye (TD), Sizes #4 to 14	**#3399, 99A, 99D, 99N** Sproat, Ball Eye (TD), Brz., Gold, 99D-Fine Wire, Sizes #9/0 -2, 4 to 20	**#57, #L057, #NT057** Sproat, Ball Eye (TD), Bronze, Sizes #4 to 16	**#TMC3769** Sproat, 1X Long, Forged, Ball Eye (TD), 2X Heavy, Bronze, Sizes #2 to 20	**#B-170** Sproat, Ball Eye (TD), Bronze, Sizes #6 to 16	**#A** Improved Sproat, 2X Fine, 1X Short, Bronze, Ball Eye (TD), Sizes #10 to 16	**#1550** Sproat, Ball Eye (TD), Bronze, Sizes #2 to 18	**#8526** Sproat, Bronze, Ball Eye (TD), Forged, Sizes #8 to 16

Pattern Application: Dry Flies

Gamakatsu	Mustad	Eagle Claw	Tiemco	Kamasan	Partridge	Daiichi	VMC
#S10-3F Sproat, 1X Fine, Black, Ball Eye (TD), Sizes #4 to 20	**#3906, #AC3906** Sproat, Tapered Eye (TD), Bronze, Sizes #2 to 20	**#57, #L057, #NT057** Sproat, Ball Eye (TD), Bronze, Sizes #4 to 16	**#TMC3761** Sproat, Forged, 1X Long, 2X Heavy, Ball Eye (TD), Bronze, Sizes #8 to 18	**#B-170** Sproat, Ball Eye (TD), Bronze, Sizes #6 to 16	**#G3A** Sproat, Forged, Heavy Wire, Ball Eye (TD), Bronze, Sizes #8 to 16	**#1550** Sproat, Ball Eye (TD), Bronze, Sizes #2 to 18	**#8526** Sproat, Forged Ball Eye (TD), Bronze, Sizes #8 to 16

Gamakatsu Selection and Substitution Chart

Gamakatsu	Mustad	Eagle Claw	Tiemco	Kamasan	Partridge	Daiichi	VMC
Pattern Application: Dry Flies							
#S10U Sproat, Black, Ball Eye (TU), Sizes #4 to 14	None	None	None	None	None	None	None
Pattern Application: Dry Flies, Wet Flies, and Nymphs							
#S10S Sproat, Black, Ball Eye (S), Sizes #4 to 14	**#3365A,** **65C, 66, 66A,** **66F, 66G, 67** Sproat, Ringed Eye (S), Nickl., Brz., Gold, Blued, Sizes #8/0 -2, 4, 6, 8, 10, 12, 14	None	None	None	None	None	**#8410** Special Sproat, Bronze, Ball Eye (S), Forged, Sizes #4 to 12
Pattern Application: Streamers and Woolly Buggers							
#S11-4L2H Sproat, 4X Long, 2X Strong, Black, Ball Eye (TD), Sizes #6 to 12	**#38941** Sproat, 3X Long, Tapered Eye (TD), Bronze, Sizes #2 to 16	None	None	None	None	None	None
Pattern Application: Salmon and Steelhead Patterns							
#S11S-3H Sproat, 3X Strong,, Bronze, Ball Eye (S), Sizes #2 to 8	**#33602** Sproat, Ringed Eye (S), Gold Plated, Sizes #5/0 to 16	None	**#TMC8089** Sproat, Forged, Wide Gape, Fine Wire, Bronze, Ball Eye (S), Sizes #2, 6, 10	None	None	None	**#8410** Special (Crystal), Forged, Ball Eye (S), Bronze, Sizes #4 to 12
Pattern Application: Streamers and Woolly Buggers							
#S11S-4L2H Sproat, 4X Long, 2X Strong, Black, Ball Eye (S), Sizes #6 to 12	**#33602** Sproat, Ringed Eye (S), Gold Plated, Sizes #5/0 to 16	None	**#TMC8089** Sproat, Forged, Wide Gape, Fine Wire, Bronze, Ball Eye (S), Sizes #2, 6, 10	None	None	None	**#8410** Special (Crystal), Forged, Ball Eye (S), Bronze, Sizes #4 to 12
Pattern Application: Wet Flies and Nymphs							
#S12S-1F Sproat, 1X Fine, Bronze, Ball Eye (S), Sizes #8 to 18	None	None	None	None	None	None	None
Pattern Application: Dry Flies, Tricos, and Variants							
#S13S-M Sproat, 1X Fine, Black, Ball Eye (S), Sizes #20 to 24	None	None	None	None	None	None	None
Pattern Application: Heavy Nymphs and Wet Flies							
#S14S-3H Sproat, 3X Strong, Bronze, Ball Eye (S), Sizes #8 to 12	**#33602** Sproat, Ringed Eye (S), Gold Plated, Sizes #5/0 to 16	None	**#TMC8089** Sproat, Forged, Wide Gape, Fine Wire, Bronze, Ball Eye (S), Sizes #2, 6, 10	None	None	None	**#8410** Special (Crystal), Forged, Ball Eye (S), Bronze, Sizes #4 to 12

Gamakatsu Selection and Substitution Chart

Gamakatsu	Mustad	Eagle Claw	Tiemco	Kamasan	Partridge	Daiichi	VMC
Pattern Application: Saltwater Patterns and Shrimp							
#SC15 Sproat, Wide Gape, Tinned, Ball Eye (S), Sizes #2/0 to 8	**#3365A, 65C, 66, 66A, 66F, 66G, 67** Sproat, Ringed Eye (S), Nickl., Brz., Gold, Blued, Sizes #8/0 -2, 4, 6, 8, 10, 12, 14	None	None	None	None	None	**#8410** Special (Crystal), Forged, Ball Eye (S), Bronze, Sizes #4 to 12
Pattern Application: Salmon and Steelhead Patterns							
#SL11-3H Sproat, 3X Strong, Tinned, Ball Eye (S), Sizes #8/0, 6/0, 5/0	**#3365A, 65C, 66, 66A, 66F, 66G, 67** Sproat, Ringed Eye (S), Nickl., Brz., Gold, Blued, Sizes #8/0 -2, 4, 6, 8, 10, 12, 14	None	None	None	None	None	**#8410** Special (Crystal), Forged, Ball Eye (S), Bronze, Sizes #4 to 12
Pattern Application: Saltwater Patterns							
#SS15 Sproat, Tinned, Ball Eye (S), Sizes #4/0 to 18	**#3365A, 65C, 66, 66A, 66F, 66G, 67** Sproat, Ringed Eye (S), Nickl., Brz., Gold, Blued, Sizes #8/0 -2, 4, 6, 8, 10, 12, 14	None	None	None	None	None	**#8410** Special (Crystal), Forged, Ball Eye (S), Bronze, Sizes #4 to 12
Pattern Application: Saltwater Patterns							
#SP11-3L3H Perfect Bend, Tinned, Ball Eye (S), Sizes #6/0 to 8	**#3365A, 65C, 66, 66A, 66F, 66G, 67** Sproat, Ringed Eye (S), Nickl., Brz., Gold, Blued, Sizes #8/0 -2, 4, 6, 8, 10, 12, 14	None	None	None	None	None	**#8410** Special (Crystal), Forged, Ball Eye (S), Bronze, Sizes #4 to 12
Pattern Application: Salmon and Steelhead Patterns							
#T10-3H Salmon, 1X Fine, Tapered Loop Eye (TU), Black, Sizes #2 to 8	**#36890, #AC36890** Limerick, Black, Looped Oval Eye (TU), Sizes #6/0 to 12	None	**#TMC7999** Salmon, Forged, Heavy Wire, Tapered Loop Eye (TU), Black, Sizes #2/0 to 12	**#B-180** Salmon, Forged, Tapered Loop Eye (TU), Black, Sizes #2/0 to 12	**#M** Salmon, Forged, 2X Heavy,Tapered Loop Eye (TU), Black, Sizes #4/0 to 1/0, 1 to 10	**#2441** Salmon, Forged, 1X Strong, Tapered Loop Eye (TU), Black, Sizes #2/0, 1/0, 1 to 8	**#8923** Limerick, Forged, 2X Long, Ball Eye (TU), Bronze, Sizes #2 to 12
Pattern Application: Salmon and Steelhead Patterns							
#T10-6H Salmon, Tapered Loop Eye (TU), Black, Sizes #1 to 8	**#36890, #AC36890** Limerick, Black, Looped Oval Eye (TU), Sizes #6/0 to 12	None	**#TMC7999** Salmon, Forged, Heavy Wire, Tapered Loop Eye (TU), Black, Sizes #2/0 to 12	**#B-180** Salmon, Forged, Tapered Loop Eye (TU), Black, Sizes #2/0 to 12	**#M** Salmon, Forged, 2X Heavy,Tapered Loop Eye (TU), Black, Sizes #4/0 to 1/0, 1 to 10	**#2441** Salmon, Forged, 1X Strong, Tapered Loop Eye (TU), Black, Sizes #2/0, 1/0, 1 to 8	**#8923** Limerick, Forged, 2X Long, Ball Eye (TU), Bronze, Sizes #2 to 12
Pattern Application: Streamers, Baitfish, Bucktails, Muddlers, Hoppers, and Stonefly Nymphs							
#Russian River Modified Limerick, Bronze, Ball Eye (TD), Size #2	**#36717** Russian River, Bronze, 1/2" Longer Shank, 5X Strong, Ball Eye (TD), Size #2	None	None	None	None	None	None

CHAPTER 4

Threads

This chapter covers the characteristics and applications
of the most frequently used threads for fly tying.

Thread Types and Sizes

In fly tying, thread is used to secure other materials to the hook. For the most part, regular sewing threads are either too bulky or weak for this purpose.

Fly-tying threads are generally made of nylon or silk fibers designed to provide strength and durability as well as a minimal amount of bulk buildup during the construction of flies. Both types are available from mail-order houses and fly-fishing shops. Which type (silk or nylon) is best is a matter of opinion and preference. Most modern threads are made of nylon, prewaxed, and available in multifilament strands (either flat or twisted). When purchasing threads, be sure to buy the best you can find from a reliable dealer.

Thread manufacturers have simplified thread diameter sizes by using the following designations: For larger-diameter threads, they use letter designators such as A, AA, D, and so forth. For smaller-diameter threads, they use 2/0, 3/0, 4/0, 5/0, 6/0, 7/0, 8/0, and 9/0, with 9/0 having the smallest diameter. Some manufacturers also name specific threads, such as Midge Thread, Monocord, and Kevlar.

The most commonly used threads are sizes A, 3/0, 6/0, 8/0, and Midge Thread. Monocord and Kevlar are also used.

THREAD APPLICATIONS	
Size / Type	**Used For**
A	Spinning hair, large bass bugs, large saltwater patterns, large streamers, hair flies
3/0	Large streamers, large nymphs, small bass bugs, small saltwater patterns
6/0	Standard dry flies, wet flies, nymphs, small streamers
8/0	Standard dry flies, wet flies, nymphs, small streamers, midges
Midge	Midges, small dry-fly patterns
Monocord	Standard dry flies, wet flies, nymphs, small streamers
Kevlar	Spinning hair, large bass bugs, large saltwater patterns, large streamers, hair flies

Thread Selection

Following are the most frequently used fly-tying threads available today.

Silk Thread: Size AA and 6/0 in white and sizes 2/0, 3/0, and 6/0 in black.
Available from most fly shops or mail-order houses. Size AA is used for large bass bugs, large saltwater patterns, large streamers, and hair flies. Sizes 2/0, 3/0, and 6/0 are used for standard dry flies, wet flies, nymphs, and small streamers. Available in 50-, 100-, and 200-yard spools.

Danville Flat Waxed Nylon: Size A. A 210-denier* prewaxed nylon floss that lies flat. Available in 100-yard spools and assorted colors. Used for large bass bugs, large saltwater patterns, shad patterns, large streamers, and hair flies.

Danville Flymaster Plus: Size A+. A prewaxed thread made of flat nylon floss with a slight twist, having a slightly larger diameter than size A thread. Used for heavy hair work and larger streamer patterns. Available in 100-yard spools and assorted colors.

Danville Prewax: Size 6/0. Also referred to as Herb Howard Flymaster or Danville's Flymaster. This thread is probably the most frequently used thread today. Made of 6/0 prewaxed nylon, it comes in 50-, 100-, and 200-yard spools in assorted colors. Used for standard dry flies, wet flies, nymphs, and small streamers.

Danville Monocord: Sizes A and 3/0. Monocord is a flat, prewaxed, continuous nylon filament thread. Size A Monocord is used for large bass bugs, large saltwater patterns, very large streamers, and hair flies. Size 3/0 is used for large to medium streamers, large nymphs, smaller bass bugs, and smaller saltwater patterns. Both sizes come in an assortment of colors in 50-, 100-, and 200-yard spools.

Danville Prewax Spiderweb Midge Thread: Size 8/0+. Ultrafine tough nylon thread that is clear (white) but can be colored using Pantone permanent markers. Used for midge and small bug patterns. Available in 100-yard spools. Also referred to as Ultra Midge Thread.

UNI-Thread: Sizes 6/0 and 8/0. Super tough, prewaxed thread that allows for little buildup. Size 6/0 has the strength of 3/0 and is ideal for standard dry flies, wet flies, nymphs, and small streamers; size 8/0 has the strength of 6/0, which is excellent for midges and small bug patterns (18 and smaller). Available in assorted colors and 200-yard spools.

A unit expressing the fineness of threads in terms of weight in grams per 9,000 meters of length (e.g., 100-denier thread is finer than 150-denier thread).

Thread Selection

Super Thread (Kevlar): Super strong, small-diameter Kevlar thread, similar in appearance to thin floss and almost impossible to break. Ideal for spinning hair, Glo-Bugs, and saltwater patterns. Available in assorted colors and 50-yard spools.

PAC Midge Thread: Size 8/0. An excellent small-diameter thread made from spun polyester that lays extremely flat and resists normal fraying. Ideal for midge and small dry-fly patterns. Available in assorted colors and 50-yard spools.

Kevlar Thread: Size 6/0. Unbelievably strong thread (*Caution:* Will cut fingers when trying to break it, and will also bend hooks when too much tension is applied.) Unbeatable for spinning hair.

Twisted Nylon D Thread: Size D. Extra strong, twisted nylon thread used for spinning hair where heavy pressure is required. Available in 50-yard spools and assorted colors.

Nylon Floss: Single Strand. In addition to threads, many tiers also use single-strand floss for spinning hair onto a hook. Single-strand floss is stronger and better than size A threads and is excellent for saltwater patterns, bass bugs, and Humpys. It is available in 100-yard spools and assorted colors.

CHAPTER 5

Feathers

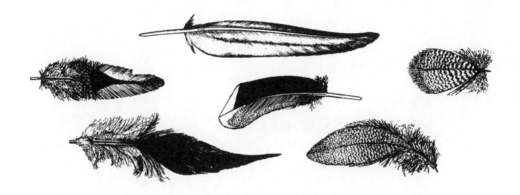

The word *feather* is defined as one of the horny, elongated structures that form the body covering of birds and provide the flight surface for their wings. A single feather consists of a hollow central shaft (*quill*) that has branch fibers on each side (*barbs*) that grow parallel upward and outward. The barbs, in turn, have smaller branches on each side (*barbules*) that collectively are called the *web* or *webbing*.

Feathers are one of the most important materials used in fly tying. They are a near perfect material that comes in many colors, shapes, sizes, and shades.

The following pages cover the more common feathers used in fly tying, including the material characteristics, selection, application, and possible sources. However, almost any feather from any bird (worldwide) can be used in one form or another in the art of creating fly-fishing patterns.

161

Sources

The primary way to obtain feathers is to purchase them through mail-order supply houses or speciality shops that cater to fly-fishing or fly-tying enthusiasts. Most shops or supply houses carry a variety of feathers that are sold as necks, capes, saddles, patches, strung hackles, or, in many cases, the entire bird. However, there are alternative sources that are often overlooked and may provide unique materials not found elsewhere. Following are a few of those alternative sources.

Hunting

If you are a hunter, or if you have friends who hunt, you can add a number of different types of bird feathers or skins to your collection, such as assorted ducks, geese, pheasants, and quail. You can skin the entire bird yourself or ask your friends to save you the feathers and wings from the birds they shoot.

Also, if you hunt at a game farm, talk to the owner. Many game farms clean the birds that are shot by clients. You may get lucky and hit a bonanza.

Chicken Farms

If you have a chicken farm nearby, give it a try. Most will be glad to give or sell you some feathers for a nominal fee.

Game Farmers

Check your local Yellow Pages for game farmers. Many raise all types of birds, including exotic species such as peacocks, guinea hens, ostriches, and various types of pheasants.

Farmers

Another possible source is local farmers. Many of them raise their own chickens, ducks, or geese for food, and many of them will sell you an entire bird for extra income.

Raise Your Own

As a last resort, if you have the room and the local ordinances allow it, you can try raising your own birds. Exotics, roosters, pheasants, ducks, or geese can be obtained from game farms or through bird breeding catalog houses.

Fly-Tying Organizations (Clubs)

If you can, join a fly-tying club. Many club members have accumulated vast collections of material over the years, as well as a lot of knowledge on how to acquire it. Some of them may be willing to give you some if they have an overabundance, or sell you some for a small fee. They can also help you find additional sources.

Skinning Birds

On occasion, you may obtain the carcass of a bird that needs to be skinned. Whether it's a roadkill, something that was shot during a hunting trip, or a specimen someone else killed and gave to you, you will want to skin and preserve it so it can be added to your material collection.

The following illustrations show the basic steps for skinning birds. The example used is a pheasant, which is easy to obtain and easy to work with.

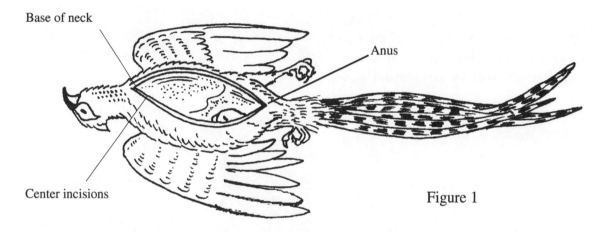

Base of neck

Anus

Center incisions

Figure 1

Step 1 (see figure 1)
Once a specimen has been obtained, the first step is to wash off all the blood and dirt using cold water. Then lay the specimen on its back on a workbench or table and part the feathers along the breastbone. With a sharp knife or scalpel, make an incision through the skin along the breastbone from the base of the neck to the anus.

Work the skin down each side of the body and push your hand through (under the back) from one side to the other

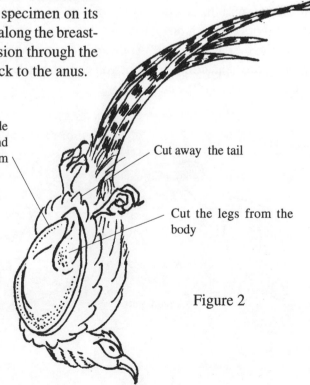

Cut away the tail

Cut the legs from the body

Figure 2

Step 2 (see figure 2)
Work the skin down each side of the body using your fingers until you reach the legs. Next, grasp a leg from the outside and push it up and out, then cut the leg from the body. Do the same with the other leg.

After freeing both legs, use your hand and the knife or scalpel to work the skin down to the tail, and cut it away from the rear of the body.

163

Skinning Birds

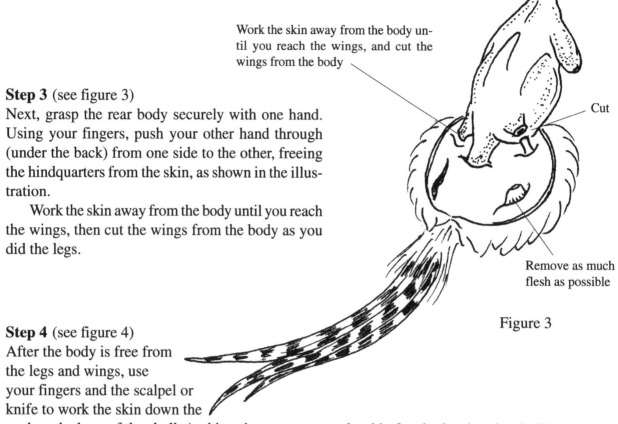

Work the skin away from the body until you reach the wings, and cut the wings from the body

Step 3 (see figure 3)

Next, grasp the rear body securely with one hand. Using your fingers, push your other hand through (under the back) from one side to the other, freeing the hindquarters from the skin, as shown in the illustration.

Work the skin away from the body until you reach the wings, then cut the wings from the body as you did the legs.

Cut

Remove as much flesh as possible

Figure 3

Step 4 (see figure 4)

After the body is free from the legs and wings, use your fingers and the scalpel or knife to work the skin down the neck to the base of the skull. At this point, you can cut the skin free by leaving the skull in the head or removing the head completely, or you can carefully cut the skin away from the skull until you reach the beak and then make the cut.

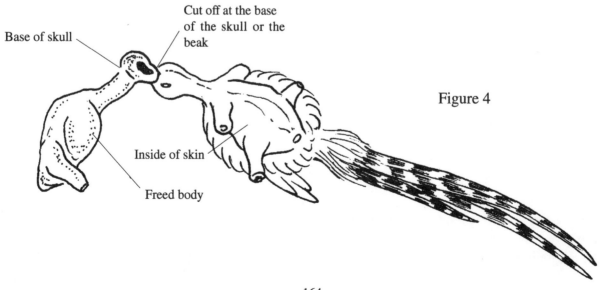

Base of skull

Cut off at the base of the skull or the beak

Inside of skin

Freed body

Figure 4

Skinning Birds

Step 5

After the skin has been removed from the body, use a dull knife to scrape away any remaining flesh or fat that you may have missed during the skinning process. Scrape small sections at a time until you can't get anymore fat or flesh off. For best results, wash the skin again in cold running water.

Step 6 (optional)

To preserve the skin, make a tanning solution of alum and salt in a 5-gallon bucket and soak the skin in it for three to ten days. After soaking, remove it from the solution, wash the skin in cold water, and allow it to dry.

Step 7

Another alternative to preserving the skin after washing is to wring out the excess water and tack it to a board (flesh side up) using small nails. Then apply a liberal amount of salt to the skin side, as well as some borax to prevent any odors, and allow it to dry for about four or five days. Once it's dry, scrape off the dried salt and borax and remove it from the board.

Game Cock or Rooster Feathers

The most commonly used feathers in fly tying come from the domesticated game cock or rooster. These birds are raised specifically for their feathers, which can be obtained through fly-tying catalog supply houses, fly shops, and most sporting goods stores that sell fishing tackle and fly-tying materials.

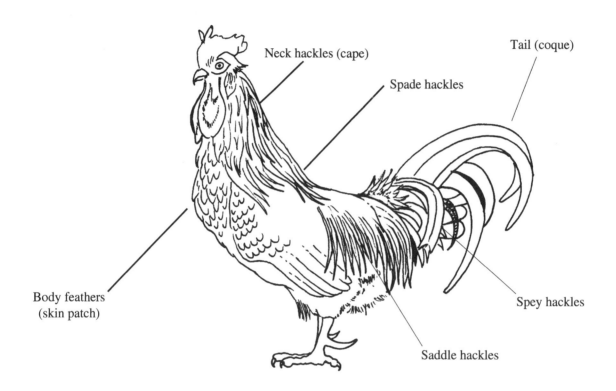

Feather Names, Characteristics, and Applications

Neck Hackles (Cape)
Stiff-quilled, narrow feathers that cover the neck and back of a rooster's head. Used both for dry and wet flies, as well as for streamers.

Spade Hackles
Short, wide hackles found on the back and shoulder. Used for bass flies and streamers.

Saddle Hackles (Saddle Patch)
Long, thin feathers with flexible stems, found on the back between the spade hackles and the tail. Used for drys, wets, bass flies, streamers, and saltwater patterns.

Spey Hackles
Short, wide hackles found near the base of the tail. Used for bass flies.

Tail (Coque) Feathers
Long feathers located at the rump. Used for saltwater streamer patterns.

Body Feathers (Body Patch)
Short, wide feathers located on the sides and belly. Used for wings or beards on drys, wets, bass bugs, streamers, and nymph patterns.

Game Cock or Rooster Feathers

Necks and Neck Hackles

One of the more frequently purchased items in fly tying is a neck (cape) from a game cock or rooster. The feathers found on the neck are used primarily to construct the wings and collars found on most dry flies. They are available in a variety of natural colors such as black, light gray (dun), medium gray, dark gray, sandy dun, barred sandy dun, cree, variant, white splash, grizzly, cream, barred cream, light ginger, barred ginger, ginger grizzly, badger, brown, sandy brown, and furnace. Following are a few tips to remember when purchasing both domestic and imported necks.

Domestic Necks

Domestic necks or capes are available through fly-tying catalog supply houses and are offered through various suppliers. The best-quality necks are sold by Metz, Keough, and Hoffman and can be expensive, depending on the grade you perchase.

Quality necks are graded, with the best being grade 1. Grade 1 necks have long, stiff hackles down to size 24 or smaller, with very little webbing. Grades 2 and 3 are slightly lower quality, with a little more webbing, and go down to about a size 16 or smaller.

Imported Necks

Many supply houses also offer imported necks from China, India, or the Philippines. When purchasing imported necks, you can identify their origin by the shape of the skin patch at the back of the neck. A few characteristics to look for are:

- Chinese necks have a bulb-shaped patch with a wide neck area.
- Philippine necks are very similar to Chinese necks, except that the neck area is very narrow.
- Indian necks have a square or rectangular patch, which makes their identification easy.

The following illustration shows the different shapes of the skin patches found on the various necks.

Phillippine
Skin patch has narrow tip cut

Indian
Skin patch has square or rectangular cut

Chinese
Skin patch has wide tip cut

Quaility Ranking

Best: Chinese necks are the best quality, with soft, narrow stems and thin, thoroughly scraped skin.

Good: Indian necks are of good quality, with thicker skin.

Fair: Philippine necks are of fair quality, with larger and sometimes twisted hackles.

Game Cock or Rooster Feathers

Neck Hackle Sizes

The illustration below shows the average number of feathers found on a typical neck and the location of feathers to be used for a specific size hook. This general rule of thumb can vary, depending on the size of the neck. The chart below can be used as a quick reference for hackle selection, based on the hook size and the type of pattern.

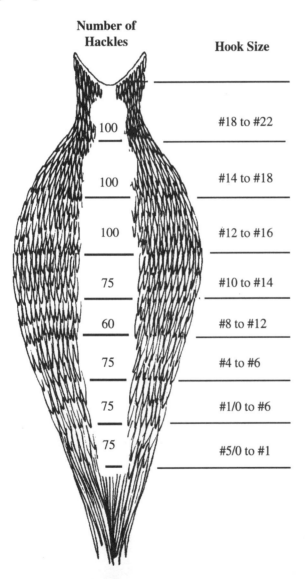

Number of Hackles	Hook Size
100	#18 to #22
100	#14 to #18
100	#12 to #16
75	#10 to #14
60	#8 to #12
75	#4 to #6
75	#1/0 to #6
75	#5/0 to #1

Typical neck (cape)

Neck Hackle Quality

Neck hackle

When selecting a neck hackle for a dry fly, the amount of webbing in the feather must be considered. Feathers with heavy webbing are generally used for wings on streamer patterns or wet flies. Feathers with little or no webbing are ideal for dry-fly patterns. The illustration below shows you what to look for.

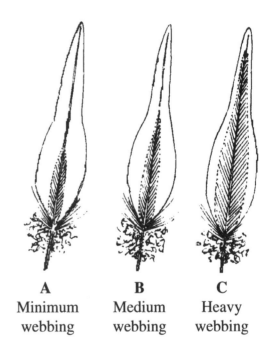

A	B	C
Minimum webbing	Medium webbing	Heavy webbing

A. Dry-fly quality: Has the least amount of webbing.

B. Dry- or wet-fly quality: Has a medium amount of webbing; can also be used for streamers.

C. Wet-fly quality: Has heavy webbing; can also be used for streamer wings and collars, nymph hackles, and saltwater patterns.

168

Game Cock or Rooster Feathers

Saddles and Saddle Hackles

In addition to necks, which are used primarly for dry flies, the game cock or rooster provides saddle hackles—long, thin feathers with flexible stems that are used for streamers, bass bugs, and larger flies. These hackles are found on the back between the spade hackles and the tail and may be sold on the skin (saddles), the same as necks (capes). Saddle hackles are also available without the skin and are sold on a string. They are available in a variety of natural colors such as black, light gray (dun), medium gray, dark gray, sandy dun, barred sandy dun, cree, variant, white splash, grizzly, cream, barred cream, light ginger, barred ginger, ginger grizzly, badger, brown, sandy brown, and furnace. They are also available in a multitude of dyed colors.

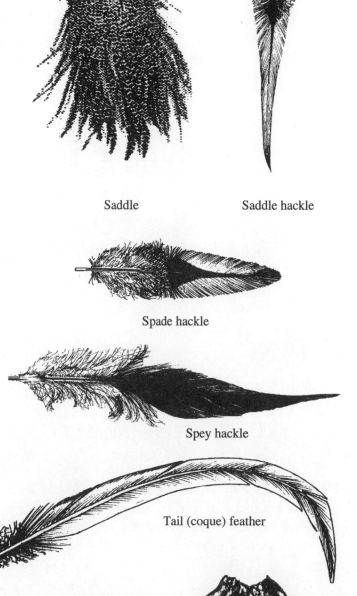

Saddle   Saddle hackle

Spade hackle

Spey hackle

Tail (coque) feather

Body feathers
(body patch)

Chicken Feathers

Hen chickens come in all types of breeds and colors, providing a variety of feathers for fly tiers. Hen feathers had limited use in the past, but today they are being used extensivly in pattern construction. Most hen feathers are not suitable for dry flies; they can be used for other applications, however, such as wet flies, bass flies, beard material, tails on nymphs, and shoulders on streamers or salmon patterns.

Hen feathers can be obtained through fly-tying catalog supply houses, fly shops, and most sporting goods stores that sell fishing tackle and fly-tying materials. They are available in sets consisting of both the neck and back—called "hen sets"—in a variety of natural colors such as black, light gray (dun), medium gray, dark gray, sandy dun, barred sandy dun, cree, variant, white splash, grizzly, cream, barred cream, light ginger, barred ginger, ginger grizzly, badger, brown, sandy brown, and furnace. They are also avaiable in a multitude of dyed colors.

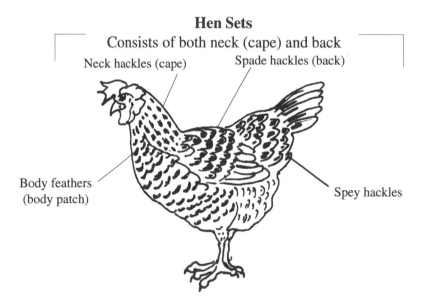

Hen Sets
Consists of both neck (cape) and back
Neck hackles (cape) Spade hackles (back)
Body feathers (body patch) Spey hackles

Feather Names, Characteristics, and Applications

Neck Hackles (Cape)
Stiff-quilled, wide feathers that cover the neck and back of a hen's head. Used for wet flies, bass flies, and streamers, as well as for nymph patterns.

Hen neck (cape) or back patch

Spade Hackles (Back Patch)
Short, wide hackles found on the back and shoulder. Used for bass flies and streamers.

Spey Hackles
Short, wide hackles found near the base of the tail. Used for bass flies.

Spey hackles

Body Feathers (Body Patch)
Short, wide feathers located on the sides and belly. Used for wings or beards on wets, bass bugs, streamers, and nymph patterns.

Body feathers (body patch)

170

Waterfowl Feathers: Ducks and Geese

Waterfowl such as ducks and geese also provide important feathers used in the construction of fly patterns. Feathers from both domestic and wild species, such as the mallard duck or the Canada goose, are used for various patterns.

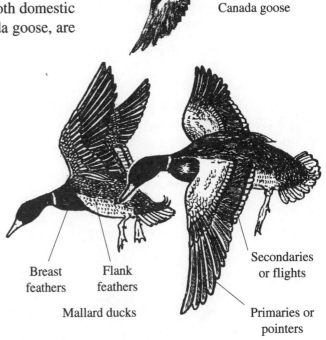

Canada goose

Secondaries or flights

Breast feathers

Flank feathers

Primaries or pointers

Mallard ducks

Duck and geese feathers can be obtained through fly-tying catalog supply houses, fly shops, and most sporting goods stores that sell fishing tackle and fly-tying materials.

Primary or pointer feathers as well as secondary or flight feathers are sold as matched pairs from both ducks and geese. Flank and breast feathers are sold as loose feathers in small packages. They can all be purchased in assorted colors.

Feather Names, Characteristics, and Applications

Primaries or Pointers

The primaries are the first six long pointer feathers found on the wing tip of both geese and ducks. They have very heavy quills. Segments from these feathers are used to make wings on most dry- or wet-fly patterns and are also used for wing cases on nymph patterns. The biots found on the leading edge of the first wing feather from a goose are also used for tails on nymph patterns.

Secondaries or Flight

The secondaries are the ten shorter feathers found on the wing nearer the bird's body. These heavy, quilled, blunt feathers are used for making wings on dry- or wet-fly patterns.

Breast

These feathers are found on ducks at the lower throat, covering the breast area of the bird. The feathers are stiff-quilled, short, wide, and curved and have barred markings. They are used for dry- and wet-fly wings and for tails and shoulders on streamer patterns.

Flank

Found along the sides of ducks, these feathers are pointed and wide, with distinctive markings. They are used for dry-fly wings, streamer shoulders, and tailing.

Pheasant Feathers

Pheasant feathers, like those of the game cock, are widely used in fly pattern construction. These feathers are obtained mostly from the ringneck pheasant, golden pheasant, Amherst pheasant, and silver pheasant. Both cock and hen pheasants feathers are used in many patterns.

Tails, crests, body feathers, and entire skins can be purchased through fly-tying catalog supply houses, fly shops, and most sporting goods stores that sell fishing tackle and fly-tying materials. Other sources include hunting for your own or buying birds from a game farm.

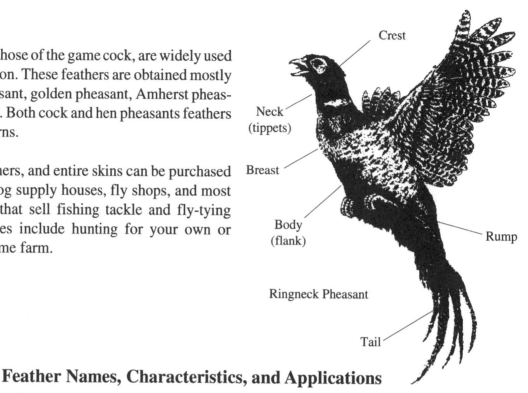

Ringneck Pheasant

Feather Names, Characteristics, and Applications

Amherst Cock Pheasant Feathers
Almost any feather on this bird can be used for various types of patterns. The center tail feathers, which have black and white markings, and the tippets, which are white with two black bars, are used mostly for salmon flies.

Tippet

Neck and crest

Silver Cock Pheasant Feathers
Silver pheasant is used primarily for streamer and salmon patterns. The white and black striped body feathers are used as shoulders on both types of patterns, and the blue crest feather is used as a topping. The tail, with its distinct markings, can also be used for wing cases and legs on assorted patterns.

Body feather

Tail

Golden Cock Pheasant Feathers
Almost any feather on this bird can be used for various types of patterns. The crest, tippets, and body feathers are used mostly for salmon flies. The tail, with its distinct markings, can also be used for wing cases and legs on assorted patterns.

Tippet

Tail

Neck and crest

Ringneck Cock Pheasant Feathers
The most common and frequently used pheasant feathers are from the ringneck. They are used for streamers, nymphs, bass flies, wets, and salmon and steelhead patterns.

Neck feathers

Tail

Breast/flank feathers

172

Peacock Feathers

Peacock

The tail feathers from the pea-cock are one of the most extensively used feathers in fly tying. Herls on the tail feathers and the swords are used for all sorts of patterns.

Peacock tail feathers come in shades of iridescent bronze, blues, and greens. The length of the herl can reach 12 inches or more. The body feathers are also iridescent, but they are difficult to obtain.

Herl from the eye of a complete tail feather offers the best-quality material. Most other herl is of lesser quality and is offered as strung prepackaged material. Herls selected from the right side of the tail feather should be wrapped clockwise, while those selected from the left side should be wrapped counterclockwise. This will give you a thicker, fuller body. Loose body feathers or entire skins are difficult to obtain.

Herl can be used for bodies on all types of patterns. Stripped herl quills are also used for dry-fly quill patterns. Swords are used for wings on streamers, and sword fibers are used as tailing. Body feathers are used as shoulders or cheeks on salmon patterns.

Tails, swords, and body feathers can be purchased through fly-tying catalog supply houses, fly shops, and most sporting goods stores that sell fishing tackle and fly-tying materials.

Peacock Eye Tail Feather Herl Selection

First twelve to fourteen herls are ideal for "quill-bodied" patterns. Herl should be removed by stripping off fibers using a razor blade edge. To make light or dark bodies, select proper side of stripped quill.

Next four or five herls can also be used for "quill-bodies," but they are not as well suited as those above.

Next eight to ten herls are most suitable for wrapping herl bodies such as those on Coachman patterns.

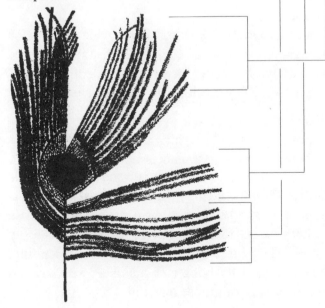

173

Ostrich Feathers

The only feathers from the ostrich used in fly tying are the plumes, which are long, thick-stemmed feathers with fibers (herls) on each side. They are used extensively by fly tiers for butts on salmon flies and as body material on midge patterns.

Ostrich herls are fragile, soft, and subtle. They are fluffier than those found on peacocks.

Ostrich feathers are available in a wide variety of colored plumes in both short (mini-plumes) and regular lengths. Entire plumes are offered by catalog supply houses. They can also be obtained through craft shops.

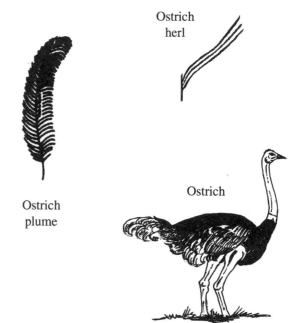

Ostrich herl

Ostrich plume

Ostrich

Grouse Feathers

Grouse are chickenlike birds with a wide distribution throughout the United States. Their feathers are used in a variety of patterns for wings, legs, collaring, and wing cases. They are ideal for legs on wet flies and nymphs.

Grouse feathers are soft and subtle and come in a wide variety of brown and gray shades. Material selection is limited, generally consisting of prepackaged loose feathers or entire skins offered by catalog supply houses. They can also be obtained through hunting, game farms, or fly-tying club members who have an overabundance of grouse material.

Grouse feather

Ruffed Grouse

Quail Feathers

Quail are relatively small birds with a wide distribution. There are a number of species of quail, with the bobwhite being the most common in the eastern and southern United States. Others include the scaled, California, and Gambel's quail.

Quail feather

Bobwhite Quail

Quail feathers are small, soft hackles that come in a wide variety of brown and gray shades. They make ideal medium dun hackles and can also be used for beards throats. The neck feathers from the California quail can substitute for jungle cock.

Selection is limited to prepackaged loose feathers or entire skins offered by catalog supply houses or obtained through hunting, game farms, or fly-tying club members.

Partridge Feathers

Partridges are relatively small birds with a wide distribution. Their feathers are used in a variety of patterns as wings, legs, and collaring. They are ideal for legs on wet flies and nymphs.

Partridge feather

These relatively small feathers are soft and subtle, with an almost speckled barring. They come in a wide variety of brown and gray shades. Selection is limited to prepackaged loose feathers or entire skins offered by catalog supply houses. They can also be obtained through hunting, game farms, or fly-tying club members who have an overabundance of material.

Hungarian Partridge

175

Turkey Feathers

Turkeys, both wild and domestic, provide a wide assortment of feathers for fly tiers. The mottled brown feathers from the wings of the wild turkey are prized for salmon fly patterns; the tail and body feathers are used for various other patterns. The domestic white turkey provides the marabou used today as a replacement for marabou stork feathers.

Wild Turkey

Turkey wing quills

The wing quills from the wild turkey are a mottled brown, and the markings vary from white speckled brown to dark oak brown. The length of the quills may be anywhere from 8 to 12 inches or longer. The tail feathers are a deep brown with blackish brown markings. The body feathers are also brown or bronze and somewhat triangular.

Wild turkey wing quills are used in the construction of classic salmon flies, muddler patterns, sculpin patterns, and hoppers. The tail and body feathers are used for tailing or wing cases on nymph patterns. The marabou feathers have a multitude of uses as wings, tails, throats, and bodies.

Wild turkey material is limited. The quills are sold as matched pairs, and the tail and body feathers are prepackaged. Domestic turkey is more abundant, with the quills, tail, and body feathers available in assorted colors. Marabou is also available in a wide range of colors.

Turkey material can be obtained from catalog supply houses or fly shops or through hunting. Also try game farms or fly-tying club members who have an overabundance of turkey material.

Guinea Fowl Feathers

The feathers from the guinea fowl have many uses. They are a good material for various applications such as legs, throats, and wings on wet flies, streamers, and nymph patterns. All the body feathers can be used on wet flies, nymphs, streamers, and salmon flies. Fibers can be used as legs, beards, and throats.

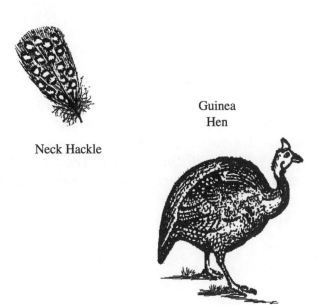

Neck Hackle

Guinea Hen

Guinea fowl feathers are small, soft hackles that are black with white spots (polka dots). The most frequently used hackles are the small neck hackles. They can be dyed or purchased prepackaged in assorted colors through catalog supply houses.

Jungle Cock Feathers

Jungle cock feathers are used extensively as the eyes, cheeks, or shoulders on classic salmon flies. Importation of the feathers was banned in 1969. Genetically-developed birds are available, but they are expensive and difficult to obtain.

Body feather

Eye feather

Jungle cock body feathers are narrow, oblong, and black with a white to creamy yellow stripe down the middle. The eye feather, which is about 1/2 to $1\frac{1}{2}$ inches long, is black with a white to creamy yellow spot near the tip of the feather.

Jungle Cock

Selection is limited to prepackaged loose feathers unless you purchase the entire skin. There is limited availability through catalog supply houses.

Parrot and Macaw Feathers

Exotic birds such as the macaw and the parrot provide colorful feathers used in the construction of various patterns. The feathers from both the parrot and the macaw are very difficult to obtain. The tail feathers from the macaw are used for topping in the construction of classic salmon flies, while parrot body feathers are used as shoulders or cheeks.

Macaw

Parrot
body feathers

Matched
macaw quills

Matched parrot quills

Macaw tail feathers are large, with colored fibers that are blue or red on one side and yellow on the opposite side. Parrot body feathers are soft and short and come in assorted colors, depending on the bird.

Selection is limited because of the difficulty of obtaining material. These feathers are sometimes offered by catalog supply houses or may be obtained through pet shops, if you ask the proprietor to save the feathers when the birds molt.

Starling Feathers

Body hackle

Because of the expense and difficulty of obtaining jungle cock, fly tiers have turned to the starling as an alternative source for eye feathers that are used on many types of patterns.

Starlings have small, soft black body hackles with a white spot near the feather tip. They are sold as pre-packaged loose feathers or entire skins through catalog supply houses.

Starling

Pigeon Feathers

Wing feather

Overlooked by fly tiers as a material, pigeon feathers can be used for almost any type of pattern. They come in all sorts of colors and are easy to obtain. Feathers from pigeons can be used for wings, tails, cheeks, shoulders, and legs.

Pigeon body feathers are small, soft hackles that come in a wide variety of colors. Unless you raise your own birds, material selection is limited. However, if you obtain a few skins, feather selection by color is excellent. Pigeon feathers are seldom offered by catalog supply houses. Your best bet is to raise your own or find someone who does and purchase them.

Common Pigeon

Crow, Raven, and Blackbird Feathers

Wing feather

Crow

Feathers from these birds are prized by fly tiers because of their true black color. No feather that has been dyed comes close to matching the black of these feathers.

These birds have deep black-colored feathers on the wings and tail with small, soft, black body hackles. The feathers make ideal medium dun hackles. They can also be used for beards and throats. Selection is limited. Find a friend who hunts, or shoot your own.

Kingfisher Feathers

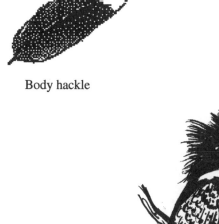

Body hackle

Kingfisher

Prized by fly tiers for their natural blue color, kingfisher feathers are used for cheeks and shoulders on Atlantic salmon patterns. Feathers that are currently available are imported into the United States because kingfishers are protected and illegal to hunt.

The small, soft hackles come in a blue shade. Prepackaged loose feathers or entire skins are available on a linited basis from catalog supply houses.

CHAPTER 6

Fur and Hair

Fur is defined as the hairy coat of a mammal or a strip or piece of any animal pelt. *Hair* is defined as a slender, threadlike outgrowth of an animal or one of the fibers or filaments that form the characteristic coat of a mammal.

What is called fur on most animals is a combination of two types of hairs (fibers or filaments) that vary in characteristics among different families of animals. The first type of hair (fiber or filament) is called the guard hair, which is long and usually straight. Guardhairs can be solid or of a cellular construction. The second type of hair is called the underfur, which is a soft, short hair (about 1/2 to 3/4 the length of the guardhair) that serves as an insulator and maintains the animal's body temperature. Underfur is usually found in a dense layer beneath the guardhairs. Some animals have no underfur, while others have a coat that consists mostly of this type of hair.

The following pages cover the furs and hairs commonly used in fly tying. However, the fur or hair from almost any mammal (worldwide) can be used in one form or another in the art of creating fly-fishing patterns.

Sources

All tiers accumulate a large assortment of fur or hair material. Most of the material they obtain is purchased through mail-order supply houses or specialty shops that cater to fly-fishing or fly-tying enthusiasts. Most shops or supply houses carry a variety of animal furs that are sold as prepackaged small pieces or patches. This limits the selection of choice or unique materials. However, there are alternative sources that are often over-looked and may provide materials not found elsewhere. Following are a few alternative sources to try when collecting fur or hair.

Roadkill (Road Hunting)

Collecting roadkill (road hunting) is not for the squeamish. In most cases, roadkill can be collected without any legal ramifications. However, hunting regulations apply to game animals as well as to endangered species, so it's a good idea to check your local or state regulations to be safe.

Most roadkills are animals in the vermin or pest class (skunks, groundhogs, squirrels, foxes, raccoons, etc.) that were hit by cars or trucks.

How long an animal has been dead or how badly it has been damaged determines whether it's worth your while to spend the time skinning and cleaning it.

If you decide to try road hunting, carry some large plastic bags, a pair of gloves, and a knife in your car or truck. After you get the carcass home, skin and clean it as soon as possible. A lot of beautiful skins can be collected road hunting.

Hunting

If you are a hunter, or if you have friends who hunt, you might be able to add some of the larger animal hides such as deer, elk, moose, or bear to your collection. Most hunters keep only the heads of the larger animals they kill (to have mounted as trophies) and discard the hide. Once you get a hide, you must clean and tan it as soon as possible, or have it done by a tannery.

Taxidermists and Furriers

Other possible sources for a variety of furs and hairs are local taxidermy or furrier shops. Most shops have scrap pieces of fur or hides from mounts or coat repairs that they will gladly give to you or sell for a minimal fee. Your local furrier may give you the name of his source for the various furs used in his business. Both are worth a try.

Sources

Slaughterhouses and Tanneries

If you have a slaughterhouse or a tannery nearby, you can get calf tails, cow hides, horse hair, and almost any type of farm animal hide for a small fee or sometimes even for free.

At a tannery, you may be able to find animal hides such as deer, elk, or moose that someone brought in to have tanned and didn't pick up. The tannery will probably let you have it for the processing fee.

Farmers and Trappers

Another possible source is local farmers. Many of them slaughter their own animals for food, and many of them trap animals for extra income.

Garage Sales and Resale Shops

Both of these sound like way-out places to go looking for fly-tying materials, but you can find some nice pieces of mink, fox, and rabbit if you're lucky. A lot of people discard old coats with fur collars or trim, fur hats, or even entire fur coats that can be purchased for a few bucks. You may be surprised at what you find.

Fly-Tying Organizations (Clubs)

If you can, join a fly-tying club. Many club members have accumulated a vast variety of materials over the years, as well as a lot of knowledge on how to acquire it. They may be willing to give you some of their extra or sell you some for a small fee. They can also help you find additional sources.

Skinning Animals

On occasion, you may obtain the carcass of an animal that needs to be skinned. It can be a large animal (such as a deer) or a small animal (such as a squirrel, rabbit, fox, or groundhog).

Whether it's a roadkill or something that was shot during a hunting trip, you will want to skin and preserve it so it can be added to your material collection.

The following illustrations show the basic steps for skinning small animals. The same principles also apply to larger animals, which require a lot more work. The example used is the common squirrel, which is found almost everywhere. It is easy to work with because of its tough skin.

Step 1 (see figure 1)
Once a specimen has been obtained, the first step is to wash off all the blood and dirt using cold water. Then lay the specimen on its back on a workbench or table and, with a sharp knife or scalpel, make an incision through the skin along the inside of each hind leg to the center of the body, as shown in the illustration. Repeat the same procedure with the front legs.

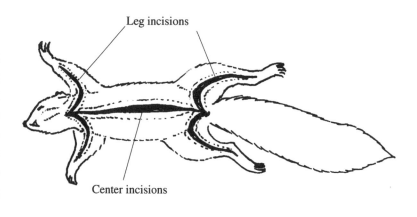

Figure 1

Step 2 (see figure 2)
Next, make an incision down the middle of the body between both the front and rear leg incisions, being careful not to cut through the stomach wall.

Using the knife or scalpel, work the skin down each side of the rear legs to the foot, and sever the foot (paw) from the body.

After freeing both rear legs, use your hand and the knife or scalpel to work the skin away from the rear of the body and the lower back toward the tail, until you can push your hand through (under the back) from one side to the other, freeing the hindquarters from the skin.

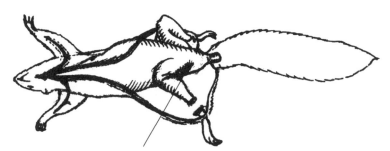

Using your hand and the knife or scalpel, work the skin away from the rear of the body and the lower back until you can push your hand under the back from one side to the other, freeing the hindquarters from the skin

Figure 2

Skinning Animals

Step 3 (see figure 3)
Grasp the rear body securely with one hand and with the other (using your fingers) pull the tail bone gently but firmly out of the tail, as shown in the illustration.

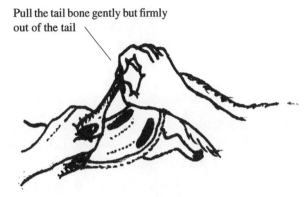

Pull the tail bone gently but firmly out of the tail

Figure 3

Step 4 (see figure 4)
After the tail bone is out, grab the hindquarters in one hand and the skin in the other. (Grab the hindquarters with a rag to keep it from slipping.) Firmly pull the skin until it peels away from the body to the upper chest or front leg area. Repeat the skinning procedure with both front legs. Once the front legs are freed, peel and pull the skin forward until you reach the head.

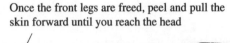

Once the front legs are freed, peel and pull the skin forward until you reach the head

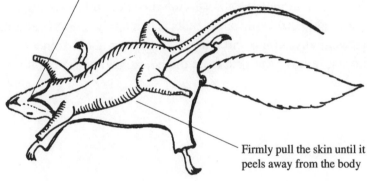

Firmly pull the skin until it peels away from the body

Figure 4

Step 5 (see figure 5)
Using the scalpel or knife, work the skin down over the skull past the ears and eyes to the lips, and cut the skin away from the skull.

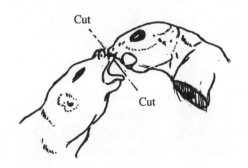

Cut

Cut

Figure 5

185

Skinning Animals

Step 6

After the skin has been removed from the body, use a dull knife to scrape away any remaining flesh or fat that you may have missed during the skinning process. Scrape small sections at a time until you can't get anymore fat or flesh off the hide. Then wash the skin again in cold running water.

Step 7 (optional)

To preserve the skin, make a tanning solution of alum and salt in a 5-gallon bucket and soak the skin in it for three to ten days. After soaking, remove it from the solution, wash the skin in cold water, and wait until it becomes almost dry or damp enough to allow rubbing it over a wooden stake. This process, known as breaking, breaks down the hide fibers, making it soft and pliable. However, it requires some effort to achieve desirable results.

Step 8

Another alternative to preserving the skin after washing is to wring out the excess water and tack it to a board (flesh side up) using small nails. Then apply a liberal amount of salt to the skin side, as well as some borax to prevent any odors, and allow it to dry for about four or five days. Once it's dry, scrape off the dried salt and borax, remove the skin from the board, and either cut it into sections or strips or leave it as a complete hide.

Deer Hair Selection Chart

The following illustration shows areas of hair to select for various pattern applications from the hide of a deer. For the most part, the same areas can be applied to elk, moose, caribou, and antelope hides.

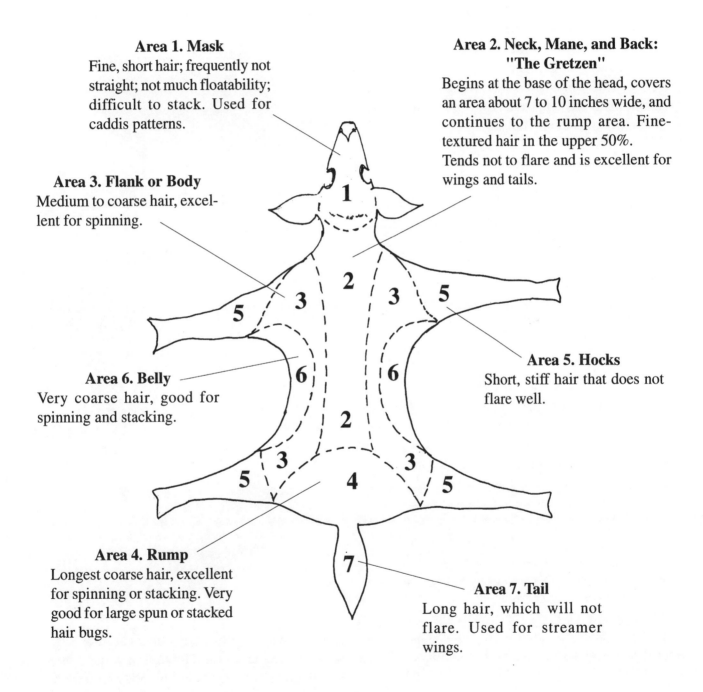

Area 1. Mask
Fine, short hair; frequently not straight; not much floatability; difficult to stack. Used for caddis patterns.

Area 2. Neck, Mane, and Back: "The Gretzen"
Begins at the base of the head, covers an area about 7 to 10 inches wide, and continues to the rump area. Fine-textured hair in the upper 50%. Tends not to flare and is excellent for wings and tails.

Area 3. Flank or Body
Medium to coarse hair, excellent for spinning.

Area 5. Hocks
Short, stiff hair that does not flare well.

Area 6. Belly
Very coarse hair, good for spinning and stacking.

Area 4. Rump
Longest coarse hair, excellent for spinning or stacking. Very good for large spun or stacked hair bugs.

Area 7. Tail
Long hair, which will not flare. Used for streamer wings.

Deer Hair

Deer hair is one of the most frequently used materials in fly tying. Most deer hair used today comes from the northern whitetail or the western mule deer. Other deer such as the southern whitetail, Florida Key deer, or coastal whitetail deer from Texas also provide excellent materials. However, they are more difficult to obtain through supply houses.

The hair fiber lengths (short to long) and textures (fine to medium to coarse) vary, depending on their location on the hide, what type of deer they came from, and the time of year they were obtained. Each of these factors also determines the tier's ability to spin or flare the material on the hook shank.

Northern
Whitetail Deer

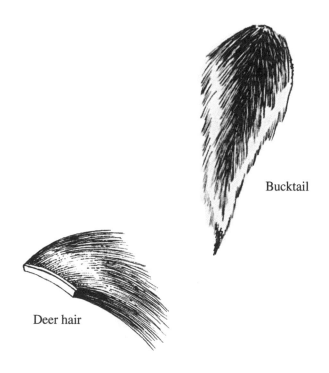

Bucktail

Deer hair

Characteristics

The key characteristics of deer hair are floatability and its ability to be spun around a hook shank. Its floatability has given rise to the false belief that the hair fibers are hollow, when in reality they are not.

For the most part, the hair (each fiber) consists of a cellular construction containing tiny air cells. The fibers containing the most cells (which are the thickest) are found on the back or sides and are frequently used for spinning. The finer white hair fibers in the belly area are cellular to a lesser degree, limiting their floatability as well as their spinning ability.

Although a deer appears to be brown or tan in color on its back and sides, the color is only on the tips of each fiber. The lower part of each fiber is almost always gray.

The tail, with its long hairs (which has the least cellular construction), is ideal for tails or wings on streamer or saltwater patterns. Both the body hair and the tail can be dyed various colors or used natural.

Deer Hair

Selection

Fine-textured hair can be found on almost any hide, but the best source is a hide from a coastal or southern whitetail (Texas coastal or Florida Key deer). Medium-textured hair is found on the neck area of a hide from an early-season or yearling deer (preferably a northern whitetail or a western mule deer), as is the coarse-textured hair found on most parts of the body of an adult buck or doe.

Application

Regardless of the locale from which the hide is obtained or the hair's location on the hide, almost every part of a deer hide can be used for various patterns. It can be used to tie dry flies, wet flies, streamers, bass bugs, poppers, nymphs, salmon flies, and saltwater patterns. It can also be used for tails, wings, bodies, heads, legs, and a multitude of other applications.

Fine-textured hair that has a limited degree of flare can be used for winging on smaller dry-fly patterns such as Wulffs, Humpys, and so forth. Medium-textured hair that has a minimal amount of flare is ideal for caddis patterns. Coarse hair that flares to 90 degrees can be used for hair-bodied bugs (bass bugs), muddlers, poppers, and some dry-fly patterns.

The key technique for applying deer hair to the hook is the tier's ability to spin or flare it around the hook shank. Once this technique is mastered, various patterns can be created using deer hair as the main material.

Sources

The first place to try is your local fly-fishing shop or tackle dealer. Many of them have sections devoted to fly-tying materials.

Another source for deer hair can be mail-order supply houses that specialize in fly-tying materials. Most supply houses carry small body patches and tails in a variety of colors.

Other possible sources are friends who hunt and would be willing to give you an entire hide to tan. Also, taxidermy shops often have scrap pieces from mounts that they discard. Finally, fly-tying club members with an overabundance of materials may be willing to give or sell some to other members.

Moose Hair

Like the hair of a deer or elk, moose hair also has a cellular construction containing tiny air cells and can be spun on a hook shank using the basic hair-spinning technique.

Moose

Characteristics

Moose hair is stiffer and less buoyant than elk or deer hair and does not flare as easily. It is a coarse, stiff hair that varies in color from black to tan to white.

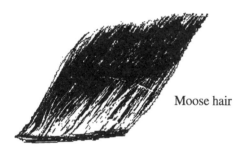

Moose hair

Selection

Selection is limited because large pieces of moose hide are difficult to obtain. Many supply houses carry moose mane as well as body patches. The hair can be purchased in natural shades such as light, medium, or dark.

Application

Moose body hair is often used for tailing on many dry or wet flies and is ideal for Wulff and Humpy patterns. Moose mane, with its long black, tan, or white fibers, can be used for tailing, extended-body patterns, and mosquito bodies. It is also used to form the wing case on nymph patterns.

Sources

The first place to try is your local fly-fishing shop or tackle dealer. Many have sections devoted to fly-tying materials.

Another source for moose hair can be mail-order supply houses that specialize in fly-tying materials. Most supply houses carry body patches or moose mane.

Other possible sources are friends who hunt, taxidermy shops that discard scrap pieces, and fly-tying club members with moose hair to spare.

Elk Hair

Elk hair is a favorite material used by many tiers in place of deer hair. Elk is finer and stiffer than deer hair, making it ideal for many purposes.

American Elk

Elk hair

Characteristics

Like the hair of a deer, elk hair also has cellular construction, giving it excellent buoyancy. Because of its stiffness and fineness, it does not flare as easily as deer hair when applied to the hook.

Selection

Elk hair can be purchased in natural shades of light, medium, or dark browns and tans. It is also available bleached (light tan) or in a variety of dyed colors. The body hair is basically a stiff hair that is used for patterns that require less flare when it's applied to the hook.

Application

Elk hair can be applied to the hook shank using the basic hair-spinning technique. It is more brittle than deer hair, requiring greater care with the thread pressure when securing it to the hook shank.
The body hair can be used to tie Paraduns, extended-body flies, backwings, Humpys, and dry-fly patterns. Elk mane is excellent for backwings on caddis patterns or stoneflies.

Sources

The first place to try is your local fly-fishing shop or tackle dealer. Many of them have sections devoted to fly-tying materials.

Another source for elk hair can be mail-order supply houses that specialize in fly-tying materials. For the most part, selection is limited because large pieces of elk hide are difficult to obtain. Some supply houses carry elk mane, elk hocks, and body patches.

Other possible sources are friends who hunt big game, taxidermy shops that discard scrap pieces, and fly-tying club members.

Caribou Hair

Like the hair of a deer, elk, or moose, caribou hair is also constructed of air cells, making it a very buoyant material.

Caribou

Caribou hair

Characteristics

Caribou hair is a light, soft hair that is more buoyant than elk or deer hair. It does not have the resiliency of deer or elk hair and does not flare as easily. It varies in color from light gray to white and is seldom sold in other dyed colors.

Selection

Selection is limited because large pieces of caribou hide are difficult to obtain. Many supply houses carry caribou mane as well as body patches. When selecting caribou mane hair, choose hair fibers that are less than 3 or 4 inches long for the best results.

Application

Caribou can be spun on a hook shank using the basic hair-spinning technique. However, the bunches must be bent and pushed up to make it flare well.
Caribou body hair is excellent for clipped body patterns and muddler or sculpin heads.

Sources

The first place to try is your local fly-fishing shop or tackle dealer. Another source for caribou hair is mail-order supply houses that specialize in fly-tying materials. Most supply houses carry caribou body patches.

Other possible sources are friends who hunt, taxidermy shops, and fly-tying club members.

192

Antelope Hair

Like the hair of a deer, elk, or moose, antelope hair has a similar cellular construction, giving it excellent floating qualities and spinning capability.

Antelope hair

Antelope

Characteristics

Antelope hair is a light, soft hair that is very buoyant, with each fiber varying in color from a light tan or white tip to a gray base. The fibers are much coarser than deer-hair fibers, but they are not as strong and resilient.

Selection

Selection is limited because large pieces of antelope hide are difficult to obtain. White pieces of the hide are excellent for dying.

Application

Antelope hair can be spun on a hook shank using the basic hair-spinning technique. Lacking the resilience of deer hair and not flaring easily, the bunches must be bent and pushed up to make it flare well.

When working with antelope hair, do not apply a lot of pressure to the thread when securing the material to the hook. Use soft wraps to prevent the thread from cutting through the soft fibers.

Antelope hair is excellent for clipped body patterns and for muddler, sculpin, and spuddler heads.

Sources

The first place to try is your local fly-fishing shop or tackle dealer. Another source for antelope hair is mail-order supply houses that specialize in fly-tying materials. Most carry antelope hair in small body patch pieces in natural shades of brown, light gray, and white.

Other possible sources are friends who hunt, taxidermy shops, and fly-tying club members.

Sheep Hair

Sheep hair (wool) can be used to make excellent bodies of a fine, soft quality preferred by some tiers.

Bighorn
Mountain Sheep

Sheep hair
(wool)

Characteristics

Sheep hair has a cellular construction that consists of air cells, giving it excellent buoyancy.

It's a fine, light, soft hair that varies in color from pure white to off-white.

Selection

Domestic sheep hair is readily available from most supply houses or fly shops in an assortment of colors. However, hair from bighorn mountain sheep or Dall sheep is very difficult to obtain and is seldom offered through supply houses or local fly shops. If you find some available, buy it. Any part of the hide is excellent for dying.

Application

Sheep hair can be spun on a hook shank using the basic hair-spinning technique, using soft wraps to prevent the thread from cutting through the soft fibers. Sheep hair is excellent for clipped body patterns; muddler, sculpin, and spuddler heads; and almost any hair fly pattern.

Sources

The first place to try is your local fly-fishing shop or tackle dealer. Another source for sheep hair can be mail-order supply houses that specialize in fly-tying materials. Most carry domestic wool, with bighorn mountain sheep or Dall sheep also available occasionally. It can be purchased in small body patch pieces in natural shades or colors.

Other possible sources are friends who hunt, taxidermy shops, and fly-tying club members.

Goat Hair

Goat hair is used in the construction of salmon flies or streamer patterns.

Goat hair

Rocky Mountain Goat

Characteristics

Goat hair texture is finer than calf tail or deer hair. It's a soft hair that varies in color from pure white to off-white.

Selection

Goat hair is seldom offered through supply houses or local fly shops. If you find some available, buy it. It can be purchased in small body patch pieces in natural shades or colors.

Application

As mentioned above, goat hair is used in the construction of salmon flies or streamer patterns.

Sources

The first place to try is your local fly-fishing shop or tackle dealer. Another source can be mail-order supply houses that specialize in fly-tying materials. A few carry domestic goat hair on occasion.

Another possibility is slaughterhouses or farmers that handle goats.

Other sources are friends who hunt, taxidermy shops, and fly-tying club members.

Cow and Calf Hair

Cow hair is seldom used, because it is difficult to obtain. However, calf tails (also known as kip or impala tails) and body hair are used extensively in fly tying. The hair and tails are obtained from the calves of domestic cows that are slaughtered and sold as veal.

Cow

Calf tail

Calf

Characteristics

Calf tails come in an assortment of natural colors, including white, black, brown, tan, and shades of beige. They are also available in an assortment of dyed colors. The tail hair fibers vary in length from short to long and are crinkly in nature. The body hair fibers are short, dense, and straight and are also available in various natural and dyed colors

Selection

Complete tails can be obtained in assorted colors and textures (hair lengths). Body hair is mostly sold in small pieces (patches).

Application

Both the tails and the body hairs are used for winging on assorted patterns. Body patch hairs are ideal for Wulff or Royal Humpy wings or almost any small dry-fly pattern.

Sources

The first place to try is your local fly-fishing shop or tackle dealer. Most supply or mail-order houses also carry both calf tails and body patches.

Another possible source is slaughterhouses that discard the calf tails or sell raw hides to tanneries. In most cases, the slaughterhouse will sell you both tails and patches in quantities for a few dollars.

Fly-tying club members with an overabundance of materials may be willing to give or sell some to other members.

Horse Hair

Horse hair is infrequently used in fly tying because it is difficult to obtain. Very few patterns require horse hair as part of their recipe, and very few tiers have experience using it.

Only the tail and mane fibers have been used as tying thread or in woven-bodied patterns that require durability or as a ribbing. Body hairs are never used, but there's no reason why they can't be.

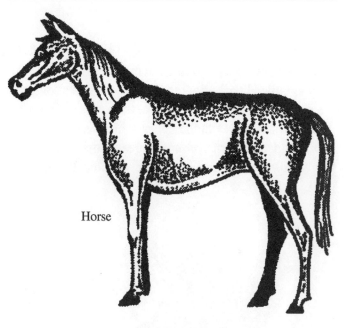

Horse

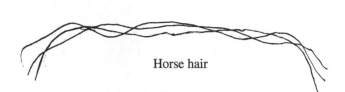

Horse hair

Characteristics

The hairs from both the mane and the tail of a horse are long, uniformly dense, and very strong. The color of the fibers can vary, depending on the animal's color. For the most part, the most common mane and tail colors are white, brown, and black. The body hairs are coarse and are seldom used.

Selection

Horse hair is seldom offered through supply houses.

Application

The mane and tail fibers can be used as a tying thread, as ribbing, or in woven-bodied patterns. Body fibers can be used as tailing or winging materials.

Sources

The first place to try is your local fly-fishing shop or tackle dealer. Only a few supply or mail-order houses carry horse hair on occasion.

Another possible source is slaughterhouses, which will probably sell you horse mane for a few dollars.

Fly-tying club members with an overabundance of materials may be willing to give or sell some to other members.

197

Bear Hair

Most bear hair used today comes from the black bear, which is common and hunted in many parts of the United States. Other bears such as the polar, brown, or grizzly are not readily available because they are considered endangered species. Polar bear hair, which was used in many of the older patterns, is no longer available anywhere. Many suppliers offer synthetic substitutes that work very well.

Black Bear

Bear hair

Characteristics

The key characteristic of bear hair is its translucent quality. The hair length varies from short to long, depending on its location on the hide and the time of year it was obtained. The guard hairs are ideal to use as a winging material for streamers or steelhead patterns. The underfur is good for blending with other materials when making dubbing.

Selection

For the most part, selection is limited because large pieces of bear hide are difficult to obtain. Most supply houses sell small body patches in natural colors (light and dark brown or black).

Application

As mentioned previously, bear hair can be used as winging material for both salmon flies and streamers. It can also be used for saltwater patterns or blended into dubbing.

Sources

The first place to try is your local fly-fishing shop or tackle dealer. Another source for bear hair can be mail-order supply houses that specialize in fly-tying materials. Bear hair can be purchased in small body patch pieces in natural shades of brown and black.

Other possible sources are friends who hunt big game, taxidermy shops, and fly-tying club members.

Seal Fur

Seal fur is used for bodies on nymph and salmon patterns, as well as dubbing for other types of patterns.

Seal

Characteristics

There are two types of seal furs: Greenland seal fur, which is coarse, glassy, and fibrous, and Pacific fur seal fur, which has a soft, velvety underfur.

Seal fur

Selection

Seal fur selection is limited. Most comes prepackaged as body patches or dubbing.

Sources

Seal fur on the skin and as dubbing can be obtained from most supply houses or mail-order houses. Another possible source to try is your local furrier, who may sell you scraps or damaged skins for a nominal fee.

Application

Seal fur is ideal as dubbing for bodies on salmon, nymph, and most other patterns.

Wild Pig Hair or Bristles

Also called a peccary or a Chinese boar, the wild pig has stiff hairs that are used for tailing and as feelers on nymph patterns.

Pig bristles

Characteristics

Wild pig hair consists of long, stiff, slender fibers.

Selection

Selection is limited to prepackaged material.

Application

Wild pig hair or bristles are ideal for mayfly or caddis tails and feelers.

Sources

Wild pig bristles come prepackaged, but they can be difficult to obtain. Check supply-house catalogs frequently.

Peccary

Coyote Fur

Coyote is a recent material used in fly tying. Not many pattern recipes call for coyote, but it can be used as a substitute for a number of furs such as fox and opossum.

Coyote body fur and tails both have a multitude of uses for such things as dubbing for dry flies, wet flies, and nymphs or winging on assorted streamer patterns.

Coyote

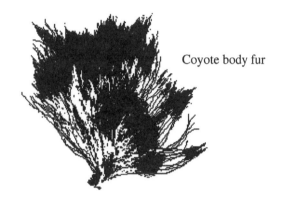

Coyote body fur

Characteristics

Coyote fur is like a light-colored version of opossum and varies from tans to reddish browns, having a hare's ear effect. The tails have long, crinkled hairs that are ideal for wings on streamer patterns.

Selection

Unless you obtain an entire hide, selection is limited, because large pieces of coyote fur are difficult to obtain.

Application

Coyote guard hairs as well as the tail fibers can be used for winging on streamers or tails on wet flies. The underfur makes excellent dubbing for a multitude of patterns.

Sources

Coyote fur is available through most mail-order houses or local fly-fishing shops that carry fly-tying materials. Another possible source is your local furrier, who may have scrap pieces or give you the name of his supplier.

If you live in a state where hunting for coyote is legal, you can hunt for yourself. Additional sources are friends or members of your local fly-tying club.

Fox Fur

Every tier should try to add fox fur and fox tails from the red, gray, silver, or arctic fox to his or her material collection. Fox body fur and tails have a multitude of uses for such things as dubbing for dry flies, wet flies and nymphs, or winging on assorted streamer patterns.

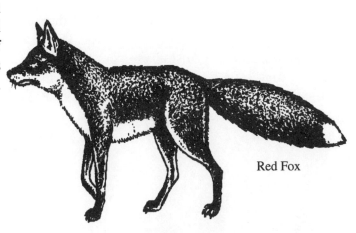

Red Fox

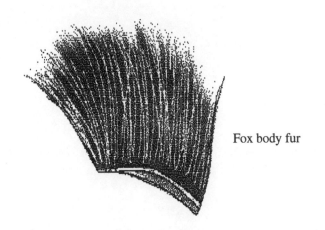

Fox body fur

Application

Fox fur guard hairs as well as the tail fibers can be used for winging on streamers or tails on wet flies. The underfur makes excellent dubbing for a multitude of patterns.

Characteristics

Fox body fur consists of a mixture of two types of hairs. One is a soft, lustrous, long-fibered hair called a guard hair, and the other is a fine, soft, silky-fibered hair (about half the length of the guard hairs) called underfur.

The color of the fibers can be pure white, gray, reddish brown, or silver, depending on the type of fox. The tails from all fox species have long, crinkled hairs that are ideal for wings on streamer patterns.

Selection

Selection is limited because large pieces of fox fur are difficult to obtain. The most frequently available fox fur is from the red or gray fox, which is often sold in small packaged pieces or as dubbing mixtures.

Sources

Red and gray fox are available through most mail-order houses or local fly-fishing shops that carry fly-tying materials. On occasion, some suppliers offer both arctic and silver fox. Other possible sources are furriers or other fly tiers.

Opossum Fur

For the most part, opossum fur is used as a dubbing material in the construction of fur bodies. The most commonly used is the Australian opossum, which is often available prepackaged from various supply houses. American opossum is rarely offered, but it also makes excellent dubbing.

Opossum

Opossum fur

Characteristics

Both the American and the Australian opossums have fine, soft fur with a lifelike luster. The Australian version varies in color from a medium gray over most of the animal to a yellow/cream underside. The American version is mostly all white.

Selection

Australian opossum fur is limited to prepackaged body patches. The American opossum offers a better selection, because entire hides can be obtained as roadkills.

Application

For the most part, opossum is used for dubbing fur bodies on dry flies, wet flies, or nymph patterns.

Sources

Austrailian opossum can be obtained from most supply houses or mail-order houses that specialize in fly-tying materials. American opossum is rarely available and difficult to obtain. The best source is roadkills.

Rabbit or Hare Fur

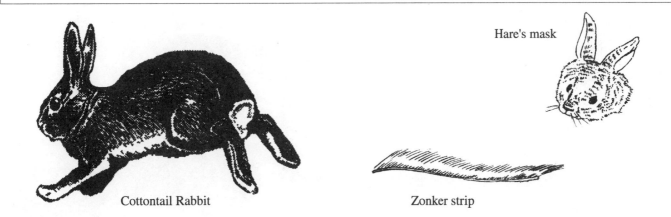

Cottontail Rabbit

Hare's mask

Zonker strip

Rabbit or hare fur is one of the most frequently used materials in fly tying. Most rabbit fur offered today comes from domestically raised rabbits or the common cottontail. Rabbit or hare can be purchased as a complete hide (in a wide range of colors), in precut strips and pieces, or as a speciality item such as a hare's mask, which is used for specific types of patterns.

Rabbit or hare fur has a multitude of uses and applications. It can be used as a dubbing material by itself or in a mixture of other types of materials, as well as in strips for Zonker or leech patterns or for streamer collars.

Characteristics

Rabbit or hare fur is a soft material that varies in both length and color. It readily absorbs water, making it ideal for many wet-fly patterns. The body hairs are longest and are generally used in strips for various streamer patterns such as Zonkers, Matukas, or leeches. The shorter hair fibers around the head and ears (hare's masks) are used to tie the popular Hare's Ear Nymph.

Selection

Summer skins from cottontails, snowshoe hares, or jackrabbits work well for hare's ear patterns if you can't find a British or Florida marsh hare's mask.

Domestic rabbit skins in a variety of colors should be the choice for patterns that require fur strips.

Application

As mentioned earlier, rabbit or hare fur makes ideal dubbing, which can be blended with other materials. It is also used to collar streamers or in strips for Matukas, Zonkers, or leech patterns.

Sources

The first place to try is your local fly-fishing shop or tackle dealer. Another source for rabbit fur can be mail-order supply houses that specialize in fly-tying materials. Most carry entire skins, hare's masks, cut strips, or body patches in assorted colors.

Other possible sources are friends who hunt, taxidermy shops, and fly-tying club members.

Beaver Fur

Beaver fur is most often used as dubbing by fly tiers. Being an aquatic animal, the beaver has fur that is basically water resistant. When wet, it has a translucent appearance.

Beaver

Beaver fur

Characteristics

Beaver fur is grayish brown in appearance and water resistant. It contains hard, shiny guard hairs with a soft, fibrous underfur. It can be dyed various colors.

Selection

Selection is limited because large pieces of beaver hide are difficult to obtain. Many supply houses carry body patches or packaged dubbing made from beaver underfur.

Application

Beaver fur is used for dubbing on many dry- or wet-fly patterns. It is often sheared from the hide and used directly as dubbing, or it can be blended with other materials such as Antron and rabbit to create dubbing for nymph patterns.

Sources

The first place to try is your local fly-fishing shop or tackle dealer. Another source for beaver fur can be mail-order supply houses that specialize in fly-tying materials. Most carry beaver body patches.

Other possible sources are friends or farmers who trap, taxidermy shops and furriers, and fly-tying club members.

Otter Fur

Otters are aquatic mammals like beavers and muskrats, with fur that is water resistant. Not many patterns call for this material.

Otter

Otter fur

Characteristics

Otter fur is basically dark brown, with light tan belly fur. The fur has coarse guard hairs with a softer underfur.

Selection

Selection is limited because large pieces of otter hide are difficult to obtain. Many supply houses carry small body patches.

Application

Otter fur is basically used as a dubbing material. When the coarse guard hairs are blended with the softer underfur, it provides a coarse dubbing. It is often sold as a blended dubbing mixed with other materials or in prepackaged pieces. It's a must for the Otter Nymph series. It can also be used for many other subsurface applications.

Sources

The first place to try is your local fly-fishing shop or tackle dealer. Another source for otter fur can be mail-order supply houses that specialize in fly-tying materials. Most carry otter body patches.

Another possible source is a local furrier. They often discard scrap pieces from coats they repair.

Other possible sources are friends or farmers who trap, taxidermy shops, and fly-tying club members.

Muskrat Fur

Like the hair of beavers, otters, and seals, muskrat fur is water resistant. It is one of the most popular furs used to make dubbing, which is used for both dry flies and nymphs.

Muskrat

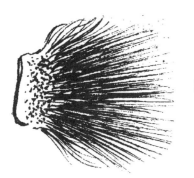

Muskrat fur

Characteristics

The natural color of muskrat fur is a medium to dark blue-gray on black, with medium to light blue-gray on the belly. It's a very soft fur with short hairs and a gray underfur that is highly water resistant.

Selection

Muskrat fur is sold mostly in small pieces or as pre-packaged dubbing. Occasionally, entire skins are available from various supply houses.

Application

Muskrat fur is used mostly as a dubbing material for patterns requiring gray fur bodies such as the Dark Cahill or Whirling Blue Dun.

Sources

The first place to try is your local fly-fishing shop or tackle dealer. Another source for muskrat fur can be mail-order supply houses that specialize in fly-tying materials. Most carry muskrat fur either in small patches or as a dubbing mixture.

Other possible sources are friends or farmers who trap, taxidermy shops and furriers, and fly-tying club members.

Squirrel Fur

The most commonly used squirrel material comes from the gray or the red fox squirrel. Others such as the pine or black squirrel are also used, but they are difficult to obtain.

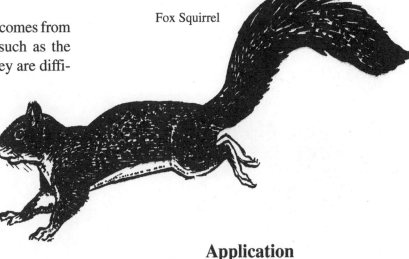
Fox Squirrel

Squirrel tail

Characteristics

Squirrel tails have long, stiff, slippery hair fibers. The body fur consists of mostly short, coarse-fibered hairs. The color and length depend on the type of squirrel.

Selection

The more common squirrels (red and gray) have the best-quality fur from hides obtained in the late fall or early spring. In most cases, the hides or material offered in shops and catalogs are obtained from animals during the fall, because that is when most states have their squirrel hunting seasons.

Application

The tails can be used for winging on assorted patterns, and the body hairs are ideal for dubbing.

Most supply or mail-order houses carry red and gray squirrel material, including entire skins or tails. Other types such as the black or pine squirrel are difficult to obtain; however, they are available occasionally. Other possible sources are roadkills or hunting.

Weasel Family Fur

The body fur and tails of all weasel family members (weasel, ermine, mink, marten, ferret, fitch) can be used in fly tying.

Ermine

Fitch fur

Characteristics

The body fur from animals in the weasel family consists of mostly short-fibered guard hairs and a thick, soft underfur. The color and length depend on which animal the fur comes from. It can vary from very short to long hairs and from pure white to various shades of brown.

Selection

Selection is limited, because only a few supply houses offer a few of the weasel family members. The most common are the ermine, mink, and fitch. In most cases, only the tail is available, as well as prepackaged dubbing.

Application

The tails can be used for winging on assorted patterns, and the body hairs are ideal for dubbing.

Most supply or mail-order houses carry ermine, mink, and fitch. Another possible source is furriers. You can also try friends who trap.

Badger Fur

Not often called for in pattern recipes because it is difficult to obtain, badger guard hairs are the primary material sought by fly tiers.

Badger

Badger fur

Characteristics

The body fur from the badger is a creamy tan, and the guard hairs are a cream color with black and white barring at the tips.

Selection

Selection is limited, because only a few supply houses offer badger. In most cases, only small body patches are available, as well as prepackaged dubbing.

Application

The tails fibers can be used for winging on assorted patterns, and the body hairs are ideal for dubbing.

Badger fur is occasionally offered by supply or mail-order houses. Another possible source is friends who trap.

Skunk Fur

Other than the tail, skunk fur is rarely used by fly tiers in the construction of fly patterns. However, it can be used as an alternative for squirrel and other wing materials on streamer patterns.

Skunk

Skunk fur

Characteristics

The body fur from the skunk consists of mostly short-fibered guard hairs and a thick, soft underfur. It can vary from very short to long hairs and from pure white to deep black. The tail has long, black or white glistening fibers.

Selection

Selection is limited, because only a few supply houses offer only tails.

Application

The tails can be used for winging on assorted patterns, and the body hairs are ideal for dubbing.

Some supply or mail-order houses carry skunk tails occasionally. Another possible source is roadkill if you have a strong stomach and want to skin it yourself. You can also try friends who trap.

Chinchilla Fur

Chinchillas are small South American rodents that are used in the fur business to make fur coats and hats. Chinchilla is a soft, smooth, short-haired, luxurious material used by many tiers for body dubbing on assorted patterns.

Chinchilla

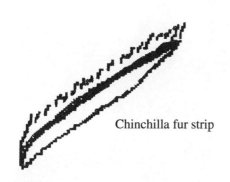
Chinchilla fur strip

Characteristics

Chinchilla varies in color from a pearly light to a medium gray. It is a very soft fur, with short hairs that have a cotton or wool texture.

Selection

The fur can be purchased in natural shades in small patches or prepackaged dubbing.

Application

As mentioned above, chinchilla fur can be used as dubbing for bodies on various patterns.

Sources

Chinchilla can be difficult to obtain from supply houses or mail-order houses. However, it is sometimes available, so check the catalogs frequently.

Another possible source is furriers. Also try getting some from fellow club members if you belong to a fly-tying club.

Woodchuck Fur

Woodchuck (also known as groundhog or marmot) is an overlooked material that is seldom used by tiers because its not readily available in most fly shops or mail-order houses.

Woodchuck

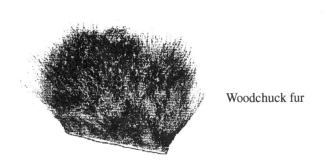

Woodchuck fur

Characteristics

Woodchuck fur varies in color from a light to a medium barred brown. It is a coarse fur with medium-length guard hairs and short, dark brown to coal black underfur.

Selection

Woodchuck fur can sometimes be purchased in natural shades in small patches.

Application

Woodchuck guard hairs found on the back or the tail hairs can be used for winging or tails on streamer patterns such as the Liama or dry-fly patterns such as the Irresistible or Wulffs. The underfur can be used for dubbing on a variety of patterns, including dry flies, wet flies, and nymphs.

Sources

Woodchuck can be difficult to obtain from supply houses or mail-order houses. However, it is sometimes available, so check the catalogs frequently.

Another possible source is roadkills if you're willing to spend the time skinning and tanning the hide.

Also try getting some from fellow club members if you belong to a fly-tying club.

Raccoon Fur

Raccoon is another overlooked material that is seldom used by tiers because it's not readily available in most fly shops or mail-order houses.

Raccoon

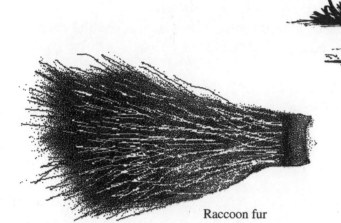

Raccoon fur

Characteristics

Raccoon fur varies in color from light to medium brown. It is a soft fur with long guard hairs and short, thick, brown underfur. The tail is ringed with black and brown fibers.

Selection

The tail and fur can sometimes be purchased in natural shades, as well as small skin patches.

Application

Raccoon tail hairs can be used for winging or tails on streamer patterns or wet-fly patterns. The underfur can be used for dubbing on a variety of patterns, including dry flies, wet flies, and nymphs.

Sources

Raccoon can be difficult to obtain from supply houses or mail-order houses. However, it is sometimes available, so check the catalogs frequently.

Another possible source is roadkills if you're willing to spend the time skinning and tanning the hide.

Also try getting some from fellow club members if you belong to a fly-tying club.

Mole Fur

Mole fur is used primarily as a dubbing material. It's a soft fur that is basically gray in color, but it can also be dyed brown or black.

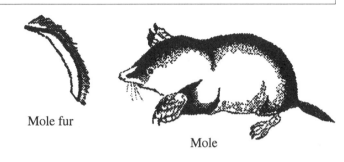

Mole fur

Mole

Characteristics
Mole is a very soft, fine-fibered fur.

Selection
Selection is limited to complete skins in natural or dyed colors. Complete skins measure approximately 4 by 6 inches.

Application
As mentioned above, mole is used as dubbing for bodies on various patterns.

Sources
Mole can be difficult to obtain from supply houses or mail-order houses. However, it is sometimes available, check the catalogs frequently.

Porcupine Quills and Bristles

Both the quills and the bristles of the porcupine are used in fly tying.

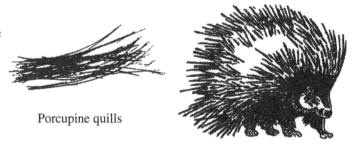

Porcupine quills

Porcupine

Characteristics
Both the quills and the bristles are stiff, hard fibers.

Selection
Selection is limited. Most are prepackaged and difficult to obtain.

Application
Porcupine material is used as tailing on various patterns, such as extended mayfly tails.

Sources
Porcupine quills or bristles can be difficult to obtain from supply houses or mail-order houses. However, they are sometimes available, so check the catalogs frequently.

CHAPTER 7

Miscellaneous Materials

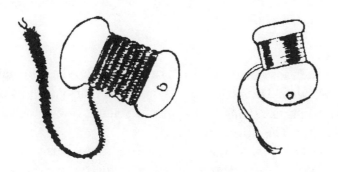

The following pages cover frequently used materials in fly tying other than fur, hair, and feathers. New materials are continually being added, making it impossible to list all of them. Included are a basic description of the material, its application or use, and possible sources to obtain it.

Miscellaneous Materials

Chenille, Yarn, and Floss

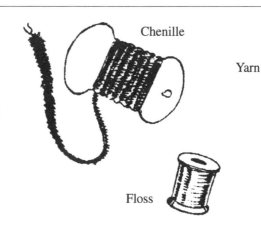

Chenille

Yarn

Floss

Chinelle, yarn, and floss are commonly used in fly tying. They are used in the construction of all types of patterns, from tiny dry flies to large saltwater streamers. They are available in a multitude of colors and sizes, giving the fly tier a vast range of possibilities.

Chenille

Common Chenille: A fuzzy, water-absorbent material, usually a rayon or silk fiber wound on a thread core, available in many sizes and colors, including fluorescent shades. It comes in ultra-fine (Vernille), fine, medium, and large diameters. Used for bodies on wet, streamer, salmon, steelhead, nymph, and saltwater patterns. Chenille can be obtained through most fly shops or catalog supply houses and is offered as variegated chenille, standard chenille, fluorescent chenille, crystal chenille, sparkle chenille, and vernille.

Tinsel, Ice, or Cactus Chenille: Strung short strands of tinsel wound on a thread core, similar to common chenille. Also comes in assorted diameters and colors and is used for bodies on assorted patterns. Can also be obtained from most fly shops or catalog supply houses.

Yarn

Yarn: Most yarns are either wool or synthetic materials available in various diameters and colors, including fluorescent shades. The most frequently used are polypropylene, sparkle poly, Mohlon, crew wool, angora yarn, Antron, and leech yarn. Yarns are used like chenille for bodies on wet, streamer, salmon, nymph, and saltwater patterns.

They are also used as tail material on a number of wet-fly patterns. Various types of yarn are available from most fly shops or catalog supply houses.

Glo-Bug Yarn: This yarn is a thick, soft material that comes in fluorescent pink, yellow, orange, and red. It is used for salmom or steelhead egg patterns.
It is available through most fly shops or catalog supply houses.

Floss

Standard Floss: A narrow and flat silk, nylon, or rayon material that is available in single, two, or four strands. Used for bodies on wet, streamer, salmon, steelhead, nymph, and saltwater patterns, as well as dry-fly patterns when multistrand floss is separated into a single strand. It is available in assorted colors and can be obtained through most fly shops or catalog supply houses.

Acetate Floss: In addition to standard floss, this type of floss is used in conjunction with an acetone solution that melts the material into a smooth mass. It is used mostly in the construction of streamer bodies or flat-bodied nymphs. It is available in assorted colors and can also be obtained from most fly shops or catalog supply houses.

Miscellaneous Materials

Tinsel, Krystal Flash, and Flashabou

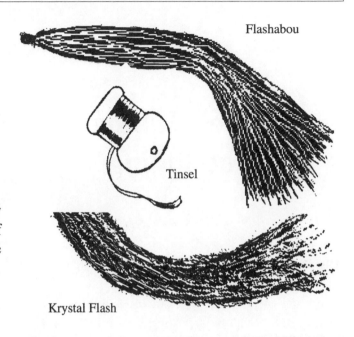

Flashabou

Tinsel

Krystal Flash

Tinsel, Krystal Flash, and Flashabou are commonly used in fly tying. They are used in the construction of all types of patterns to give them a little flash. All are available in various colors.

Tinsel

Tinsel is a metallic material used extensively in all types of pattern construction and manufactured worldwide. French tinsel, which is coated with a protective covering of varnish to keep it from tarnishing, is the best and most widely used in fly tying, but it is difficult to obtain. Mylar tinsel, which is made from a synthetic material, is most frequently offered through fly shops and catalog houses.

Both types are offered in gold and silver in sizes ranging from 1/32 to 1/16 of an inch and are listed as fine, medium, or wide. Tinsel is also available as flat, embossed, or oval shaped, which is wound around a cotton core.

Tinsel is basically used for ribbing bodies on streamers, wet flies, and salmon and saltwater patterns. It can also be used for other types of pattern construction, including nymphs and lures.

Krystal Flash

Krystal Flash is a synthetic, stiff material similar to Flashabou manufactured in 10- to 12-inch lengths of thin, spiraled strands. It is highly reflective. It can be purchased from most fly shops or catalog houses in a wide range of colors, including fluorescents. It is used to enhance patterns by adding flash to wings, bodies, and tails.

Flashabou

Flashabou is a form of mylar cut into fine, hairlike strands about 10 to 12 inches long. It's considered a fine substitute for marabou and can be used on a number of patterns.

It comes in a fairly wide range of colors, including black, purple, orange, silver, green, light green, blue, light blue, gold, red, olive, copper, and pearl. It can be purchased from most fly shops or catalog houses. Holographic Flashabou is also available, adding a holographic effect to the Flashabou strands.

Flashabou is excellent for both saltwater and freshwater patterns, adding flash and action to any fly in the water. It can be used for bodies, wings, and tails on any type of pattern.

Miscellaneous Materials

Tubes, Tubing, and Piping

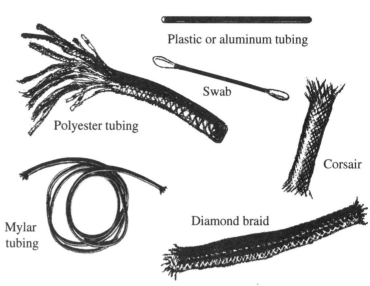

A number of different types of tubes, tubing, and piping are available for fly tying. Some are made of stiff plastic, like the straw types used for tying tube flies; others are braided and flexible, like diamond braid or mylar tubing, which can be used to form great bodies on streamer or lure patterns.

Plastic or Aluminum Tube Fly Tubes

As the name implies, these tubes are used in place of hooks to construct salmon or streamer patterns that are used with treble hooks. Generally, a stiff plastic or aluminum tube similar to a small straw or coffee stirrer is slid above the hook on the tippet or leader.

These tubes are available in various diameters and lengths or as kits from most fly shops or catalog houses. Possible alternatives are straws, coffee stirrers, or the tubes used in the manufacture of some ear swabs, which can be used by removing the cotton from the ends.

Mylar Tubing

Mylar tubing is a synthetic form of tinsel strands that are braided or interwoven around a cotton core. Available in silver and gold colors and diameters from 1/8 to 1 inch, mylar tubing is used for bodies on streamer and lure patterns. It is sold through most fly shops and catalog houses under various names such as Flash-A-Bou Minnow Body, Everglo Tubing, and EZ Body or Fishscale Woven Tubing.

Polyester Tubing

Pearlescent tubing is the same as mylar, except that it is made of a strong polyester, giving it an iridescent pearl color. It is available in the same sizes as mylar tubing.

Diamond Braid

Diamond braid is a new braided synthetic material that stretches and is similar to both mylar and polyester tubing. Used for saltwater, streamer, and nymph bodies, it is available in various colors; however, it's not readily available from most fly shops or catalog supply houses.

Corsair

Corsair tubing is a new tubular mesh made from very tough nylon in a loose weave. Used for saltwater patterns such as eels and baitfish imitations, it can be twisted and pulled into many shapes.

Corsair comes in white, silver/white, silver, gold, gold/black, black, and translucent colors and 1/3-, 1/4-, and 1/2-inch diameters. It is not readily available from most fly shops or catalog supply houses.

Miscellaneous Materials

Synthetic Hairs and Furs

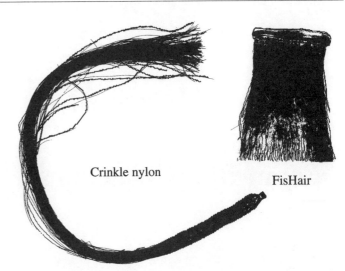

Crinkle nylon

FisHair

In recent years, synthetic hair has become popular with many fly tiers. It has been used extensively in the construction of both new saltwater patterns and freshwater creations.

Artificial Fur

Artificial fur is made from very soft, furlike acrylic fibers that are attached to a cloth backing and dyed to resemble various types of furs.

Artificial furs are sometimes offered by catalog houses, but generally they can be obtained from resale shops or garage sales on old garments, where they are used as collars or for entire coats. Artificial fur can be used on almost any type of pattern for wings or tails where fur is called for.

FisHair

FisHair is a synthetic nylon fiber with a lustrous sheen, available in $2\frac{1}{2}$-, 4-, 6-, and 10-inch lengths. It comes in assorted colors, including fluorescents, and is used as wings, tails, and beards on streamers and saltwater patterns.

Ultra Hair

Ultra Hair is a translucent fiber with a slight crinkle that has flash and sparkle as it moves through the water. It comes in 11-inch lengths and assorted colors and is used for saltwater patterns.

Super Hair (Crinkle Nylon)

Super Hair is similar to FisHair but is a tougher material that's available in various colors and lengths. It is also used as wings, tails, and beards on streamers and saltwater patterns.

Polar Aire

Polar Aire is a synthetic polar bear material that is shiny, supple, and a substitute for original polar bear.

It is excellent for parachute posts or hairwing and spinner wing patterns. It is available from most catalog houses in various colors.

Angel Hair

Angel Hair is another synthetic winging material that is very limp and flashy and provides a lot of action with little bulk. It is available in 10-inch lengths in assorted colors and is used on both freshwater and saltwater patterns.

Neer Hair

Neer Hair is another synthetic with long, soft fibers that can be used as wing material on streamers and saltwater patterns. It is available from most catalog houses in various colors.

Miscellaneous Materials

Wing Materials, Popper Bodies, and Foam Body Materials

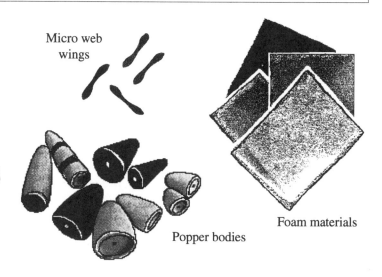

Micro web wings

Popper bodies

Foam materials

Wing Materials

Micro Fibetts: Ultra-thin synthetic fibers used as legs, tails, feelers, and wings on spinner patterns. Available in various colors through most fly shops or catalog houses.

Micro Web Sheets: A thin, flat, porous material laced with a geometric webby design resembling wing venations on insects. Also available in various colors through most fly shops or catalog houses.

Popper Bodies

Cork Bodies: Available as straight cylinders or in a bullet shape. Used for popper patterns and cemented onto kinked hooks and painted. They can be obtained in various sizes, and some supply houses offer them prepainted in various colors and pattern designs.

Sandal Plug Bodies: Made from a dense open-cell foam. Most tiers make their own by cutting out the plugs from old beach sandals and then shaping them. They can vary in color or color combinations, depending on the sandal used. In addition, kits consisting of various-diameter metal tubes are available that allow the tier to make plugs either by hand or with a hand drill. Preshaped plugs and plug-making kits can be obtained through some catalog supply houses.

Foam Body Materials

Foam materials come in two types: open cell and closed cell. Both are sold under various names and are available through most fly shops, catalog supply houses, and craft supply stores. The following are only a few of the products available.

Craft Foam: A soft open-cell foam available in sheet form and assorted colors from most craft supply stores. Used for bodies on various patterns.

Fantafoam: A soft open-cell foam in a very thin sheet form, available in a wide range of colors and used for bodies on emerger and dry-fly patterns.

Furry Foam: A thick, porous, elastic foam material covered on both sides with fuzzy fibers. Available in assorted colors and used for bodies on nymph and wet-fly patterns.

Evosite: A closed-cell foam that is extremely buoyant. Used for bodies on various types of patterns.

Miscellaneous Materials

Wire, Lead, Tape, and Foil

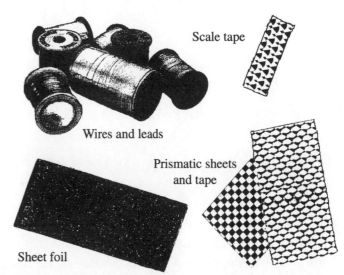

Scale tape

Wires and leads

Prismatic sheets and tape

Sheet foil

All the items listed can be obtained through most fly shops or catalog supply houses. Another possible source for some of the items (wires, foils, or prismatic sheets) is craft shops.

Wire

Wire is used extensively in fly tying as a ribbing or reinforcement for other materials, such as peacock or ostrich herls. It is available in fine or medium sizes and various colors such as gold, silver, copper, red, and green.

Lead Wires

Lead wire is used mostly on nymph and streamer patterns as additional weight when wrapped along the hook shank or tied in along the sides. It is available on spools in various diameters in extra-fine, fine, medium, or large.

Zonker Tape (Lead Tape)

As the name implies, Zonker Tape is used to create the beer belly on Zonker patterns. It is a thin, adhesive-backed lead foil that can be folded around a hook shank and cut to shape.

Foil

Sheet Foil: Thin, adhesive-backed metal material available in gold, silver, and copper that can be cut to any desired shape using scissors. Used mostly for bodies on saltwater patterns.

Prismatic Sheets: A metallic, synthetic, iridescent material used primarily on streamers, lures, or bass bugs. The adhesive backing allows easy attachment to the hook. Can be cut with scissors to any desired shape. Available in various iridescent colors such as orange, green, gold, silver, purple, blue, and yellow.

Prismatic Tape: Same as the sheet material, except sold in tape form.

Scale Tape: A new 2- by 3-inch clear, sticky-backed material with a printed scale pattern that allows the colors underneath to come through. Used over popper bodies to give them the scaled airbrush effect. Available in silver, gold, and copper.

Miscellaneous Materials

Eyes

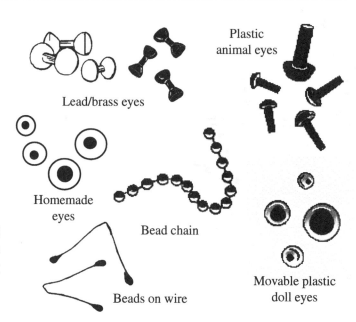

Lead/brass eyes

Plastic animal eyes

Homemade eyes

Bead chain

Beads on wire

Movable plastic doll eyes

Eyes are a proven trigger on many patterns in enticing fish to strike. The following is a listing of the various types available from fly shops, catalog houses, and craft shops.

Plastic Eyes

Animal Eyes: Solid plastic eyes in various colors and sizes with black pupils attached to a stem. The stems are cut off prior to attaching the eyes to streamers, lures, or hair or saltwater patterns.

Doll Eyes: Clear plastic eyes that come in various sizes with colored pupils. Used on streamers, lures, bass bugs, and saltwater patterns.

Metal Eyes

Lead Eyes: Hourglass- or dumbbell-shaped eyes made of lead and available in various sizes. Used as eyes and weights on nymphs, streamers, lures, and saltwater patterns.

Brass Eyes: Same as lead eyes, except made of brass and nickel plated.

Bead Eyes

These types of eyes can be made in a multitude of colors and sizes by attaching glass or plastic beads to different lengths of copper wire using epoxy cement.

Bead Chain Eyes

In addition to catalog houses or fly shops, bead chains are available in various sizes, colors (gold or silver), and lengths from most hardware stores or electrical supply houses. The eyes are made by snipping or pulling off a pair of the beads from the chain using wire cutters or pliers. The paired beads are then attached to the hook shank with thread by wrapping between the beads. They can be used on nymph, steelhead, streamer, lure, and saltwater patterns.

Homemade Eyes

Styrofoam Eyes: These eyes can be made by painting the pupil onto a piece of Styrofoam from an egg carton or cup and then punching out the desired outer diameter with a hand punch or leather punch.

Colored Plastic Sheet Eyes: Same as above, except the material used is thin, colored plastic sheets.

Prismatic Eyes: Same as above, except the material used is thin, colored prismatic sheet material.

Miscellaneous Materials

Rubber Items, Beads, and Colored Markers

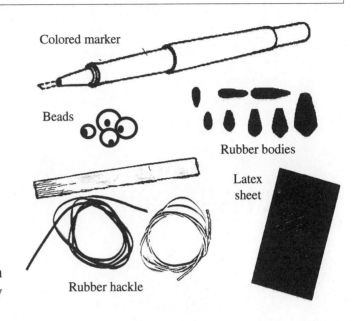

The following items are often used in the construction of various patterns and are available through most fly shops or catalog supply houses.

Rubber Items

Rubber Hackle: Round or square rubber threads in ribbon form that are prescored and can be separated into single strands. Available in black, gray, white, yellow, green, and orange. Used as tailing, wings, antennae, feelers, and legs on wet flies, streamers, poppers, lures, and saltwater patterns.

Latex Sheets: A thin rubber material that can be cut to desired sizes (strips). Comes in assorted colors and is used as a body material on various patterns, as well as for wing cases on nymphs.

Rubber Bodies: Preshaped bodies made of rubber that are glued onto a hook. Used for nymph and terrestrial patterns. Available in various sizes and colors.

Beads

Glass Beads: Assorted sizes and colors are used for bead head patterns. The bead is slipped over the hook shank and secured in position as the pattern head.

Metal Beads: Same as glass beads, except made of brass, copper, and aluminum, with some plated gold. Metal beads also add weight to the pattern.

Marking Pens

Permanant markers are available in various colors and are used to color threads, hair, foil, and tubing on various types of patterns.

Miscellaneous Materials

Straws
and
Plastic Lacing

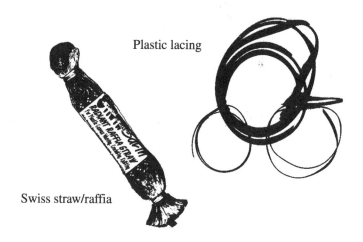

Plastic lacing

Swiss straw/raffia

Straws

Raffia: A dried leaf stalk from a palm tree cut into ribbon lengths and dyed various colors. Used for bodies on dry flies, wet flies, and nymphs, where it is also used for wing cases. Available through craft sores, fly shops, and catalog houses.

Swiss Straw: Similar in appearance to raffia, but a synthetic material that comes in assorted colors and is used for the same applications as raffia. It is also available through craft stores, fly shops, and catalog houses.

Plastic Lacing

Swannundaze: A soft, vinyl-type plastic lacing material that is flat on one side and slightly curved or oval on the other. Used as a body material on nymphs and larvae patterns, as well as ribbing on streamer or steel-

head patterns. Available through most fly shops or catalog houses and comes in a variety of sizes and colors, including some translucent shades as well as clear.

Larva Lace: Similar to Swannundaze, except that it stretches. Available in clear, black, olive, green, brown, orange, and yellow from most fly shops or catalog houses.

V-Rib (Vinyl Rib): A half-round vinyl material similar to Swannundaze and Larva Lace except that it has controllable stretch to a narrow diameter. Comes in small and medium thicknesses and various colors. Great as a ribbing on nymphs and scuds and can also be used as body material on saltwater patterns.

Dubbing

Assorted types of packaged dubbing

One of the more widely used materials in fly tying, dubbing is basically a mixture or blend of materials such as fur fibers, yarns, and other synthetics used in the construction of pattern bodies. It is available in a variety of mixtures, blends, and colors from most fly shops and catalog houses. Many tiers make their own. Following are some of the more popular prepackaged dubbing materials available today.

Synthetic Blends

Fly Rite: A blend of light, nonporous, polypropylene fibers available in 40 colors and used for bodies on various types of patterns. Sold prepackaged from fly shops or catalog houses.

Antron: A DuPont product with frosted, sparkling fibers that dubs easily. Used to form bodies on nymph patterns. Sold prepackaged in various colors from fly shops or catalog houses.

Ligas Ultra Translucent: A coarse, high-sheen material that has the translucent sparkle of seal fur. Ideal as a seal fur substitute. Can be used on dry flies, wet flies, and nymph patterns. Available in 24 colors from most fly shops or catalog houses.

Lite Brite: Consists of super-fine shreds of Flashabou that can be dubbed plain or combined with other materials. Available in 21 colors from most fly shops or catalog houses.

Spectrum: Made from very fine polyester. Available in assorted colors from most fly shops or catalog houses.

Synthetic/Fur Blends

Hare-Tron: A blend of synthetic Antron and natural rabbit underfur fibers. Great for dry flies as well as nymph patterns. Available from most fly shops or catalog houses.

Hare's Ear Plus: Hare's ear blended with Antron fibers in 10 different colors. Available from most fly shops or catalog houses.

Fur Blends

Natureblend: A blend of natural furs with colors that imitate the body colors of most aquatic insects. Available from some fly shops or catalog houses.

Masterblend: A blend of natural furs. Available from most fly shops or catalog houses.

Natural Fur Dubbings

In addition to the various synthetic or blended dubbings, the following fur dubbings can be purchased prepackaged from some fly shops or catalog houses or used directly from the animal hide:

- Rabbit
- Otter
- Mink
- Beaver
- Opossum
- Nutria
- Mole
- Badger
- Seal
- Fox

Miscellaneous Materials

Cements, Adhesives, Thinners, and Solvents

Cements, thinners, solvents, and adhesives

Following are some of the more common cements, adhesives, thinners, and solvents used for fly tying. Head cements are the most frequently used and are sold under various names. It is the tier's choice which product works best and produces the best results. Most of the items listed can be obtained through local fly shops or catalog houses.

Lacquer Head Cement

Most head cements are lacquers that dry quickly and are used to coat the thread head on fly patterns. They are sold under various names:

Hunter's Best Head Cement: Penetrates quickly, dries hard, and is easily thinned.

Wapsi Celluloid Head Cement: A high-quality celluloid lacquer available in clear and colors (black, white, red, and yellow).

Cellaire: Made in England and considered the ultimate head lacquer, it penetrates deeply and dries clear, hard, and smooth. Available in clear, yellow, black, and red.

Griffin's Thin Head Cement: A very thin cement that penetrates deeply and rapidly and dries hard.

Dave's Flexament: Not a glossy cement; dries to a rubbery, flexible finish. Excellent as a single coat.

Von Schlegell Head Cement: A lacquer cement that comes in a patented flow-control valve applicator.

Water-Based Head Cement

Loon Water-Based Head Cement: A polyurethane emulsion head cement that can be thinned with water. Penetrates well; dries fast and hard.

Vinyl Head Cement

A new type of head cement made with a vinyl base. Penetrates well, dries clear, and is waterproof.

Cements and Adhesives

Five-Minute Epoxy: A two-step adhesive used for epoxy fly patterns as well as a head cement. After mixing, it dries to a hard, clear finish.

Goop: A rubberlike adhesive used for mounting eyes to hair patterns. Remains flexible after drying.

Zap-A-Gap: A superglue used for attaching eyes to streamers and hair patterns.

Flex-Coat: A two-hour epoxy used for saltwater epoxy patterns and coating heads.

Alpha Glue: A superglue that forms the strongest bond with stainless steel. Used for saltwater popper pattern construction.

Pliobond: A Goodyear product that bonds anything to anything. Dries quickly to a rubberlike consistency.

Pliobond Thinner: A solvent used to cut or thin Pliobond.

Buglaze: A deep-penetrating, thick cement that dries to a glossy one-coat finish. Excellent for painted heads, poppers, and shellbacks.

Thinners and Solvents

Lacquer Thinner: A solvent used to thin lacquer-based head cements.

Water-Based Thinner: A solvent used for polyurethane emulsion head cement rather than water.

Vinyl Head Cement Thinner: A solvent used for thinning vinyl head cement.

Acetone: A solvent used to melt acetate floss.

CHAPTER 8

Techniques

This chapter contains information on the basic techniques used to attach various types of materials to a hook. Also included are instructions for the two principal knots used in fly tying. Learning how to make these knots and mastering these techniques will improve your tying ability, as well as the quality of your finished fly patterns.

Warning: Many tiers have the habit of moistening material that they are applying to the hook with their mouths. This is not a safe practice, even if you think the material is clean. Almost all materials are treated with some sort of chemicals or preservatives, which can be dangerous if taken internally. They can also contain parasites that can cause severe health problems. If you need to moisten material during the tying process, use a small dish of water rather than your mouth.

Basic Knots

The half hitch and the whip finish are the two most important knots to master in fly tying.

Half Hitch

Step 1.
Catch the thread with two fingers.

Step 2.
Form a loop by flipping your hand over and opening your fingers.

Step 3.
Bring the thread to the hook shank and slip the eye of the hook into the open loop.

Step 4.
Place your index finger on the shank over the thread and pull the thread tight with your bobbin.

Whip Finish

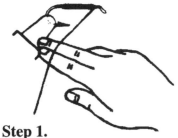

Step 1.
Catch the thread with two fingers.

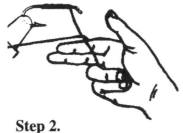

Step 2.
Form a loop by flipping your hand over.

Step 3.
Bring the thread to the hook shank and open the loop by spreading your fingers.

Step 4.
Pass the loop to the back, over the hook shank (shank into open loop), and close your fingers.

Step 5.
Rotate the loop from the back forward, and repeat steps 4 and 5 three or four times.

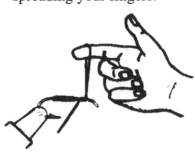

Step 6.
Stop the loop at the top of the hook and pull the thread tightly with your bobbin, releasing the loop as you pull.

Thread and Tail Attachment

Hook and Thread Attachment

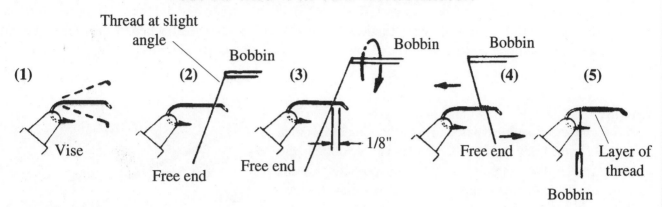

Step 1.
Always level the hook in the vise and hide as much of the point and barb as possible.

Step 2.
Hold the free end of the thread with one hand and the bobbin with the other hand, and place the thread against the hook shank at a slight angle.

Step 3.
Start the thread about 1/8 inch behind the hook eye and make a half turn around the shank while maintaining tension with both hands.

Step 4.
Continue wrapping the thread with the bobbin to the rear while moving the free end forward to the eye, causing the thread to wrap over itself.

Step 5.
After you've made about six wraps, snip off the excess or free end and continue to wrap until you have a layer of thread just short of the bend of the hook.

Tying in Tails

Various patterns call for many different materials to be used as tails, but they are all attached in the following fashion.

Step 1.
Select the material for the tail, place it between your fingers, and lay it firmly at the back of the hook on top of the shank. Also, grab the shank with your fingers to keep the material from turning and to keep it in position. Hold this position until the entire sequence of wraps is completed.

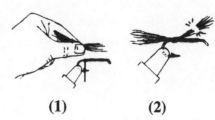

Step 2.
Make three wraps over the material toward the back and one wrap under the material. Bring the thread forward and make an additional three wraps over the top of the material, going forward. Make a half hitch and snip off the excess material at the front.

Material Variations

Yarn Hackle tips

Peacock (sword or herl) Quill

Fur Hair

Techniques-Bodies

Tying in Bodies

Various patterns call for many different materials to be used when tying in a body. Some patterns call for two or three different materials in the body construction. Nevertheless, they are all attached to the hook in the same basic manner. A basic body construction found on most streamer or wet-fly patterns is shown below.

Body Construction

Step 1.
After laying down a thread base, tie in the base material (yarn or floss) for the body at the back of the hook. Next, tie in the ribbing (tinsel, for example) at the same spot and snip off the excess. Then bring the thread forward to within 1/8 inch of the hook eye.

Step 2.
Form a tapered body with the yarn or floss material by wrapping forward and then back until the body is cigar shaped. Secure the material with your thread and snip off the excess.

Step 3.
Starting at the back, give the tinsel a single wrap at the back of the hook. Then wrap the tinsel forward over the yarn or floss, creating a candy-stripe effect and keeping the spaces equal. Secure the tinsel behind the eye with a half hitch and snip off the excess.

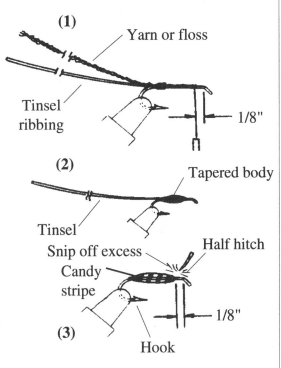

Body Variations

Egg Sac (Butt)
Tie in a strand of peacock herl at the back of the hook. Make four to six wraps with the herl (one on top of the other) and secure it with your thread.

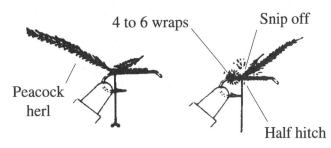

Palmered Hackle
Tie in a piece of yarn or floss and a hackle feather at the back of the hook. Form the body with the yarn or floss and secure it with your thread. Next, wrap the hackle over the body, forward to the hook eye. Snip off the excess and secure with a half hitch.

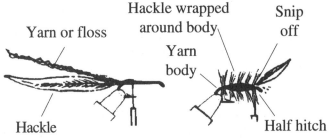

Techniques-Dubbing

Applying Dubbing

Dubbing consists of furs or various materials cut and blended together to form a matting to be used for body construction. Most dubbing is applied to the thread with a twisting motion, which creates a furry strand that is then wrapped around the shank of the hook. The following illustrations show a few ways to apply the dubbing to the thread.

Conventional Method

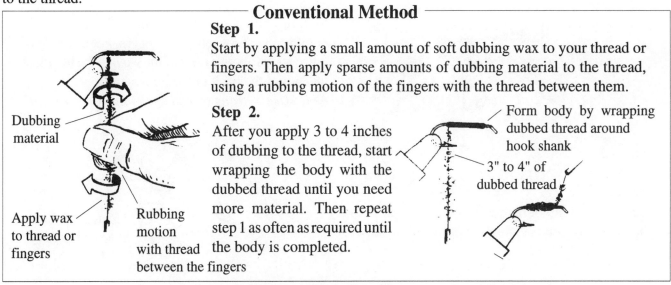

Step 1.
Start by applying a small amount of soft dubbing wax to your thread or fingers. Then apply sparse amounts of dubbing material to the thread, using a rubbing motion of the fingers with the thread between them.

Step 2.
After you apply 3 to 4 inches of dubbing to the thread, start wrapping the body with the dubbed thread until you need more material. Then repeat step 1 as often as required until the body is completed.

Dubbing material

Apply wax to thread or fingers

Rubbing motion with thread between the fingers

Form body by wrapping dubbed thread around hook shank

3" to 4" of dubbed thread

Dubbing Loop Method

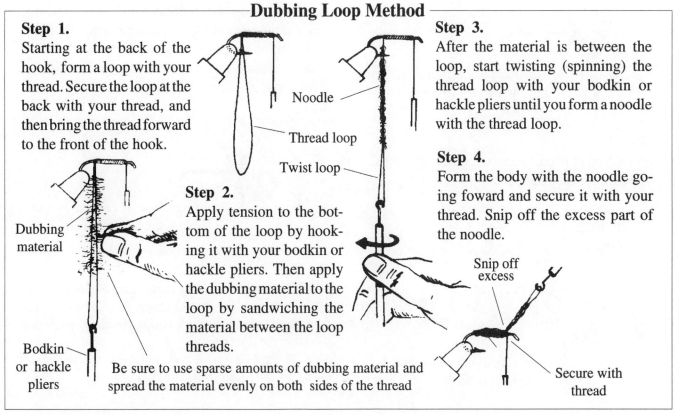

Step 1.
Starting at the back of the hook, form a loop with your thread. Secure the loop at the back with your thread, and then bring the thread forward to the front of the hook.

Step 2.
Apply tension to the bottom of the loop by hooking it with your bodkin or hackle pliers. Then apply the dubbing material to the loop by sandwiching the material between the loop threads.

Be sure to use sparse amounts of dubbing material and spread the material evenly on both sides of the thread

Noodle

Thread loop

Twist loop

Dubbing material

Bodkin or hackle pliers

Step 3.
After the material is between the loop, start twisting (spinning) the thread loop with your bodkin or hackle pliers until you form a noodle with the thread loop.

Step 4.
Form the body with the noodle going foward and secure it with your thread. Snip off the excess part of the noodle.

Snip off excess

Secure with thread

231

Techniques-Spinning Hair

Applying Hair

The following illustrations show the basic steps used to spin hair onto a hook shank.

Instructions

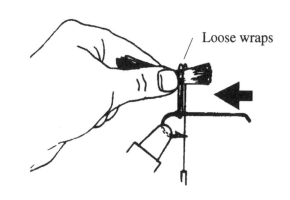

Loose wraps

Step 1.

Starting with a clump of hair that you can hold comfortably between your fingers, put a couple of loose wraps about a third of the way up the length of the hair at the back of the hook shank.
Note: Use a strong thread like Monocord or size E.

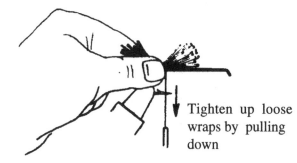

Tighten up loose wraps by pulling down

Step 2.

Bring the clump of hair down on the shank of the hook and tighten the loose wraps by pulling down.

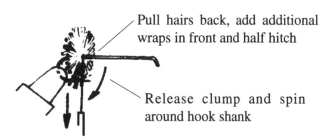

Pull hairs back, add additional wraps in front and half hitch

Release clump and spin around hook shank

Step 3.

When the wraps start to tighten, release the clump and continue to add a few additional wraps through the clump as it turns around the hook shank. With your free hand, pull back the hairs at the front of the clump, and add some additional wraps and a half hitch.

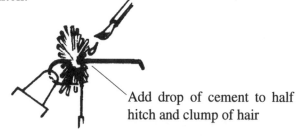

Add drop of cement to half hitch and clump of hair

Step 4.

Put a drop of head cement over the half hitch and at the front of the clump.

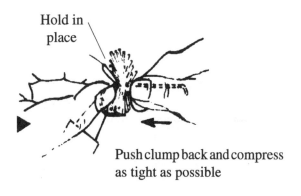

Hold in place

Push clump back and compress as tight as possible

Step 5.

Repeat steps 1 through 4 for each clump of hair you add to the hook shank; after each clump is added, press it to the back of the hook shank by using your fingernails, as shown in the illustration.
Note: The tighter you press the clumps of hair together, the better the result when you trim your fly.

Techniques-Wings

Attaching Wings

Wing Materials

Many types of materials can be used for wings, such as hair fibers, hackle tips, quill segments, and the like. For the most part, they are all applied to the hook in the same fashion. Depending on the type of fly you are tying (dry, wet, or streamer) and the position of the wings, however, some variations in application will be necessary.

Down-Wing Position

The following illustrations show the basic steps required to attach wings. They show quill segments used for the pattern in what is called a down-wing position.

Upright Wings

Upright wings are tied in the same way as the basic wing attachment, except that the butt end of the material is held at the front of the hook rather than at the back. In addition, after the loose wraps are tightened, the wing is pulled upright and a few wraps are made at the front and back of the material to keep it in the upright position.

The following illustrations show how to tie in the wings in the upright position using quill segments or hair fibers for most dry-fly patterns.

Basic Wing Attachment

Step 1.

Position the material in its proper location, holding it tightly and grasping the hook at the same time with the same fingers. Give it two loose wraps with the thread.

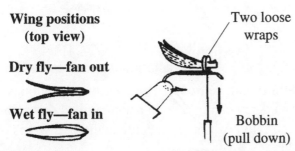

Wing positions (top view)

Dry fly—fan out

Wet fly—fan in

Two loose wraps

Bobbin (pull down)

Step 2.

Pull down with your bobbin, tightening the two wraps. Add an additional wrap behind the material and three more at the front.

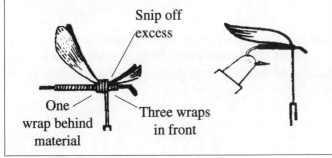

Snip off excess

One wrap behind material

Three wraps in front

Quill or Hackle Wings

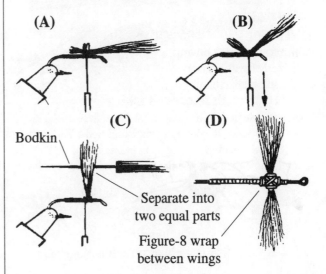

(A) Pull upright

(B)

(C)

Few wraps at the back   Few wraps at the front

Hairwings

The same application described above applies for hairwing patterns. If you want to separate the hairs into two wings, apply the following procedure.

(A) (B)

(C) (D)

Bodkin

Separate into two equal parts

Figure-8 wrap between wings

Techniques-Hackling

Applying Hackles (Hackling)

When a pattern calls for a hackle to be used for a collar, beard, or palmered body, proper hackle selection can be important. Listed below are a few characteristics to consider when selecting the hackle for your fly.

1. Hackles used for dry flies are selected by the length of the barbules (which should be one and a half times the gap of the hook) and by the lack of webbing in the feather. Most dry-fly hackles come from a rooster or male bird.
2. Hackles for wet flies and streamers should be softer, webby-type feathers. These feathers absorb water readily. They generally come from a hen or female bird.
3. Most dry flies use saddle or neck hackles; in wet-fly patterns, the spade or spey hackles are used.
4. Hackles to be used for collars (spun) should have as little webbing as possible.
5. Hackles used for beards or palmering can be either a wet- or dry-fly type of feather.

Hackle Preparation

One of the following ways of preparing a hackle should be done before tying it onto the hook.

Strip off soft fluffy material at the bottom of the feather

Trim off soft fluffy material at the bottom of the feather with scissors, leaving stubblelike barbs

Palmered Hackles

When a hackle is tied in at one point (**A**) on the hook shank and is then wound (**B**) along its length and tied off at another point (**C**), the hackle is called a palmered hackle. This technique is called palmering and is used in a variety of patterns.

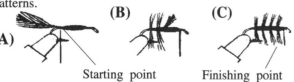

(**A**)   (**B**)   (**C**)

Starting point   Finishing point

Hackling Techniques

Hackle Collar

When a hackle is wound in at the same location on the hook shank, it is called a spun hackle. Most spun hackles are used on dry flies or streamers when the pattern calls for a hackle collar. The hackle can be tied in by the tip end (**A**) or by the butt end (**B**) and then spun around the hook shank, as shown below (**C, D**).

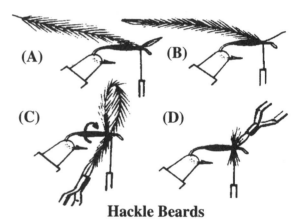

(**A**)   (**B**)

(**C**)   (**D**)

Hackle Beards

Beards can be tied in using various techniques.
(**A**) They can be a spun hackle pulled down and tied into position with some additional wraps of thread.
(**B**) They can be loose hackle barbules tied in under the hook shank.
(**C**) They can be a hackle tip cut into a "V" notch and then tied in and pulled into position.

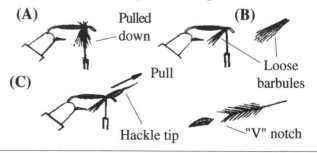

(**A**)   Pulled down   (**B**)

Pull   Loose barbules

(**C**)   Hackle tip   "V" notch

Techniques-Weighting Hooks

Weighting Hooks

Certain types of patterns require additional weight besides the hook to work properly and to be effective under certain conditions and in their presentation. For fly fishers who tie their own patterns, this doesn't present a problem, because they can tie a number of the same pattern in various weights for different conditions. For the most part, nymph patterns and streamers are weighted using lead wire wrapped around, under, or on both sides of the hook shank and secured with thread. The amount and size of the lead wire determine how deep the pattern will sink below the surface. Following are examples of weighted hooks with the wire wrapped around the hook shank.

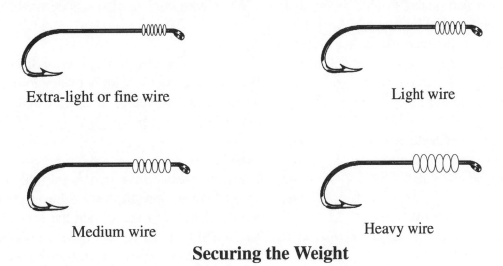

Extra-light or fine wire

Light wire

Medium wire

Heavy wire

Securing the Weight

Once enough wire has been wrapped around the hook shank for the desired weight, do not cut the end off with scissors. Rather, pull it off with your fingers and tuck the loose end down. Using thread, secure the wire by wrapping over it. Then at both ends, build a small ramp from the lead to the shank for an even transition when adding materials over the lead wire.

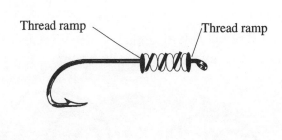

Thread ramp   Thread ramp

Weight Variations

Strip of lead wire secured
under the shank

Strips of lead wire secured on both
sides of the shank

Dyeing Materials

After you accumulate various tying materials, you may find that your collection doesn't include a specific color you need for some of the patterns you would like to tie. To get the proper color, most tiers dye their own materials. Following are a few tips.

Dyeing Process

Step 1.
Prepare the materials for the dye bath.
A. Mix a solution of detergent (Woolite or any dishwashing detergent) and warm water.
B. Soak the materials in the solution to soften the fibers and remove any grease, grime, or dirt. Soaking time depends on the type of materials.
 The following is a general rule of thumb.

Necks, capes, and poultry feathers	2 Hrs.
Ducks, geese, or oily-feathered birds	4 to 6 Hrs.
Deer, elk, moose, and calf tails	2 Hrs.
Most other furs	2 Hrs.

C. After soaking, rinse the materials in lukewarm water.

Step 2.
Take an empty plastic milk bottle (gallon size) and cut off the top, as shown in the illustration.

Empty gallon
milk bottle

Cut off top
portion of bottle

Step 3.
Add the dye (powder or liquid) to the milk bottle and add two teaspoons of glacial acetic acid.

Step 4.
Turn on the water tap and let it run until the water is hot. Fill the gallon bottle with hot water to mix the dye. If you're using powdered dye, give it a few stirs to dissolve the powder.

Step 5.
Place the presoaked materials into the dye bath and swish them around with a stick. Leave the materials in the dye bath until you obtain the desired color. The shade will look darker while the materials are wet.
Note: Don't mix different materials in the dye bath. Dye unlike materials such as poultry and deer separately.

Step 6.
Remove the materials from the dye bath and rinse them under cool running water until the water runs clean. Squeeze out any excess water (do not wring).

Step 7.
Place the dyed materials on newspaper (skin side down or skin side to skin side) and allow them to dry. Occasionally fluff up the materials during the drying process.

Bleaching and Burning

Bleaching Materials

There are a few simple rules to remember when bleaching materials.

Rule 1.
Don't use household bleach. The proper bleaching agent is hydrogen peroxide—a 20 percent volume mixture used full strength.

Rule 2.
Never bleach feathers. Bleaching feathers destroys the texture of the fibers. The only time to use bleach on feathers is for "burning" or de-flueing feathers for Spey fly patterns.

Rule 3.
Bleach fur only when the natural shade is unobtainable.

When bleaching fur, check it frequently. The length of time to leave the material in the bleach depends on the type of fur and its original color. The time can vary from a few hours to a few days. Experiment by trying a little at a time until you learn from experience.

"Burning" Feathers

The following process is used to de-flue feathers for various patterns such as Spey flies or Quill Gordons.

Step 1.
Dilute household bleach by 50 percent with warm water.

Step 2.
Immerse the feathers in the solution and swish them around until the feathers pucker up (you can see the difference).

Step 3.
Watch the feathers closely until the desired effect is reached.

Step 4.
Remove the materials from the bleach solution and soak them in a solution of baking soda and water to neutralize the bleach.

Step 5.
Remove the feathers from the baking soda solution, rinse in clean water, and allow them to dry.

CHAPTER 9

Material Storage and Inventory

After accumulating a large variety of materials, the next challenge is to store it and protect it from infestation. The following pages offer a few suggestions on how to store, protect, and catalog or inventory materials.

Material Storage

A number of methods can be used to store your materials, depending on the amount of materials you have, the space available, and the amount of time or effort you put into setting up a storage system.

If you are a dedicated tier, you will want to inventory your materials and store them in a convenient fashion, making them easy to locate when you're in the process of creating or tying patterns.

The following storage containers can be useful.

Glass Jars: Glass jars with screw-on lids are available in various sizes. They allow you to see the material and prevent anything from entering the container. The drawback with glass jars is the room and shelves required to store them.

Plastic Bags (Zip-Loc Bags): These bags are available in various sizes and have a seal to prevent infestation. However, they are not as secure as glass jars. They can be kept in file cabinets, hung on wall hooks, or stored on a homemade storage rack.

Plastic Storage Boxes (Shoe Boxes): These boxes can be purchased from any general merchandise store for a few dollars.

They come with snap-on lids, and can be stacked one on top of the other on shelves or in a storage cabinet.

Infestation Prevention

Whether you purchase your material from a local fly shop or catalog supply house or collect it from other sources, it can be infested with bugs or other creatures that will destroy it within a short time, as well as any other materials stored close to it.

Isolation/ Microwave: To prevent infestation, one of the best methods is to isolate new materials in a glass jar and zap them in a microwave for a few seconds. This will destroy any adult insects, larvae, or their eggs.

Moth Nuggets or Crystals: Another option is to add a few paradichlorobenzene nuggets or moth crystals to your storage containers and keep the containers in a cool, well-lighted, open area if possible. Most insects prefer warm, dark, closed areas.

Material Inventory

Following is an example of an inventory list that can be used to locate materials and maintain a record of the amount, color, and quality of various items. It can also be used as a shopping list for materials that you plan to obtain in the future.

Bird Materials

Chicken (Game Cock)

Item #   **Location**   **Description**   **Quantity:** ❑ Good   ❑ Low
    ❑ Jar ❑ Bag ❑ Box   Chicken (Game Cock)—Rooster Neck Hackles (Capes)
    ❑ Metz Grade#__   ❑ Keough Grade#__   ❑ Hoffman Grade#__
    Colors: ❑ Black   ❑ Lt. Gray (Dun)   ❑ Med. Gray (Dun)
    ❑ Grizzly   ❑Cream   ❑ Lt. Ginger   ❑ Barred Ginger
    ❑ Brown   ❑ Other_____

Item #   **Location**   **Description**   **Quantity:** ❑ Good   ❑ Low
    ❑ Jar ❑ Bag ❑ Box   Chicken (Game Cock)—Rooster Saddles
    ❑ Metz Grade#__   ❑ Keough Grade#__   ❑ Hoffman Grade#__
    Colors: ❑ Black   ❑ Lt. Gray (Dun)   ❑ Med. Gray (Dun)
    ❑ Grizzly   ❑Cream   ❑ Lt. Ginger   ❑ Barred Ginger
    ❑ Brown   ❑ Other_____

Item #   **Location**   **Description**   **Quantity:** ❑ Good   ❑ Low
    ❑ Jar ❑ Bag ❑ Box   Chicken (Game Cock)—Dyed Necks
    Colors: ❑ Orange   ❑ Red   ❑ Yellow   ❑ Green   ❑ Blue
    ❑ Purple   ❑ Olive   ❑ Brown   ❑ Chartreuse
    ❑ Other_____

Item #   **Location**   **Description**   **Quantity:** ❑ Good   ❑ Low
    ❑ Jar ❑ Bag ❑ Box   Chicken (Game Cock)—Strung Saddle Hackles
    Colors: ❑ Orange   ❑ Red   ❑ Yellow   ❑ Green   ❑ Blue
    ❑ Purple   ❑ Olive   ❑ Brown   ❑ Chartreuse
    ❑ Other_____

Item #   **Location**   **Description**   **Quantity:** ❑ Good   ❑ Low
    ❑ Jar ❑ Bag ❑ Box   Chicken (Game Cock)—Strung Neck Hackles
    Colors: ❑ Orange   ❑ Red   ❑ Yellow   ❑ Green   ❑ Blue
    ❑ Purple   ❑ Olive   ❑ Brown   ❑ Chartreuse
    ❑ Other_____

Material Inventory

Bird Materials

Chicken (Hen Sets)

Item #   **Location**   **Description**   **Quantity:** ❑ Good   ❑ Low

❑ Jar ❑ Bag ❑ Box   Chicken—Hen Sets (Hen Necks and Backs)

Colors: ❑ Black   ❑ Brown   ❑ Furnace   ❑ Ginger

       ❑ Grizzly   ❑ White   ❑ Other_____

Duck

Item #   **Location**   **Description**   **Quantity:** ❑ Good   ❑ Low

❑ Jar ❑ Bag ❑ Box   Duck—Paired Wing Quills

❑ Mallard ❑ Pintail ❑ Domestic ❑ Other_____

Colors: ❑ Natural Gray   ❑ Lt. Gray (Dun)   ❑ Yellow

       ❑ Orange ❑ White ❑ Red ❑ Olive

       ❑ Brown ❑ Other_____

Item #   **Location**   **Description**   **Quantity:** ❑ Good   ❑ Low

❑ Jar ❑ Bag ❑ Box   Duck—Drake Barred Breast Feathers

❑ Mallard ❑ Pintail ❑ Domestic ❑ Other_____

Item #   **Location**   **Description**   **Quantity:** ❑ Good   ❑ Low

❑ Jar ❑ Bag ❑ Box   Duck—Drake Barred Flank Feathers

❑ Mallard ❑ Pintail ❑ Domestic ❑ Other_____

Item #   **Location**   **Description**   **Quantity:** ❑ Good   ❑ Low

❑ Jar ❑ Bag ❑ Box   Duck—Mallard Hen Feathers

❑ Mallard ❑ Pintail ❑ Domestic ❑ Other_____

Item #   **Location**   **Description**   **Quantity:** ❑ Good   ❑ Low

❑ Jar ❑ Bag ❑ Box   Duck—Wood Drake Feathers

Goose

Item #   **Location**   **Description**   **Quantity:** ❑ Good   ❑ Low

❑ Jar ❑ Bag ❑ Box   Goose—Paired Wing Quills

❑ Canada ❑ Snow ❑ Domestic ❑ Other_____

Colors: ❑ Black   ❑ White ❑ Other_____

Material Inventory

Bird Materials

Item #   **Location**   **Description**   **Quantity:** ❑ Good   ❑ Low

❑ Jar ❑ Bag ❑ Box   Goose—Body Feathers

❑ Canada ❑ Snow ❑ Domestic ❑ Other_____

Colors: ❑ Natural ❑ White ❑ Other_____

Item #   **Location**   **Description**   **Quantity:** ❑ Good   ❑ Low

❑ Jar ❑ Bag ❑ Box   Goose—Biots

Colors: ❑ Black ❑ White ❑ Other_____

Pheasant

Item #   **Location**   **Description**   **Quantity:** ❑ Good   ❑ Low

❑ Jar ❑ Bag ❑ Box   Cock Pheasant—Ringneck (Entire Skin)

Item #   **Location**   **Description**   **Quantity:** ❑ Good   ❑ Low

❑ Jar ❑ Bag ❑ Box   Cock Pheasant—Ringneck (Skin Pieces, Tail Feathers)

Item #   **Location**   **Description**   **Quantity:** ❑ Good   ❑ Low

❑ Jar ❑ Bag ❑ Box   Hen Pheasant—Ringneck (Entire Skin)

Item #   **Location**   **Description**   **Quantity:** ❑ Good   ❑ Low

❑ Jar ❑ Bag ❑ Box   Hen Pheasant—Ringneck (Skin Pieces, Tail Feathers)

Item #   **Location**   **Description**   **Quantity:** ❑ Good   ❑ Low

❑ Jar ❑ Bag ❑ Box   Cock Pheasant—Golden (Entire Skin)

Item #   **Location**   **Description**   **Quantity:** ❑ Good   ❑ Low

❑ Jar ❑ Bag ❑ Box   Cock Pheasant—Golden (Crests, Body Pieces, Tail Feathers)

Material Inventory

Bird Materials

Item #   **Location**   **Description**   **Quantity:** ❏ Good   ❏ Low
❏ Jar ❏ Bag ❏ Box   Cock Pheasant—Amherst (Entire Skin)

Item #   **Location**   **Description**   **Quantity:** ❏ Good   ❏ Low
❏ Jar ❏ Bag ❏ Box   Cock Pheasant—Amherst (Crests, Body Pieces, Tail Feathers)

Item #   **Location**   **Description**   **Quantity:** ❏ Good   ❏ Low
❏ Jar ❏ Bag ❏ Box   Cock Pheasant—Silver (Entire Skin)

Item #   **Location**   **Description**   **Quantity:** ❏ Good   ❏ Low
❏ Jar ❏ Bag ❏ Box   Cock Pheasant—Silver (Crests, Body Pieces, Tail Feathers)

Peacock

Item #   **Location**   **Description**   **Quantity:** ❏ Good   ❏ Low
❏ Jar ❏ Bag ❏ Box   Peacock—Tail Feathers

Item #   **Location**   **Description**   **Quantity:** ❏ Good   ❏ Low
❏ Jar ❏ Bag ❏ Box   Peacock—Body Feathers

Item #   **Location**   **Description**   **Quantity:** ❏ Good   ❏ Low
❏ Jar ❏ Bag ❏ Box   Peacock—Herl

Item #   **Location**   **Description**   **Quantity:** ❏ Good   ❏ Low
❏ Jar ❏ Bag ❏ Box   Peacock—Swords

Ostrich

Item #   **Location**   **Description**   **Quantity:** ❏ Good   ❏ Low
❏ Jar ❏ Bag ❏ Box   Ostrich Plumes—Herl
Colors: ❏ Orange   ❏ Red   ❏ Yellow   ❏ Green   ❏ Blue
❏ Purple   ❏ Olive   ❏ Brown   ❏ Chartreuse
❏ Other_____

Material Inventory

Bird Materials

Partridge

Item #	Location	Description	Quantity: ❑ Good ❑ Low
	❑ Jar ❑ Bag ❑ Box	Partridge	

Turkey

Item #	Location	Description	Quantity: ❑ Good ❑ Low
	❑ Jar ❑ Bag ❑ Box	Turkey—Tail, Wing, and Body Feathers	

Colors: ❑ Orange ❑ Red ❑ Yellow ❑ Green ❑ Blue ❑ Purple ❑ Olive ❑ Brown ❑ Chartreuse ❑ Other_____

Item #	Location	Description	Quantity: ❑ Good ❑ Low
	❑ Jar ❑ Bag ❑ Box	Turkey Marabou	

Colors: ❑ Orange ❑ Red ❑ Yellow ❑ Green ❑ Blue ❑ Purple ❑ Olive ❑ Brown ❑ Chartreuse ❑ Other_____

Guinea Fowl

Item #	Location	Description	Quantity: ❑ Good ❑ Low
	❑ Jar ❑ Bag ❑ Box	Guinea Fowl	

Jungle Cock

Item #	Location	Description	Quantity: ❑ Good ❑ Low
	❑ Jar ❑ Bag ❑ Box	Jungle Cock	

Macaw/Parrot

Item #	Location	Description	Quantity: ❑ Good ❑ Low
	❑ Jar ❑ Bag ❑ Box	Exotic Birds—Macaw Feathers, Parrot Feathers	

Starling

Item #	Location	Description	Quantity: ❑ Good ❑ Low
	❑ Jar ❑ Bag ❑ Box	Starling	

Material Inventory

Bird Materials

Grouse

Item #	Location	Description	Quantity:
	❑ Jar ❑ Bag ❑ Box	Grouse	❑ Good ❑ Low

Quail

Item #	Location	Description	Quantity:
	❑ Jar ❑ Bag ❑ Box	Quail	❑ Good ❑ Low

Pigeon

Item #	Location	Description	Quantity:
	❑ Jar ❑ Bag ❑ Box	Pigeon	❑ Good ❑ Low

Crow, Raven, Blackbird

Item #	Location	Description	Quantity:
	❑ Jar ❑ Bag ❑ Box	Crow, Raven, Blackbird	❑ Good ❑ Low

Kingfisher

Item #	Location	Description	Quantity:
	❑ Jar ❑ Bag ❑ Box	Kingfisher	❑ Good ❑ Low

Material Inventory

Fur and Hair Materials

Deer

Item #   **Location**   **Description**   **Quantity:** ❑ Good   ❑ Low
❑ Jar ❑ Bag ❑ Box   Deer, Whitetail—Body Pieces (Natural)

Item #   **Location**   **Description**   **Quantity:** ❑ Good   ❑ Low
❑ Jar ❑ Bag ❑ Box   Deer, Whitetail—Body Pieces (Colored)
Colors: ❑ Orange   ❑ Red   ❑ Yellow   ❑ Green   ❑ Blue
        ❑ Purple   ❑ Olive   ❑ Brown   ❑ Chartreuse
        ❑ Other_____

Item #   **Location**   **Description**   **Quantity:** ❑ Good   ❑ Low
❑ Jar ❑ Bag ❑ Box   Deer, Whitetail—Bucktails (Natural)

Item #   **Location**   **Description**   **Quantity:** ❑ Good   ❑ Low
❑ Jar ❑ Bag ❑ Box   Deer, Whitetail—Bucktails (Colored)
Colors: ❑ Orange   ❑ Red   ❑ Yellow   ❑ Green   ❑ Blue
        ❑ Purple   ❑ Olive   ❑ Brown   ❑ Chartreuse
        ❑ Other_____

Item #   **Location**   **Description**   **Quantity:** ❑ Good   ❑ Low
❑ Jar ❑ Bag ❑ Box   Deer, Mule—Body Pieces (Natural)

Item #   **Location**   **Description**   **Quantity:** ❑ Good   ❑ Low
❑ Jar ❑ Bag ❑ Box   Deer, Coastal—Body Pieces (Natural)

Moose

Item #   **Location**   **Description**   **Quantity:** ❑ Good   ❑ Low
❑ Jar ❑ Bag ❑ Box   Moose—Body Pieces (Natural, Light, Dark, Moose Mane)

Elk

Item #   **Location**   **Description**   **Quantity:** ❑ Good   ❑ Low

❑ Jar ❑ Bag ❑ Box   Elk—Body Pieces (Natural, Light, Dark)

Caribou

Item #   **Location**   **Description**   **Quantity:** ❑ Good   ❑ Low
❑ Jar ❑ Bag ❑ Box   Caribou—Body Pieces (Natural)

Material Inventory

Fur and Hair Materials

Antelope

Item #   **Location**   **Description**   **Quantity:** ❑ Good ❑ Low

❑ Jar ❑ Bag ❑ Box   Antelope—Body Pieces (Natural, Light, Dark, White)

Sheep

Item #   **Location**   **Description**   **Quantity:** ❑ Good ❑ Low

❑ Jar ❑ Bag ❑ Box   Sheep, Domestic, Big Horn, Dall's

Goat

Item #   **Location**   **Description**   **Quantity:** ❑ Good ❑ Low

❑ Jar ❑ Bag ❑ Box   Goat, Domestic, Rocky Mountain

Cow

Item #   **Location**   **Description**   **Quantity:** ❑ Good ❑ Low

❑ Jar ❑ Bag ❑ Box   Cow

Calf Tail

Item #   **Location**   **Description**   **Quantity:** ❑ Good ❑ Low

❑ Jar ❑ Bag ❑ Box   Calf Tails

Colors: ❑ Orange ❑ Red ❑ Yellow ❑ Green ❑ Blue
        ❑ Purple ❑ Olive ❑ Brown ❑ Chartreuse
        ❑ Other_____

Horse Tail

Item #   **Location**   **Description**   **Quantity:** ❑ Good ❑ Low

❑ Jar ❑ Bag ❑ Box   Horse Tail

Bear

Item #   **Location**   **Description**   **Quantity:** ❑ Good ❑ Low

❑ Jar ❑ Bag ❑ Box   Bear, Black, Brown

Seal

Item #   **Location**   **Description**   **Quantity:** ❑ Good ❑ Low

❑ Jar ❑ Bag ❑ Box   Seal

Material Inventory

Fur and Hair Materials

Wild Pig

Item #	Location	Description	Quantity: ❏ Good ❏ Low
	❏ Jar ❏ Bag ❏ Box	Wild Pig—Peccary, Chinese Boar	

Coyote

Item #	Location	Description	Quantity: ❏ Good ❏ Low
	❏ Jar ❏ Bag ❏ Box	Coyote	

Fox

Item #	Location	Description	Quantity: ❏ Good ❏ Low
	❏ Jar ❏ Bag ❏ Box	Fox	

Opossum

Item #	Location	Description	Quantity: ❏ Good ❏ Low
	❏ Jar ❏ Bag ❏ Box	Opossum	

Rabbit

Item #	Location	Description	Quantity: ❏ Good ❏ Low
	❏ Jar ❏ Bag ❏ Box	Rabbit	

Beaver

Item #	Location	Description	Quantity: ❏ Good ❏ Low
	❏ Jar ❏ Bag ❏ Box	Beaver	

Otter

Item #	Location	Description	Quantity: ❏ Good ❏ Low
	❏ Jar ❏ Bag ❏ Box	Otter	

Muskrat

Item #	Location	Description	Quantity: ❏ Good ❏ Low
	❏ Jar ❏ Bag ❏ Box	Muskrat	

Material Inventory

Fur and Hair Materials

Squirrel

Item #	Location	Description	Quantity: ❑ Good ❑ Low
	❑ Jar ❑ Bag ❑ Box	Squirrel	

Mink, Ermine, Marten, Ferret, Fitch

Item #	Location	Description	Quantity: ❑ Good ❑ Low
	❑ Jar ❑ Bag ❑ Box	Mink, Ermine, Marten, Ferret, Fitch	

Badger

Item #	Location	Description	Quantity: ❑ Good ❑ Low
	❑ Jar ❑ Bag ❑ Box	Badger	

Skunk

Item #	Location	Description	Quantity: ❑ Good ❑ Low
	❑ Jar ❑ Bag ❑ Box	Skunk	

Chinchilla

Item #	Location	Description	Quantity: ❑ Good ❑ Low
	❑ Jar ❑ Bag ❑ Box	Chinchilla	

Woodchuck

Item #	Location	Description	Quantity: ❑ Good ❑ Low
	❑ Jar ❑ Bag ❑ Box	Woodchuck	

Raccoon

Item #	Location	Description	Quantity: ❑ Good ❑ Low
	❑ Jar ❑ Bag ❑ Box	Raccoon	

Mole

Item #	Location	Description	Quantity: ❑ Good ❑ Low
	❑ Jar ❑ Bag ❑ Box	Mole	

Porcupine

Item #	Location	Description	Quantity: ❑ Good ❑ Low
	❑ Jar ❑ Bag ❑ Box	Porcupine	

Material Inventory

Miscellaneous Materials

Chenille

Item #   **Location**   **Description**   **Quantity:** ❑ Good   ❑ Low

❑ Jar ❑ Bag ❑ Box   Variegated Chenille—Medium

Colors: ❑ Black/Yellow ❑ Black/Orange
❑ Dark Olive/Yellow ❑ Black/Olive ❑ Black/Coffee
❑ Brown/Yellow

Item #   **Location**   **Description**   **Quantity:** ❑ Good   ❑ Low

❑ Jar ❑ Bag ❑ Box   Standard Chenille ❑ Fine ❑ Medium ❑ Large

Colors: ❑ White ❑ Red ❑ Yellow ❑ Orange ❑ Olive
❑ Burnt Orange ❑ Gray ❑ Ginger ❑ Green
❑ Black ❑ Purple ❑ Dark Olive ❑ Tan ❑ Pink
❑ Brown ❑ Other_____

Item #   **Location**   **Description**   **Quantity:** ❑ Good   ❑ Low

❑ Jar ❑ Bag ❑ Box   Fluorescent Chenille ❑ Fine ❑ Medium ❑ Large

Colors: ❑ Red ❑ Yellow ❑ Orange ❑ Green
❑ Fire Orange ❑ Pink ❑ Other_____

Item #   **Location**   **Description**   **Quantity:** ❑ Good   ❑ Low

❑ Jar ❑ Bag ❑ Box   Crystal Chenille ❑ Fine ❑ Medium ❑ Large

Colors: ❑ Red ❑ Gold ❑ Silver ❑ Pearl
❑ Royal Blue ❑ Copper ❑ Rainbow ❑ Green
❑ Black ❑ Purple ❑ Blue ❑ Lime

Item #   **Location**   **Description**   **Quantity:** ❑ Good   ❑ Low

❑ Jar ❑ Bag ❑ Box   Sparkle Chenille—Medium

Colors: ❑ White ❑ Yellow ❑ Orange ❑ Dark Olive
❑ Gray ❑ Black ❑ Brown ❑ Other_____

Item #   **Location**   **Description**   **Quantity:** ❑ Good   ❑ Low

❑ Jar ❑ Bag ❑ Box   Vernille Chenille—Ultra-Fine

Colors: ❑ White ❑ Black ❑ Red ❑ Yellow ❑ Orange ❑ Olive
❑ Brown ❑ Other_____

Material Inventory

Miscellaneous Materials

Chenille

Item #   **Location**   **Description**   **Quantity:** ❏ Good   ❏ Low
❏ Jar ❏ Bag ❏ Box   Tinsel Chenille ❏ Fine ❏ Medium ❏ Large
Colors: ❏ Silver ❏ Gold

Item #   **Location**   **Description**   **Quantity:** ❏ Good   ❏ Low
❏ Jar ❏ Bag ❏ Box   Cactus Chenille ❏ Fine ❏ Medium ❏ Large
Colors: ❏ Pearl ❏ Red ❏ Yellow ❏ Orange ❏ Olive ❏ Purple
❏ Brown ❏ Other_____

Yarn

Item #   **Location**   **Description**   **Quantity:** ❏ Good   ❏ Low
❏ Jar ❏ Bag ❏ Box   Poly Yarn
Colors: ❏ White ❏ Cream ❏ Gray ❏ Beige ❏ Amber ❏ Red
❏ Olive ❏ Green ❏ Brown ❏ Black

Item #   **Location**   **Description**   **Quantity:** ❏ Good   ❏ Low
❏ Jar ❏ Bag ❏ Box   Antron Yarn
Colors: ❏ Fl. White ❏ Purple ❏ Gray ❏ Claret ❏ Gold ❏ Red
❏ Olive ❏ Dk. Olive ❏ Caddis Green ❏ Lt. Brown
❏ Dk. Brown ❏ Black ❏ Burnt Orange ❏ Fl. Pink
❏ Fl. Lime Green ❏ Fl. Orange ❏ Fl. Yellow

Item #   **Location**   **Description**   **Quantity:** ❏ Good   ❏ Low
❏ Jar ❏ Bag ❏ Box   Wool Yarn
Colors: ❏ White/Cream ❏ Lt. Gray ❏ Med. Gray ❏ Orange
❏ Med. Brown ❏ Dk. Brown ❏ Red ❏ Med. Olive
❏ Green ❏ Black

Item #   **Location**   **Description**   **Quantity:** ❏ Good   ❏ Low
❏ Jar ❏ Bag ❏ Box   Fluorescent Yarn
Colors: ❏ Red ❏ Yellow ❏ Orange ❏ Fire Orange
❏ Green ❏ Pink

Material Inventory

Miscellaneous Materials

Item #   **Location**   **Description**   **Quantity:** ❑ Good   ❑ Low
     ❑ Jar ❑ Bag ❑ Box   Glo-Bug Yarn
Colors: ❑ Fl. Pink   ❑ Fl. Orange   ❑ Fl. Yellow   ❑ Fl. Green
❑ Fl. Red   ❑ Salmon

Item #   **Location**   **Description**   **Quantity:** ❑ Good   ❑ Low
     ❑ Jar ❑ Bag ❑ Box   Leech Yarn
Colors: ❑ Rust   ❑ Olive ❑ Black   ❑ Gold   ❑

Floss

Item #   **Location**   **Description**   **Quantity:** ❑ Good   ❑ Low
     ❑ Jar ❑ Bag ❑ Box   Rayon, 4-Strand Floss
Colors: ❑ White   ❑ Orange   ❑ Yellow   ❑ Burnt Orange   ❑ Blue
❑ Gold   ❑ Red   ❑ Lt. Brown ❑ Red   ❑ Dark Red
❑ Olive   ❑ Chartreuse ❑ Green   ❑ Dk. Brown   ❑ Black
❑ Pink   ❑ Purple

Item #   **Location**   **Description**   **Quantity:** ❑ Good   ❑ Low
     ❑ Jar ❑ Bag ❑ Box   Nylon, Single-Strand Floss
Colors: ❑ Red   ❑ Orange   ❑ Yellow   ❑ Fire Orange   ❑ Green
❑ Pink

Item #   **Location**   **Description**   **Quantity:** ❑ Good   ❑ Low
     ❑ Jar ❑ Bag ❑ Box   Acetate, Single-Strand Floss
Colors: ❑ Red   ❑ Burnt Orange   ❑ Yellow   ❑ White   ❑ Brown
❑ Kelly Green   ❑ Pink   ❑ Scarlet

Tinsel

Item #   **Location**   **Description**   **Quantity:** ❑ Good   ❑ Low
     ❑ Jar ❑ Bag ❑ Box   Mylar Tinsel ❑ Flat ❑ Embossed ❑ Oval
❑ Fine ❑ Medium   ❑ Wide
Colors: ❑ Silver ❑ Gold ❑ Silver/Gold

Material Inventory

Miscellaneous Materials

Krystal Flash

Item #	Location	Description	Quantity:	☐ Good	☐ Low

☐ Jar ☐ Bag ☐ Box

Krystal Flash 10"–12" Hank

Colors: ☐ Silver ☐ Gold ☐ Copper ☐ Red ☐ Green
☐ Dark Blue ☐ Silver ☐ Pearlescent Lt. Blue ☐ Black
☐ Pearlescent ☐ Pearlescent Hot Yellow
☐ Pearlescent Orange ☐ Pearlescent Hot Purple
☐ Pearlescent Dk. Blue ☐ Rainbow
☐ Pearlescent Peacock ☐ Pearlescent Olive
☐ Pearlescent Lime Green

Flashabou

Item #	Location	Description	Quantity:	☐ Good	☐ Low

☐ Jar ☐ Bag ☐ Box

Flashabou 10"–12" Hank

Colors: ☐ Silver ☐ Gold ☐ Bronze ☐ Red ☐ Ocean Green
☐ Blue ☐ Silver ☐ Pearlescent Lt. Blue ☐ Black
☐ Pearl ☐ Fluorescent Chartreuse ☐ Yellow
☐ Purple ☐ Pink

Tubing

Item #	Location	Description	Quantity:	☐ Good	☐ Low

☐ Jar ☐ Bag ☐ Box

Tubing

☐ Mylar ☐ Polyester

Size: ☐ Fine ☐ Medium ☐ Large

Colors: ☐ Silver ☐ Gold ☐ Pearlescent

Synthetic Hair

Item #	Location	Description	Quantity:	☐ Good	☐ Low

☐ Jar ☐ Bag ☐ Box

FisHair 2-1/2", 4", 6", and 10" Lengths

Colors: ☐ Silver ☐ Gold ☐ Bronze ☐ Red ☐ Ocean Green
☐ Blue ☐ Silver ☐ Pearlescent Lt. Blue ☐ Black
☐ Pearl ☐ Fluorescent Chartreuse ☐ Yellow
☐ Purple ☐ Pink

Material Inventory

Miscellaneous Materials

Wing Material

Item #   **Location**   **Description**   **Quantity:** ❑ Good   ❑ Low
❑ Jar ❑ Bag ❑ Box   Micro fibetts and Micro Web Sheets

Popper Bodies

Item #   **Location**   **Description**   **Quantity:** ❑ Good   ❑ Low
❑ Jar ❑ Bag ❑ Box   Cork and Sandal Plug

Foam Materials

Item #   **Location**   **Description**   **Quantity:** ❑ Good   ❑ Low
❑ Jar ❑ Bag ❑ Box   Craft Foam, Fantafoam, Furry Foam, Evosite

Lead Wire

Item #   **Location**   **Description**   **Quantity:** ❑ Good   ❑ Low
❑ Jar ❑ Bag ❑ Box   Lead Wire ❑ X-Fine   ❑ Fine ❑ Medium   ❑ Heavy

Wire

Item #   **Location**   **Description**   **Quantity:** ❑ Good   ❑ Low
❑ Jar ❑ Bag ❑ Box   Wire ❑ Fine   ❑ Medium   ❑ Heavy
Colors: ❑ Gold   ❑ Silver   ❑ Copper   ❑ Red   ❑ Green

Tape and Foil

Item #   **Location**   **Description**   **Quantity:** ❑ Good   ❑ Low
❑ Jar ❑ Bag ❑ Box   Zonker Tape/Prismatic Tape/Scale Tape
Sheet Foil/Prismatic Sheets

Rubber Items

Item #   **Location**   **Description**   **Quantity:** ❑ Good   ❑ Low
❑ Jar ❑ Bag ❑ Box   Rubber Hackle/Latex Sheets/Rubber Bodies

Beads

Item #   **Location**   **Description**   **Quantity:** ❑ Good   ❑ Low
❑ Jar ❑ Bag ❑ Box   Glass and Metal—Assorted Sizes

Material Inventory

Miscellaneous Materials

Eyes

Item #	Location	Description	Quantity:
	❑ Jar ❑ Bag ❑ Box	Eyes	❑ Good ❑ Low

Types: ❑ Plastic Animal ❑ Plastic Doll ❑ Lead Eyes ❑ Brass Eyes ❑ Bead Chain ❑ Styrofoam

Colored Markers

Item #	Location	Description	Quantity:
	❑ Jar ❑ Bag ❑ Box	Permanant Markers	❑ Good ❑ Low

Colors: ❑ Red ❑ Black ❑ Green ❑ Yellow ❑ Orange ❑ Blue ❑ Brown ❑ Pink

Straw Material

Item #	Location	Description	Quantity:
	❑ Jar ❑ Bag ❑ Box	Swiss Straw or Raffia	❑ Good ❑ Low

Colors: ❑ Cream ❑ Black ❑ Olive Green ❑ Yellow ❑ Orange ❑ Brown

Plastic Lacing

Item #	Location	Description	Quantity:
	❑ Jar ❑ Bag ❑ Box	Swannundaze/Larva Lace/V-Rib	❑ Good ❑ Low

Colors: ❑ Cream ❑ Med. Brown ❑ Caddis Green ❑ Dark Olive ❑ Pink ❑ Dark Gray ❑ Light Olive ❑ Ginger ❑ Beige ❑ Dark Brown ❑ Olive Dun ❑ Med. Amber ❑ Yellow ❑ Silver Gray ❑ Light Amber ❑ Dark Green ❑ Tan ❑ Clear ❑ Brown ❑ Orange ❑ Black ❑ Smoke ❑ Red ❑ Olive ❑ Amber

Material Inventory

Miscellaneous Materials

Dubbing

Item #   **Location**   **Description**   **Quantity:** ❏ Good   ❏ Low

❏ Jar ❏ Bag ❏ Box   Dubbing—Fly Rite

Colors: ❏ Black ❏ Dark Olive ❏ Rust ❏ Blue-Wing Olive
❏ Cream ❏ Rusty Orange ❏ Cahill Tan ❏ Adams Gray
❏ March Brown ❏ Dark Reddish Brown ❏ Quill Gordon
❏ Dk. Olive Brown ❏ Lt. Hendrickson ❏ Inchworm Green
❏ Pale Morning Dun ❏ Pale Watery Yellow ❏ Gray Fox
❏ Caddis Pupa ❏ White ❏ Orange ❏ Bright Yellow
❏ Dark Tan ❏ Dark Gray ❏ Olive Sulfur ❏ Orange Sulfur
❏ Ginger Cream ❏ Med. Dun ❏ Choc. Brown
❏ Golden Yellow ❏ Claret

Item #   **Location**   **Description**   **Quantity:** ❏ Good   ❏ Low

❏ Jar ❏ Bag ❏ Box   Dubbing—Ligas

Colors: ❏ Lt. Hare's Ear ❏ Dark Hare's Ear ❏ Med. Hare's Ear
❏ Caddis Green ❏ Olive Brown ❏ Black ❏ Muskrat
❏ March Brown ❏ Dark Rust ❏ Olive ❏ Pale Olive
❏ Orange Scud ❏ Golden Brown ❏ Pale Sulfur
❏ Pink Fox ❏ Cream Fox ❏ Amber ❏ Black Drake
❏ Cinnamon ❏ Yellow ❏ Shrimp ❏ Light Beige
❏ Gill Red ❏ Olive Gray

Item #   **Location**   **Description**   **Quantity:** ❏ Good   ❏ Low

❏ Jar ❏ Bag ❏ Box   Dubbing—Hare-Tron

Colors: ❏ Golden Brown ❏ Lt. Olive Brown ❏ March Brown
❏ Dark Dun ❏ Pale Yellow ❏ Yellow ❏ Golden Stone
❏ Creamy Gray ❏ Olive Dun ❏ Olive ❏ Pale Olive
❏ Ginger ❏ Caddis Green ❏ Dark Brown ❏ Gray
❏ Burnt Orange ❏ Dark Olive ❏ Cahill ❏ Seal Brown
❏ Olive Tan ❏ Cinnamon ❏ Olive Brown ❏ Black

Material Inventory

Miscellaneous Materials

Dubbing

Item #	Location	Description	Quantity: ❏ Good ❏ Low
	❏ Jar ❏ Bag ❏ Box	Dubbing—Natural Furs	

Animal: ❏ Rabbit
❏ Otter
❏ Mink
❏ Beaver
❏ Opossum
❏ Nutria
❏ Mole
❏ Badger
❏ Seal
❏ Fox

INDEX